A Dirty Little War

'Of all the works published so far on East Timor's brutal passage to independence, and there have been many, *A Dirty Little War* is the most useful for anyone wanting to understand what went on.'

Jon Greenaway, *Sydney Morning Herald*

'*A Dirty Little War* is a major contribution... an intensely and movingly personal chronicle of the dreadful suffering of brave people... It should be widely read and contemplated.'

Merle Ricklefs, *Age*

'Martinkus's book simmers with controlled emotion... *A Dirty Little War* is a riveting eyewitness account by an Australian freelance journalist of East Timor's 1997–2000 agony.'

Tony Kevin, *Australian Financial Review*

'*A Dirty Little War* is the best book in English about East Timor since James Dunn published his revised history, *Timor: A People Betrayed* in 1996... the narrative is sustained at thriller-like pace from the first page to last.'

Brian Woodley, *Weekend Australian*

'For anyone with more than a passing interest in East Timor, Martinkus's book is essential. It will tell you more about what really happened in East Timor in the lead-up to the 1999 ballot, and afterwards, and why, than any other book I know.'

Damien Kingsbury, *Australian Book Review*

'This is a vivid, searing account of 'one of the great crimes of the century' that left the witness-author sometimes 'too inarticulate with rage to say anything.' What he has told is extraordinary—shocking, inspiring, and rich in insights and lessons. It's an impressive achievement, in the finest tradition of the best journalism.'

Noam Chomsky

A Dirty
Little War

John Martinkus

RANDOM HOUSE AUSTRALIA

Random House Australia Pty Ltd
20 Alfred Street, Milsons Point, NSW 2061
http://www.randomhouse.com.au

Sydney   New York   Toronto
London   Auckland   Johannesburg

First published by Random House Australia 2001

National Library of Australia
Cataloguing-in-Publication Entry

Martinkus, John.
A dirty little war.

Includes index.
ISBN 1 74051 016 X.

1. Political atrocities – Indonesia – Timor Timur. 2.
Timor Timur (Indonesia) – Politics and government. 3.
Timor Timur (Indonesia) – Autonomy and
independence movements. I. Title.

320.95986

Cover and text design by Greendot Design
Typeset by Midland Typesetters, Maryborough, Victoria
Printed and bound by The SOS Printing Group Pty Ltd

Historical details in introduction courtesy of Parliament of Australia
Senate Committee inquiry report into East Timor, October 1999.

10 9 8 7 6 5 4 3

contents

Foreword

When reading this book it is important to try to under-stand what the effect of the violence catalogued here has had upon the East Timorese people today. Remember that the violent consequences of Indonesian military rule of East Timor in the period covered here were only the final stages of a 25-year brutal occupation. Far worse atrocities than those detailed here were carried out against the East Timorese people in the late seventies and eighties. Sadly for us, these were not well documented. The international media were largely silent because of foreign governments' concern for their relations with Indonesia and the great impossibility of anyone gaining physical access to East Timor.

Until 1989, East Timor was barred to all outsiders and the internal conflict, which all Timorese knew very well, was largely unknown beyond our prison-island. In 1991 the brave Youth resistance led a massive demonstration that had an extraordinary political impact. The dramatic footage of Indonesian forces murdering unarmed East Timorese civilians opened the world's eyes to the violence that until then had been kept hidden.

Despite the widespread international attention the footage aroused, only a very small number of journalists and politicians continued to pay close attention to, report, and speak out about the continuing repression inside East Timor. Although I often said we were alone in our struggle we were not; there were people all over the world who worried about us and helped us.

The work of journalists, such as John Martinkus, in East Timor became increasingly important throughout the nineties. Comprehensive and impartial documentation of incidents of violence conducted against the East Timorese people paved the way for the international pressure on the Indonesian government to allow the United Nations to conduct the ballot in August of 1999.

When the Indonesian military and their militia proxies embarked on the campaign of killing, depopulation and the destruction and theft of property in East Timor in response to the independence result, it looked as though East Timor and the suffering of its people would once again be hidden from the outside world. It was only a handful of internationals who remained to try and document the final crimes of the Indonesian military that took place before international peacekeepers were allowed into the country. This book is one such document.

John Martinkus covered our conflict from inside East Timor through the period of armed struggle by our heroic Falintil guerrillas, the years of brave youth and clandestine resistance, to the violence before and after the ballot as well as the eventual arrival of the peace-keepers and the departure of the Indonesian forces. The stories he wrote about the atrocities helped to bring international attention to the genocide the world was ignoring.

This book provides a first-hand account of some of the key events that led to the long awaited independence of

East Timor. The violence that it documents illustrates the cruel and violent tactics so long applied to our people. We are still trying to recover from these manipulations to our society. Freedom has a sour taste for some trying to overcome all that has been perpetrated on them and cope with the huge social and economic problems that exist in our country. A complex political process awaits us over the next year: civil registration, civic education, setting up of an electoral system, nation-wide elections, the drafting of a constitution and the setting up of democratic institutions. We want a harmonious transition and for that we need wise and thoughtful leadership and support.

I hope his book goes some way towards making people understand the very recent violent history of our homeland and the current and long-term effects this will have on our society. I hope readers of the book will be better able to empathise with us in our continuing struggle to overcome our tragic past and create a peaceful, just and democratic society. We still need our friends to support and understand us in our new struggle.

Xanana Gusmão

Map of East Timor

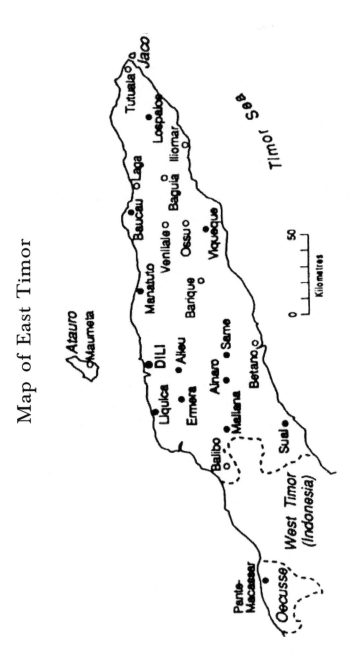

Historical introduction

The declaration of the independence of East Timor by Xavier do Amaral on 28 November 1975 brought to an end the period of colonial rule by Portugal which had begun in 1701 with the appointment of the first Governor, Antonio Coelho Guerreiro. Portuguese association with Timor went back to 1512, when Portuguese adventurers arrived from Malacca, which had been conquered by Alfonso de Albuquerque the year before, in search of the island's sandalwood.

During the 16th and 17th centuries, Timor and the neighbouring islands of Flores and Solor were the scenes of imperialist and missionary rivalry between the Portuguese, Dutch, Spanish and English, with the Dominican order of missionary friars acting as the principal agents of the Portuguese. By 1701, the Dutch had succeeded in driving most of their rivals out of the eastern parts of the archipelago—except for the Portuguese, who had been forced to move their base to Oecusse in the western region of Timor. In 1769, Dutch pressure forced a further move to Dili, which then became the Portuguese capital, although Oecusse remained a Portuguese enclave.

*Xavier do Amaral, the first president of independent East Timor, was the president of Fretilin (*Frente Revolucionaria de Timor Leste Independente*) in 1975. Fretilin had won more support than any other political grouping in the elections* *for village chiefs organised by the Portuguese administration in early 1975—the first democratic elections ever held in the territory. These elections were a consequence of the changes that had swept through Portugal and the Portuguese empire following the Lisbon coup of 25 April 1974, which caused the overthrow of the dictatorial regime that had ruled for the previous 50 years. Portugal was preparing to grant independence to all its overseas provinces, and was encouraging the formation of political parties in East Timor. Fretilin's main rival was the UDT (*União Democratica Timorense*). In January 1975, the two formed a coalition for national independence. A third party, Apodeti (Associacão Popular Democratica Timorense), pressed for integration with Indonesia.*

The Fretilin-UDT coalition broke down at the end of May 1975, and on 11 August, the UDT attempted to take over the administration of the province by force. This was resisted by Fretilin, who had the support of most of the East Timorese troops in the Dili barracks. The last two weeks of August saw armed conflict between supporters of Fretilin and UDT, while the Portuguese governor withdrew with the officers of his administration to the island of Atauro.

By mid-September Fretilin was in control of the province and had set up a provisional administration. Many of the defeated UDT leaders and their supporters took refuge in West Timor. By this time, those in Indonesia opposed to the creation of an independent East Timor were gaining ascendancy. Operasi Komodo, designed to bring about the incorporation of East Timor into Indonesia by subversive means, was formulated by General Ali Moertopo, deputy chief of the intelligence agency Bakin, and adopted in October 1974.

Opponents of Fretilin from among the supporters of Apodeti and the UDT who had gone to West Timor, such as João Tavares and João Carrascalão, cooperated with Kopassus, the Indonesian Special Forces, after September 1975 in operations designed to destabilise the Fretilin regime.

On 16 October 1975, five journalists and cameramen who were working for Australian television were shot and killed during an Indonesian attack on the town of Balibo, near the border with West Timor. Despite knowing, even in advance, of the killings through monitored Indonesian military transmissions, the Australian government denied any knowledge of the fate of the newsmen and actively cooperated with the Indonesians to obscure the details of their murder. It was at this point the Indonesians knew there would be no resistance from Australia for their planned incorporation of East Timor into Indonesia.

Indonesian attacks increased over the following weeks. On 20 November the important mountain base of Atabae came under sustained attack, leading to its capture two weeks later. The fall of Atabae precipitated the Fretilin leadership's decision to declare the independence of East Timor on 28 November.

On 7 December 1975, just 10 days after East Timor declared independence, Indonesia launched a combined military, naval and airborne invasion of East Timor, commencing with an assault on Dili by a force of 10,000. Along with the capture of Dili came massacres, wholesale looting, rape and indiscriminate destruction, setting the pattern of conduct for the Indonesian armed forces over the next 24 years. The only foreign reporter who stayed to try report the invasion, Australian Roger East, was killed by the Indonesians.

On 16 July 1976, the Indonesian parliament passed a bill (signed into law the following day) incorporating East Timor into the unitary State of Indonesia as its 27th province.

>—+—◦—◦—+—<

THE MASSACRE at the Santa Cruz cemetery in Dili on 12 November 1991, and the killings and repression in the follow-

ing days, are the best-known examples of the regime of terror to which East Timor was subjected. Film of the atrocities, captured by Max Stahl, became a catalyst for a new wave of international condemnation of Indonesia and inspired thousands of activists to work to end East Timorese repression by the Indonesian military.

Amnesty International Australia reported that at least 100 people were killed in the shootings in the cemetery and that up to 200 more disappeared after being taken away by the Indonesian security forces. Neither the graves of the dead nor the fate of those who disappeared were ever clarified by the Indonesian government.

This dramatic and tragic incident in 1991 did not occur in a vacuum. Indonesia committed serial human rights violations between the years of 1975 and 1997—restrictions on peaceful expression of political views, the widespread use of torture and ill-treatment of detainees, the 'disappearance' of people taken into military custody, extrajudicial executions, unfair trials and restrictions on human rights monitoring were all catalogued by Amnesty International.

They found the abuses most severe at times of political tension or heightened military activity; attacks on Indonesian forces frequently led to widespread arrests and ill-treatment of people suspected of sympathy with the resistance movement.

According to Amnesty International, there were few reported cases of Indonesian police or soldiers being held accountable for abuses, and the sentences given by military courts were inadequate compared to sentences given by Indonesian civil courts for equivalent misdemeanours. In most cases, only low-ranking soldiers were held accountable, most of them East Timorese.

For much of the period, Indonesian forces viewed the collection of information about human rights abuses as a serious offence. Torture victims were routinely warned not to make their experiences public.

Indonesian forces used civilian 'ninja' groups of pro-integration East Timorese to harass or detain suspected supporters of independence from at least 1990; increasingly after 1995 they utilitised groups such as Gadapaksi and Halilintar. Informants were widely used. New militias—paramilitary groups—were formed in late 1998. They were given much greater freedom of action and encouraged to intimidate pro-independence supporters.

A THIRD *of the East Timorese population had perished by the early 1990s as a direct result of the Indonesian military's efforts to secure the island. These people had died in the fighting or due to its consequences, many as victims of the famine induced by their forced relocation away from the interior of the island. Of a population of 750,000, more than 250,000 had died. This was the highest per capita death toll of any conflict in the 20th century. When I returned to Australia from East Timor in 1994 and then again in 1995, I was told by a string of editors from every major daily in the country that the ongoing killings by the Indonesians were not news. 'Look, we are not going to publish anything on East Timor. Can you stop bothering us . . .' said the foreign editor of one major Australian daily newspaper.*

I WAS *told by an Australian lecturer in journalism that the Australian press had a 'Finland complex'—we dared not criticise our powerful neighbour, Indonesia. But the rest of the world was moving faster than Australia; it had begun to notice the conflict only 500 kilometres to Australia's north.*

I went back to East Timor in early 1997.

Glossary

General

APODETI   *Associaocão Popular Democratica Timorense*
                (Timorese Popular Democratic Association),
                pro-Indonesian integration party established in
                May 1974.

BRIMOB   *Brigada Mobil:* (Indonesian riot police).

CNRT   *Concelho Nacional de Resistençia Timorense*
                (National Council of Timorese Resistance).

FALINTIL   *Forcas Armadas de Libertação de Timor Leste*
                (Armed Forces for an Independent East Timor).

FRETILIN   *Frente Revolucionaria de Timor Leste Independente*
                (Revolutionary Front for an Independent East
                Timor).

FORCAREPETIL Pro-referendum East Timorese intellectuals' forum.

FPDK   *Forum Persatuan Demokrasi Dan Keadilan*
                (Forum for Unity, Democracy and Justice,
                political wing for pro-Indonesian militia).

GRPTT   *Gerakan Rekonsiliasi dan Persatuan Rakyat Timor
                Timu* (Movement for Reconciliation and Unity
                of the People of East Timor).

UDT   *União Democratica Timorense* (Timorese
                Democratic Union).

ICRC   International Committee of the Red Cross.

INTERFET   International Force East Timor.

IFET   International Federation for East Timor.

GPK	*Gerombolan Pengacau Keamanan* ('security disturbance groups'), the term used by the Indonesian military for the guerrillas.
KODAM	(Indonesian regional military command); under Indonesian rule, East Timor was divided into 17 Kodams.
KODIM	(District Military Command).
KONTRAS	organisation to investigate political disappearances and killings.
KOPASSUS	(Indonesian Special Forces).
KORAMIL	(Sub-district Military Command).
KOREM	(Sub-regional Military Command).
KOSTRAD	(Strategic Reserve Command of the Indonesian Army).
UNAMET	United Nations Assistance Mission in East Timor.
UNTET	United Nations Transitional Administration in East Timor.
SGI	(Indonesian Combat Intelligence Unit), dominated by Kopassus.
TNI	*Tentara Nasional Indonesia* (Indonesian Regular Army).
YAYASAN HAK	Organisation of Rights, the East Timorese legal aid foundation and human rights monitor led by East Timorese lawyer Aniceto Guterres.

Militia Groups

ABLAI	Based in Same.
AITARAK	'Thorn', based in Dili and led by Eurico Guterres.
AHI	'Fire', based in Aileu.
BESIH MERAH PUTIH	'Red and White Iron', based in Liquiça and led by Manuel de Sousa.
DARAH MERAH	'Red Blood', based in Ermera.
DADURUS MERAH PUTIH	'Red and White Tornado', based in Maliana.
HALI LINTAR	'Thunder', based in Maliana and led by João Tavares.

LAK SAUR 'Flying Eagle', based in Suai.

MAHIDI 'Live or Die for Integration', based in Ainaro, Cassa and Zumalai, and led by Cançio Lopes De Carvalho.

TEAM 59/75 JUNIOR Named after the unsuccessful Indonesian-led rebellion against the Portuguese administration in 1959, based in Viqueque.

Paramilitary Groups

TEAM ALPHA, TEAM SERA, TEAM SAKA Formed by Kopassus in the early 1990s as East Timorese auxiliary groups to serve in operations against the guerrillas with the Indonesian military. Based in Baucau and Lospalos in the east. Fully armed and trained by the Indonesian military, similar to regular military units.

GADAPAKSI Forerunner to the militia units, set up as 'civil defence' by Indonesians in mid 1990s. Based in urban areas. Long-term association with political 'disappearances' and night-time 'ninja' attacks on pro-independence figures, particularly in Dili in the mid '90s.

RATIH Generic term for a people's unit trained by the Indonesian army.

CHAPTER ONE

January 1997

Dili, East Timor

AT THE DESERTED beach, with its crumbling concrete shelters, swaying palms and clear water lapping white sand, it was obvious what the Timorese man had urged me to come and see: a headless body, no hands, no feet, was lying in the water, moving with the tide. It looked like the sides and the backs of the legs had been eaten by fish, or dogs. I had never seen a corpse like that before; I just thought that was how a dead person looked after a few days in the sea. But this wasn't normal; for there to be no head, only a torso, arms and legs. And from the shape of the muscles you could tell the corpse had once been a strong young man. It turned out the body had been hacked to pieces, not eaten.

In another country this would have been a crime scene, cordoned off while the authorities investigated then removed the horrible spectacle. In East Timor at that time, it was the authorities themselves who were responsible.

Their point was blunt: support independence and this is what will happen.

East Timorese people had told me what happened to those who 'disappeared'. The Indonesian authorities would take them to SGI (the Indonesian Combat Intelligence Unit) headquarters, a walled compound near Dili's centre, where they would be tortured and then killed. In a matter of fact way, the East Timorese would explain the routine, knowing they might be next: when dead, the bodies were dumped in the harbour or left on gruesome display in some other public area.

The man whose body I was looking at had been killed in retaliation; an East Timorese corporal in the Indonesian army had tried to shoot Bishop Carlos Belo as he returned to Dili after collecting the 1996 Nobel Peace prize in Oslo, but the thousands of East Timorese there to meet Belo had beaten the would-be assassin to death. Two days after the crowd had killed the corporal, three headless corpses were found in the Dili suburb of Tacitolu; another body was found a week or so later, dismembered, wrapped in plastic bags and dumped. The body I saw floating on the tide was just one more. I didn't even think to report it.

The taxi I'd taken to the beach was gone by the time I got back to where I'd left it waiting, so I had no choice but to start walking back to town in the hot sun along the road that ran next to the sea. I didn't see anyone else until I reached the military post that overlooked this route out of Dili. Indonesian soldiers sat in the shade of their veranda, shirtless, holding guns. One yelled out something to me. They all laughed. I walked on, past the restaurants scattered along the beach road where the men who commanded those soldiers enjoyed lavish meals of barbecued fish and squid. It was one of the benefits of being stationed in Dili in those days.

I had been in one of those restaurants myself just the day before, getting drunk with an English doctor I'd met. Chris was an interesting man. Recently in Bali, where he had been busy bragging about his war-zone exploits, he had been approached by an East Timorese-born Australian who had heard him talking about his experiences as a combat surgeon in Angola, Bosnia and Zaire. The man, who Chris wouldn't name, had asked him to come to East Timor to treat one of the Falintil guerrilla commanders who had been sick for some time. Chris, for reasons partly to do with ego and adrenaline and partly to do with a genuine desire to help, had agreed.

'Two weeks I've been waiting, and they keep saying "tomorrow". It's fucking always tomorrow with these people,' Chris complained. 'I mean, it was all supposed to be arranged. Their commander is sick, and I was supposed to be in and out of here in a week. Straight up to the bush, then back to Bali.' He went on and on.

I had arrived in Dili two days before, determined to write about the conflict. I was intending to freelance stories to whichever newspapers would buy them. During my two previous visits, in 1994 and 1995, I had been convinced that there was a story here. But because of the kind of hidden counter-insurgency terror being perpetrated by the Indonesians, it was difficult to pin down and report.

Reports of the violence in East Timor were always met with blanket denials from the Indonesian authorities. If they did acknowledge any particular incident had occurred, the pro-independence Falintil guerrillas were routinely blamed. So an unidentified mutilated body floating on the tide near Dili wouldn't be enough to interest a sceptical foreign editor back in Australia.

Since he'd arrived, Chris had been stuck out at Pedro Lebre's house-cum-hotel waiting to be contacted by the guerrillas. Pedro lived out in Becora, an eastern suburb of Dili, in an area far from the three main hotels on the waterfront. Indonesian security operatives, from Intel, watched the main hotels like hawks, trying to make sure foreigners kept away from the East Timorese people.

'They beg me to come here and see their commander,' Chris continued, 'but then they put me in this house and tell me to wait. You can't do anything here. At night there are those fucking ninjas, and Pedro barricades the house. In the day the place is crawling with military and they keep telling me not to do anything, or talk to anybody or even go out.'

Unfortunately, Becora was also home to a large Indonesian military base and, at that time, was not safe at night. The Indonesians were very jumpy and sent patrols through the East Timorese-dominated area; they were often in the process of arresting someone.

But Chris's time in East Timor hadn't all been spent indoors and without event. He told me about what I'd missed the week before, at the attempted assassination of Bishop Belo. Thousands of East Timorese had flocked to the airport to welcome him home and, like any large public gathering in Dili, it was a slap in the face to the Indonesian authorities, especially since Belo had won the prize for protesting the abuse of the East Timorese at the hands of the Indonesian military. There was also always the chance that the Indonesian military would repeat their Santa Cruz cemetery crowd control methods of 1991—by shooting the people.

At the airport, a group of Indonesians pushed their way through the crowd towards Bishop Carlos Belo. An East Timorese soldier in the Indonesian military, Corporal Alfredo Do Santo Siga, forced his way to the front and revealed a handgun. Seeing it, the crowd, thousands thick around the bishop, beat him to death. Eleven of his

Indonesian minders were also recognised by the crowd and severely beaten as they ran for their lives.

Surprising everyone, there was no immediate Indonesian response, which encouraged people to celebrate the event as a victory. A little of the sense of euphoria was still in the air when I arrived. Unlike my earlier experiences, the East Timorese people smiled and responded to my greetings in the street. Previously, they had been too terrified of being seen communicating with a foreigner by the Indonesians—a sure invitation for interrogation, or worse. Some people were still openly wearing BISHOP BELO NOBEL PRIZE T-shirts. But the feelings of euphoria were to be short-lived, and the antic-ipated Indonesian response to the crowd's actions would soon be felt. As night approached, the mood changed and people became tense again. Crammed onto minibuses and taxis, riding bicycles and motorbikes, they fled from the streets. By the time it was dark, the city appeared dead.

The crackdown had been going for several days when I arrived. Humiliated by the failed assassination attempt on Belo, the Indonesian military intelligence unit, the SGI, reverted to proven methods of repression: the ninjas. Formed around 1995, the name came from the black fatigues and balaclavas they wore as they crept around town at night armed with M-16s.

In 1995 I had seen them surrounding a house silently at night as I drove past in a car. They all froze as our lights passed over them, but moved on into the dark alleys and thick tropical foliage that surrounds most East Timorese houses as we drove away.

When these groups operated, they followed a regular routine: a family would suddenly find men armed with guns inside their house late at night. The masked men (usually Indonesian military or their East Timorese hirelings) would take away the man of the house and often rape the mother or daughters. Young men, particularly those with an education, were almost always taken away. Often they were never heard of again; sometimes their mutilated remains were discovered weeks later, by the roadside or dumped on some vacant land or the beach.

━━◦━━

CHRIS'S ACCOUNT of what had been going on in East Timor hadn't surprised me. What did interest me was what he was doing there—and who he was going to see. Only a handful of journalists had been able to meet with the guerrillas since 1975 when the Indonesian army invaded. The only journalist who tried to stay at that time, Australian Roger East, was executed on the Dili waterfront—along with over 1,000 East Timorese—on the first day of the invasion by Indonesian troops.

Because of Chris's experience, and the complete lack of medical care available to the Falintil guerrillas, they were very keen for him to visit. However, the crackdown in town had made things difficult, and with every passing day Chris spent wandering around Dili, attracting attention, the chance that the Indonesians would start following him grew.

Pedro knew exactly what was going on and became more nervous every day. When we had arrived back from drinking on the beach after dark, he had been furious. 'What do you think this is, a holiday? Do you know there was shooting tonight in Santa Cruz? Do you think those bloody Indonesian bastards will just say good night to you if they see you on the street when they are shooting? Fucking hell.'

Pedro spoke English with an Australian accent and in a way that reflected the time and place he'd learnt it: in the mining camps of Far North Queensland in the early 1970s. He'd returned to East Timor before the invasion and was led by his natural flair for business and sense of patriotism to establish the only East Timorese-owned accommodation for foreigners in Dili. A precarious position for him, but for foreign journalists, his was the obvious place to stay, away from the prying staff at the other three hotels in town, which in those days were mostly full of Indonesian military officers and businessmen who tended to ask a lot of leading questions, or were just downright hostile.

'Here come the bloody Indonesian bastards,' Pedro would say as the police and immigration officials arrived daily to check on who was staying at his run-down house. Then he'd walk out into the blazing sun and laugh and make jokes with the officials as they checked us out from behind mirrored sunglasses. 'Please have a beer, it is so hot today,' Pedro would say, inviting them to join us on the veranda, which was equally hot in the heavy wetness of January in Dili.

And every day they would join us, sweating in their polyester safari suits, drink a few beers and ask the same questions: 'Where are you from? Why don't you holiday in Bali? Why have you stayed so long here?' Chris always said that he was heading for Bali, but had been too sick to travel. And they always responded that if he was sick, he should not drink beer and they could arrange for him to see a doctor. The conversation went on like this for a while, then they'd leave, telling us when the next ferry left and how to get a bus to West Timor, just in case we didn't know.

JOHN MAULANO was one of Pedro's large extended family who hung around the house. A young man who hardly ever spoke and only revealed his understanding of English when one of us cracked a joke and he'd laugh, he was a nephew of Pedro from the Baucau region. East Timor's second-largest town is about 130 kilometres east of Dili.

In the mid-1990s, Baucau had been more of a hotspot than Dili. Local youths had rioted in late 1994 and '95, with the Indonesian troops firing into the crowd. Government officials in the town told me as many as 25 people were killed on one occasion in January 1995, but the whole thing passed without much international notice.

There was also frequent conflict between the traders from the Indonesian island of Sulawesi and the youth in the town. Stabbings and the razing of the Sulawesi market stalls and shops had a political edge. The Sulawesis had come in with the Indonesians; they were Muslim, the Timorese were Catholic, and the Indonesian authorities tried to pass the conflict off as a religious one. But the local youths would say they just wanted to get rid of the Indonesians. The ratio of East Timorese to Indonesians was higher in Baucau than Dili and, as a result, the local population caused more trouble for the Indonesians there.

John Maulano was our contact with the guerrillas, and from his self-control you knew he wasn't one of those angry youths fighting Sulawesis or charging Indonesian troops in a riot. He fought in other ways.

Pedro knew of our plan to meet the Falintil guerrillas, but ignored it. The less he knew, the less he could tell, he said. Three days later, everything was finally organised and I was included in the plan. A friend of Pedro's in Australia, who had once translated some smuggled videos for me, had vouched for my credentials.

Two Indonesian government four-wheel drives, complete with civil-service plates and blacked-out windows, pulled into the driveway and went straight around the back. 'Be fucking careful. Don't let the bloody bastards catch you, they'll bloody kill you,' was all Pedro said as he watched the road for Indonesians while we jumped into the car.

The suburb of Becora stretches out along the main road from Dili's centre. At that time it was a densely populated area, with mainly East Timorese living in a jumble of shacks and houses sprawling off narrow tracks that led from both sides of the road.

In the middle of the suburb was a large military barracks for Indonesian Battalion 745. Further along the main road was the prison and, past that, the market and bus station. At all or any one of these places there were usually military checkpoints where traffic heading east was routinely searched. That day, our guides had timed our departure well: the checkpoints were all empty.

As the vehicle climbed the hills that surround Dili, I saw a man by the side of the road wearing nothing but shorts and a hat briefly lift his hand and say something into a radio he was trying to hide in this hand. The sharp, distorted sound of a two-way radio came from the front seat of our car and the guide in the passenger seat answered the man on the road.

We drove east along the spectacular coast road. In places, it is cut into the mountains that rise straight from one of the deepest stretches of sea in Asia to form the north coast of the island. Nestled between the steep mountains, the flat country looks like parts of Northern Australia, with gum trees and open areas of dry grass.

The Falintil guides in the front seat pointed out the Indonesian military posts to us. I had driven along this road many times but had never noticed the low grass huts on every commanding height as the road rises and falls around the coastline. They were positioned almost within sight of each other along the entire 130 kilometres of road between

Dili and Baucau. The guides told us that each post contained at least 10 Indonesian troops at all times, and at night they moved out and patrolled the surrounding villages.

Just before we entered one town, the other four-wheel drive, which had been travelling in front of us, stopped. The guides jumped out and started waving us off the road frantically. A column of 15 Indonesian military trucks, each carrying at least 40 armed soldiers—their faces hidden behind black balaclavas—roared past in the opposite direction. They came so close I could see one soldier was wearing Australian Army-issue boots. Probably from his training in Queensland, I thought.

I saw one of our guides reach for the pistol he was carrying, and thought how useless that would be against a truck-load of Indonesians with M-16s. They passed without stopping.

Outside Baucau, on the high plain near East Timor's largest airport, we slowed to dodge the petrol drums in the middle of the road—a roadblock. A Kopassus (Indonesian Special Forces) soldier seemed to look straight into my eyes as he peered blindly through the tinted rear window of the four-wheel drive.

We were driven through the town of Baucau to a seminary, where we were bundled into a side room and told to wait.

Hours later, when it was dark, we were driven to a hillside. We followed our guides as they disappeared up the hill on foot. I could hear the noise of heavy trucks nearby, and dogs barking and people yelling. I knew we hadn't travelled very far from Baucau; I also knew that there were around 5,000 Indonesian soldiers in Baucau. My legs were very shaky as I tried to step in the guides' footsteps through the loose rock that rattled down the hillside, causing dogs to bark. A few times we stopped dead and the guides gestured for total silence.

We reached a high plain illuminated by moonlight and the guides bent low and moved in a half run. Trying to do the same and keep up with them was difficult. When Chris fell heavily, they stopped and stood like statues. Moments later, they giggled quietly at the sight of Chris, and John took his bag to help him. It was a relief to move into the cover of thick bush in a valley.

Faces underlit by weak torches started appearing ahead of us. Then, after squeezing through a hole cut in a dense wall of bush, we were surrounded by men with guns. The Falintil commander, David Alex, wearing a captured Indonesian uniform, stepped forward with his hand extended and welcomed us. We were in a series of tiny shelters lined with tarpaulins slung so low you had to walk bent double. Equipment, guns, ammunition, radios and uniforms were crammed into tiny spaces that were basically hollows surrounded by dense bush and covered by low tarps and foliage. Eight men, all laughing silently at our condition made space for us to sit and handed us cups of thick, strong Timorese coffee.

One of the men leaned forward and spoke to me in English: 'I know you from Sydney last year. You were at that conference.' It was Jose Belo. I couldn't believe it, I had spoken to him six months earlier when he was shivering in a Sydney winter. He had laughed then because I had mistaken him for someone else. And when he'd said, 'Of course, we all look alike to you,' what he really meant was: you stupid white fool. He laughed again to see me sweating from fear and exertion, crouching uncomfortably in the awkward, low shelter. But this time he laughed noiselessly. 'The Indonesians are too close, we must be quiet,' he whispered, still smiling at the shock of seeing me there.

I knew about Jose's life. When he had told me all about it back in Sydney, it had seemed so appalling, and I was sure he wouldn't go back to East Timor. But there he was, surrounded by men whose lives had probably been worse. As a young boy he had fled to the mountains when the Indonesians invaded. In 1978 he was captured during the Indonesian offensives in the east, when they tried to wipe out the guerrillas and relocate the subsistence farming population to Indonesian-controlled areas. He had been forced to watch as they raped, and then killed, his elder sister.

During the next 17 years, Jose was arrested by the Indonesian authorities seven times and jailed for a total of nine years. Each time, he was beaten and tortured. When he was arrested at a demonstration at Dili University in 1995, three Australians witnessed the beating he received. 'They were beating him so hard, the police truck was rocking wildly, like a washing machine,' one of them said later, after they had all been expelled from East Timor for witnessing the demonstration. That time he was not given food or water for four days. His arms and legs were bound and he was hung upside down overnight. He was then beaten severely with truncheons, cigarettes were extinguished on his chest and arms, and electric shocks were administered to his genitals.

〰〰◦〰〰

THE NEXT morning, after the area had been checked for any Indonesian presence at first light, we could finally talk. Jose started telling me what had happened since I last saw him. When he had left for Australia, he had promised his SGI interrogators that he would not return to East Timor, but that he would study in Jakarta. When he returned in June

1996, despite the pleas of many East Timorese for him to stay in Australia for his safety, he was constantly detained, beaten and questioned. 'The situation in the towns, it made me crazy. Sometimes I was only with my family two weeks and [then] I [would] have to go to the prison or to another place to hide. The pressure from the Indonesians ... always looking for me, informing on me. I received information from my friends that it was very dangerous for me and I had to get out of town.' That was in November. Jose was laughing when I asked him what he thought of Australia. 'On the way back, in Bali, the Australian women, they don't wear any clothes,' he whispered with a wide-eyed look of shock. 'Of course as a young man I would like to enjoy my life as the other young people in other countries like Australia, Canada and Japan—but it's hard for us Timorese because since 1975 we are in this crisis. We are in this massacre.'

I didn't need to ask him why he'd come back. It was obvious: his English-speaking skills were essential, and the commander communicated with us through him. Underneath the low-slung canopy that was now becoming like an oven as the sun moved up in the sky, Chris examined the 12 fighters present. All except for two of them had bullets inside their bodies. They all had malaria and they all had kidney infections from the bad drinking water.

This unit, as the commander was to explain to me later, contained men who, like himself, had been fighting since 1975 in these mountains. A few of these men were among the last of the 2,500 East Timorese who had experience in the Portuguese army in colonial times. They had formed the backbone of the Falintil forces that grew to around 20,000 fighters after the Indonesians invaded. For the first three years of the conflict they managed to control eighty percent of East Timor. They had been bombed, shot and starved by the Indonesians ever since. Only 600 remained as active Falintil fighters in the mountains and many of those had joined since the Indonesian offensives of the late 1970s.

They operated in bands of no more than 20 from small camps like this one throughout the island. A larger group would be too much of a target, could have led to them being wiped out. On several occasions, when they had tried to group their forces for meetings, they had been attacked. There were many informers and spies—the Indonesians paid well, and threatened people's families for information.

They had fought their lonely war like this since the big battles of the late 1970s, when the Indonesians surrounded and bombed them. At that time, the Falintil had been forced to order the surrender of the civilian population, because they could no longer help them. Famine followed for East Timor, with its people relocated away from the mountains and the main food-producing areas.

For Falintil in the mountains, just to survive through that was a victory. 'In the decade of the '80s, we were lacking in everything—food, clothing, medicines. It was really very hard to live,' said David Alex. 'Many died then. We had to keep our force small to survive.'

His small, wasted body was testament to the hardship. He couldn't digest food; he'd developed a stomach ulcer as a result of long periods of not eating. This was why Chris had been called in, but there wasn't a lot he could do.

Chris went to work. He thought he could remove some of the bullets that were lodged in the men's bodies, although on the others, some he wouldn't even consider, like the guy who pulled out his lower lip to reveal the grey metal fragments of shrapnel visible in his gums. Chris laid down a plastic groundsheet and poured disinfectant all over it. He gave one of the men a shot of local anaesthetic. Jose and the others positioned themselves to hold him down, as Chris wasn't sure if the local anaesthetic would work deeply enough. Bending awkwardly over the man because of the low canopy, Chris sliced into his leg with a scalpel blade held in pliers. After cutting into the calf muscle, he dug in and pulled out a bullet that had been lodged there since November 1995.

Suddenly, everybody laughed. The bullet was out. A doctor was there. Another fighter with an old leg wound pushed himself forward to be next. Chris pushed him back, to give himself time to wash the blood off the groundsheet and bandage and sew up the leg.

The next procedure proved more difficult. A bullet was lodged in the thigh of a 27-year-old. It was between the bone and a main tendon, but this wasn't discovered until after his leg had been sliced open. We all sat around watching, including the man whose leg was open, and a friend who was sitting on his chest to help him deal with the pain. Chris explained to the commander that if he cut the tendon to remove the bullet, it would be at least three months before the man would be able to walk again.

'The bullet stays,' said Alex. If he were to be immobile for that long, the Indonesians would almost certainly catch, torture and kill him. Lead poisoning from the bullet would probably kill the guy eventually, Chris told me later, but 'hell, if three months of not being on your feet will kill you, then there's not much of an option, is there?' He still didn't feel right sewing him back up without fixing it, though.

That night we realised why the commander wouldn't allow a man to be immobilised. A message came through on the Indonesian military radio they had purchased from a corrupt officer; a battalion-sized patrol of Indonesian troops was moving through the area.

The relaxed atmosphere quickly dissipated; possessions were packed, ammunition distributed and lights extinguished.

The two fighters who just hours before had had their legs cut open were dispatched to join the lookouts that had been doubled from four to eight. The rest of us sat in silence, the fighters with M-16s in their hands, as everybody strained to hear the tread of the Indonesian troops. David Alex tried to listen to the radio pressed up against his ear, the volume on its lowest setting. The slightest noise made by any of us in the main tent drew a sharp look from the commander, whose neck muscles looked like taut wire. He made a sign to Jose, 20 metres away, who reached over and wrote on my notepad that Chris and I must keep absolutely quiet.

Two more of the fighters slipped away silently. Jose, Chris, David Alex and I sat in the dark, too frightened to wave away the mosquitoes buzzing around us.

An hour passed and still we sat in total silence, until Chris whispered very close to my ear: 'If there is shooting, we stand up and surrender straight away.' This infuriates me. From what I've heard, that would probably be the worst thing to do. If they found us and didn't kill us, they would definitely kill the others, whose position we would have given away. Besides, it was pitch black in this undergrowth—they wouldn't be able to tell if we were white or not.

I whispered something to that effect to Chris, earning a warning 'shut up' look from Alex.

Sometime later I fell asleep—then woke being shaken violently with someone's hand over my mouth. It was Chris; I'd been talking in my sleep. Looking around I saw Jose and the commander still holding their guns and the radio still at the commander's ear. It was 3 am. Jose offered me a cigarette, and the commander nodded. We were allowed to smoke again—things must have improved.

IN THE morning, things were more relaxed. Local villagers brought bread, coffee and processed cheese. The fighters, who had been awake all night, gathered around to enjoy the meal. For the first time I saw that there were 12 or so men there, armed with a machine gun, M-16s, Mauser rifles and pistols. Everyone seemed relaxed after the tense night; even the noise of a low-flying Indonesian military helicopter didn't seem to bother them.

The fighters said the Indonesians had come within 20 metres of the camp during the night, and had passed back and forth numerous times. Chris said he'd heard their footsteps, and one of the men on lookout duty said that an Indonesian soldier had been walking directly toward him, but for some reason went the other way at the last minute.

The commander said he wasn't surprised the Indonesians had been sweeping this area, as they knew he was somewhere nearby and could have found out there were foreigners with them. But he didn't seem particularly bothered by the Indonesians' proximity: 'It's normal for us to be so close to the enemy—we can survey and monitor their movements. Often it is only 30 or 40 metres from where they are camped, and they pass less than 15 to 20 metres above us. But it is better to be close to monitor the enemy's movements than to be far away and not know what the enemy is doing.'

A HEAVY monsoonal downpour allowed everyone to relax a little more. It rained so hard and loud, they were able to play music and collect water as it streamed off the side of the tarpaulins. Alex told us about the recent killings in this area and what else had been happening. The East Timorese treated the guerrillas as a sort of parallel government; the people reported everything that the Indonesians were doing as it happened.

'There have been a lot of massacres and killing, but I will cite only a few,' he said, before giving me a comprehensive run-down of deaths that had occurred due to Indonesian reprisals. The families of some of his men had been killed, as well as villagers from near where they were operating— and some totally innocent people about whom the commander knew nothing. He rattled the names, dates and places off the top of his head. Every now and then he checked some detail or another with one of the other men. Someone always knew the answer.

The commander told the story of an old friend who had joined the Indonesian Army after surrendering in the late '70s. He and this former friend—Julio Fraga—found themselves commanding troops on opposite sides in the same area. A major, Fraga was the most senior East Timorese officer in the Indonesian Army in East Timor. In October of 1996, he had been killed in Baucau by the Indonesian Special Forces, Kopassus, because he had refused to assassinate Bishop Belo. According to Alex, Fraga's enraged wife had ripped the Indonesian flag from his coffin as the Army was burying him, and East Timorese conscripts from Fraga's Team Saka unit had fired large amounts of ammunition into the air to prevent the flag being replaced. An armed stand-off with other Indonesian units had ensued, with the conscripts eventually returning to their barracks.

As Alex's stories usually did, this one ended in a state-ment about the cause: 'In the case of Fraga ... who worked so hard for the promotion of [his] Indonesian officers, in the end [he was] killed. Why don't those who collaborate with the Indonesians open their eyes and see that, despite their collaboration, when they lose their enthusiasm they will kill you because you know too much?'

Often, the conscripts in the Indonesian paramilitary groups were former guerrillas who had been captured or had surrendered. Forced to move ahead of the Indonesian soldiers, they frequently came up against their former guerrilla colleagues. The month before, one of these conscripts had literally fallen into the Falintil hiding place. The guerrillas just told him to be quiet and let him go—with his weapon—so that he wouldn't raise the alarm. Some paramilitaries supplied ammunition, radios and uniforms to the guerrillas, and they often defected back to the Falintil.

Ambushes provided other weapons. Alex pointed to the pistol on his belt and laughed. They had surprised an Indonesian officer riding a motorcycle near Venilale the previous November: 'He was extremely frightened, shaking like a leaf. He expected to die. He had only been in East Timor for one month.' They let him go after disarming him.

Alex also spoke of the time they killed two Indonesian soldiers at an ambush in August 1996—English cameraman Dominic Rotheroe had been present and shot some footage that was used in a documentary.

Dominic's gear still lies in the corner. After the Indonesian soldiers were killed, he had to leave in a hurry—word had got out that there was a *malae* (foreigner) with the guerrillas. His film was smuggled out by someone else. Soon after, two civilians were killed in retaliation, and all transport was checked by the military.

I asked David Alex how frequently these kinds of clashes happened. 'Do you want to see some combat?' he asked, raising himself up.

'No, no, no ... not at all,' I stammered, thinking he was about to organise a shooting incident for me.

━━•━○━•━━

OUR LONG talk was interrupted by the arrival of an *estafeta* (messenger). Two young East Timorese men had been shot dead in a Dili suburb while walking home. One had died instantly with five bullet wounds. The other, shot four times in the chest, was taken by the Indonesian soldiers to the military hospital, where he died. They were both 20 years old. One had been wearing a BISHOP BELO NOBEL PRIZE T-shirt and that, the commander suggested, was probably why they had been shot.

Not long after that, another message came in, this time from the Baucau jail. All 71 prisoners incarcerated there had requested the Falintil commander's permission and assistance to organise their escape. Subject to torture and terrible conditions at the hands of the Indonesian authorities, they wanted to break out and join the Falintil to fight in the mountains.

David Alex vetoed the plan. A prison breakout would have played directly into the Indonesians' hands. It would have given them an excuse for a crackdown; more troops could be called into the area, and more arrests and the occasional killing could be justified to make a point to the population. The jail would be full again in a week, this time not with the men, but with their wives and families. He sent a message back to the men in the prison—the breakout was off.

His men, who sat around him in the small hole in the scrub we had all lived in for four days, couldn't look him in the eye. Many of them had been in jail and knew what it was like. At that moment, I could see how much they hated him and this hideout and the whole thing. Sitting there,

I could also see that it would just keep going on like this until all these men were dead.

⊱━◦━⊰

ALEX'S BODYGUARD started dismantling and cleaning his rifle, snapping the parts together loudly. Ceits, an older man who recorded all the communications, wiped away the muck from his eyes—most of us had conjunctivitis from washing in the same bucket of water—and began writing something. Chris mouthed the words: 'We've got to go.' And suddenly I felt very trapped.

Leaving didn't turn out to be simple. There were many other wounded men from other groups who needed medical attention, and they had been moving slowly at night across the mountains to get to David Alex's camp.

In a mix of bad Portuguese and Spanish, Chris spoke to David Alex. 'We're out of medicine,' he told the commander. 'I can't do anything else until we get more, and John is out of film—he can't do anything, he needs to get back to send his report.' It felt like he was pleading for our release. Alex went into a long explanation with his men and messengers were sent off to organise transport and secure a way out.

In the meantime, he gave Chris money to buy and send back more medicine from Dili. They settled into a long discussion about how to use certain drugs for particular ailments, and what needed to be bought from the Indonesian pharmacies in Dili.

The money Chris took from the commander was a great wad of tattered small-denomination notes, donated to the fighters by the East Timorese people. Although poor, these people wanted to support the guerrillas, and did so with food and what little money they could spare. Some families could give as little as 500 rupiah—equivalent to about 30 cents at that time.

⊱────◦────◦────◦────◦⊰

WE EMERGED from the claustrophobic hole in the scrub after four days and nights. After a few steps out onto the bright moonlit plateau, I turned around and looked at where we'd come from. There was no trace of the 12 armed men and their camp that I knew were just behind me.

⊱────◦────◦────◦────◦⊰

THREE HOURS later we arrived, drenched in sweat, at a series of bamboo houses. Dogs started barking and our guide—Jose Belo—disappeared. When he returned, we followed him in the darkness to one of the huts, trying to walk as quietly as possible past the other houses, as he did. We couldn't risk being seen because, in this tiny group of five or six huts, there was a family the Falintil didn't trust; the father was an East Timorese who worked for the Indonesian civil service.

Inside the hut we'd been taken to we were welcomed by a bright electric light and a table set for a meal. Traditional woven East Timorese fabric was tacked onto the wall to stop any light showing through the thin bamboo slats. Three women stood to one side of the table, beaming as Jose introduced us in whispers. They nodded and gently shook our hands.

Although it was 2 am, they served us a generous meal of rice, noodles and kuru—a cucumber-like vegetable. While we ate, the husband of one of the women came in, tense and exasperated. He rushed over to his wife who was standing to one side, as all women do in rural East Timor when the men eat. I observed the conversation, thinking it was about us.

'Don't worry,' said Jose, 'he's talking about their baby—it is sick. We are safe here, don't worry,' he said, continuing to eat.

'What's wrong with the baby?' asked Chris, also between mouthfuls of food.

Jose asked the woman, who wouldn't answer. She told us not to worry, but to eat. She knew Chris was a doctor. They had just been introduced. The husband told us that the baby had been vomiting black blood.

'Kidney failure, maybe,' said Chris. 'I might be able to do something.'

'Where is the baby?' he asked them. 'Can we go there?'

He stood up to grab his bag, causing a commotion.

'No, no. You must finish your meal,' they whispered. 'You can't go out. Wait here. Sit down, sit down.'

Jose told us to be quiet, but Chris, annoyed at what he thought was the excessive politeness of these people, wanted to go to the baby. He thought he could help; he had to, he should. Just like me, he was feeling trapped and claustrophobic.

But the reason they didn't want Chris to go to the baby had nothing to do with politeness; it was about the survival of the whole village. A lumbering white man turns up in the middle of the night to help a sick child. Where had he come from? What was he doing here? If the Indonesians had found out—perhaps from an untrustworthy neighbour—the next day the soldiers would have come and burned down the village, arrested the men and done whatever they liked with the women. It was simply too high a price to pay for one child's life.

A compromise was reached: the husband would go and make sure the way was clear, come back, and then Chris could go and see the child. An hour later the husband returned.

'The baby is dead,' he said, facing Chris, not his wife. Jose translated, but he hadn't needed to. Chris looked more distraught than the parents.

When there is a death in an East Timorese family, the body is traditionally laid out in the family's house. Relatives and friends gather to see the body, and the wailing and singing of the women goes on for hours. The wailing, called *lelir*, is like a combination of sobbing and mournful singing.

Later, when the people were openly opposing the Indonesians, reporters like me were always ushered to the front of the crowd. Ears full of the horrible cries, we would photograph or write down the name of the victim laid out in front of us. Usually, in these situations, the body was a bloody mess; often, the skull was smashed, a military bullet having ripped through it. And despite the condition of her son's body, the mother would still embrace the bloody remains—a pulped mess of hair and bone and tissue—and the family would not shy away. They would make us photograph it, to document it, to show how their son or husband or brother had died. That was how the Timorese honoured their dead and dealt with the grief—openly and loudly.

But there would be no such ceremony for the baby who died that night. Because of us, they couldn't have risked it. The others in the hut just stood and stared, watching for Chris's reaction with concern. They didn't know what the unpredictable foreigner might do. But they did know what would happen if we were discovered in their house. Jose looked somehow relieved that the baby had died. He'd had orders to keep us in this house; he didn't want Chris running around the village in the darkness.

THE NEXT morning, Jose was suffering with malaria. His eyes were streaming, his nose was running, and he was sweating profusely. A car was being arranged for the next leg to Dili, and we weren't allowed to go outside. In an error of judgment, I can see now, I did a wide-ranging interview with Jose about his experiences, to pass the time. He whispered into my tape recorder.

Listening to it later, I was disturbed. I could just hear the chickens in the yard and the occasional passing motorbike in between grabs of the loud Portuguese soccer commentary from the radio our hosts had turned on to camouflage our voices. And then, there was Jose's weakly whispered dialogue. In between sniffs and weak coughs, he said things such as: 'We here know we are going to die—but at least we die knowing we fight for peace and justice.' A pause. A laboured breath. 'Those of you who have left, who jump the walls of embassies, who will stop the Indonesians raping our women, I want to tell you to return to fight. If we here die, we must be replaced. In the prisons they still kill us, they still torture us, they still violate us ...'

Jose continued in this way for the full 90 minutes' duration of the tape, sometimes not making any sense, other times lucid, delivering heroic phrases. I asked him what his plans for the future were, when East Timor was free.

'I will seek asylum in another country or stay in the mountains,' he said, either not understanding the question, or having no concept of an East Timor where to live in the towns was to live without being terrorised by the Indonesians.

The car arrived and we drove back to Dili at dusk. But that journey was without fear of confrontations at the Indonesian military posts—we were just dirty tourists who had scored a lift with a car full of young men. Dirty tourists on our way to Bali.

PEDRO WAS ecstatic. We were back in Dili. We were safe. He was safe. The 'immigration officials' had only visited once after we left and accepted that we had gone travelling around. He hid the films I gave him gleefully.

'This'll bloody shit the Indonesians. No guerrillas here my bloody arse, mate,' he said, laughing.

We washed and sent Pedro's son for beers, then spent the evening drinking. It had all gone fine. No-one had been hurt. No-one had been caught. I had a good story and could afford to relax a little. Chris, instead of racing back to resume his holiday in Bali, talked about organising medical supplies.

AFTER A few days in Dili, I headed off to Ermera on a public bus, then got a lift on a truck to Letefoho, high up in the central mountains. The parish priest there—Father Domingos Soares—was known to be outspoken, and I went to see him. It was late in the day, so he invited me to stay the night. The village was beautiful. It reminded me of Nepal, with its low, squat buildings and thatched roofs. It was cool in the mountains and the mist rolled in late in the afternoon. There seemed to be no Indonesian troops in the area; quite a contrast to Baucau and Dili at that time.

Over dinner, Father Soares quizzed me about who I knew and who I was. After a few beers, he loosened up. 'What the people need here are guns to defend themselves,' he said angrily, his manner changing after I'd admired the new computer the church had sent him.

He talked about the troops who came through the

villages at night and pretended to be guerrillas. They would knock on the door and ask for food. If the villagers helped, uniformed soldiers would return the next day and arrest them. The previous few nights, the Indonesians had been killing the village dogs because the people had stopped answering their doors after dark.

I headed back to Dili the next day.

CHRIS CAME out to meet me as I walked up the road to Pedro's. He was agitated.

'It's fucked. They've got photos of you and me with the guerrillas. I just missed them yesterday, they've been here asking questions.'

'They came twice yesterday. I've been at the ICRC. Your stuff is packed—I'll see you at the Resende,' he said, referring to a hotel in the centre of Dili.

Pedro had already fended off two lengthy visits from Intel agents looking for us. 'I told them I had no idea you were not tourists,' he said. 'Let's face it, all you did here in Dili was drink beer. I told them that.' He was joking, but he was nervous—about what they could do to his family. I said goodbye, grabbed my films and left.

Chris was sitting in the restaurant at the Resende. It was the best restaurant in town and in those days full of wealthy Indonesian businessmen. At night, the Indonesian officers would perform karaoke there. He had already bought a ticket to Denpasar, and was leaving in an hour.

Somehow, one of the guides or the locals who had visited the camp had taken photos of us and then tried to have them developed in Dili, and the Indonesians had intercepted them. At least that was what Chris thought. I just thought it was a spy paid off by the Indonesians. Either way, Chris wasn't sticking around to find out. (After we'd left, Pedro was called in for questioning and was shown the photos; they did exist.)

A car pulled up outside the Resende and Chris froze. It was the same one that had been outside Pedro's the day before when the Intel had been there. Two men got out and headed for the door. We ran out the back, hailed a cab and went a short way. Chris got out and hailed another cab. I went to the bus station and he went to the airport.

That night at the West Timor border the guard lost interest in me after I'd bought him a beer. He spent his time checking the other passengers and baggage. Chris was followed from the airport in Denpasar and roughed up in town by some men with short military haircuts. They told him never to go to East Timor again.

CHAPTER TWO

31 May 1997
Jakarta, Indonesia

THE US EMBASSY official was excited: 'It's the Timorese Tet. They've shown that no matter what they do, the Indonesians can't control the guerrillas. They attacked right in the centre of Dili. I think that was a very significant attack.'

Edmund McWilliams was essentially assigned to watch the situation in East Timor and the Indonesian democracy movement. At a function at his house in Jakarta, surrounded by American democracy activists who had just attempted to monitor yet another Suharto win in the Indonesian general elections, he was comparing the current conflict to Vietnam. When the communists in Vietnam attacked urban targets, including the US Embassy, in downtown Saigon on the last night of January 1968, it showed the world that the US and conventional military power could not win a guerrilla war. That was what had happened with the Falintil raid in the centre of Dili, said

McWilliams, and he went on to speculate how the Indonesians would respond.

'They can only increase the pressure to stop these attacks, which will only increase the resentment and prolong the conflict,' he said loudly, speaking over the Janis Joplin CD his wife was playing on the stereo—it enhanced the US college politics atmosphere of the gathering.

The guerrillas had attacked the Dili headquarters of Brimob—the Indonesian riot police—in Bairo Pite the night before the elections. Two Indonesian police were killed and four wounded in a gun battle which lasted for several hours and ranged across Dili. It was the first time they had attacked in the city since the early '80s and there was further violence at the poll booths in the central town of Ermera on election day.

Andrew McNaughtan, an Australian doctor who had been thrown out of East Timor several times when trying to document human rights abuses, joined our conversation to say that he'd heard from East Timorese people in Darwin that a further 17 Indonesian police and one soldier had been killed in a grenade attack on a police truck near the town of Baucau that day.

I knew that such an attack in that particular area could only have been carried out with the authority of David Alex.

Even though there were no journalists in East Timor to report the situation, the guerrillas' strategy had worked. Knowing there was a large contingent of international media in Jakarta covering the election and its predictable outcome, it was a good time for the pro-independence movement to get some attention. Despite the price they were going to have to pay.

▷┄◄▷┄◇┄◁┄◄

I'D HAD a few late-night reverse-charge phone calls from Jose to my house in Sydney with news of an arrest or some shootings, and a note from Pedro telling me not to come back because of the photos taken of myself with Falintil. Aside from that, I hadn't had any contact with the resistance since I'd left in January.

East Timor was officially closed to journalists. The resident Jakarta correspondents had been denied permission by the Indonesian authorities to travel with Australian Ambassador John McCarthy during his upcoming visit to the province.

The next day, after arranging with Andrew McNaughtan to do what he could to inform the resistance people, I left for East Timor.

⊱━◦━⊰

ATAMBUA HAD never been a pleasant place for foreigners. The last major town in Indonesian West Timor before the border, it served as a military base for the Indonesian military campaign—three months of border incursions and attacks—that preceded the December 1975 invasion.

And it had stayed a military town since then, complete with the ominous series of huge statues of Indonesian troops charging east towards the border. Standing at major intersections in the flat, sprawling town, they looked like the work of a stray Soviet social-realist sculptor.

During the day, school children marched in formation and sang the Indonesian national anthem. The red and white Indonesian flags hung from buildings and poles everywhere. The place had an air of aggressive overcompensation about it, putting its Indonesian identity on constant display. But that hadn't stopped the mainly Indonesian-Chinese shop-owners from trading across the border. Over in East Timor, goods were always overpriced and in short supply.

⊷⊶⊙⊷⊶

THE NIGHT bus from the West Timor capital of Kupang stopped in Atambua at 3 am to wait until dawn. In the small wooden shack where passengers waited and drank coffee, a group of belligerent young men questioned and baited me: 'What are you doing in Dili? You are a journalist—the guerrillas will kill you. They are killing people again. Why you go there?' And on and on.

I was tired and walked outside. 'When you get to Dili, speak to Eduardo at the polytechnic—he has much information.' The voice was coming from inside the stationary bus.

When I asked the man what he'd said, he just repeated it through the window in an even more earnest whisper, then turned away and pretended to be asleep. I went back to the shack to get more coffee and face more questions.

⊷⊶⊙⊷⊶

'WHAT'S WRONG—what's happened?' was all the man at the Hotel Dili said. 'Uh, nothing. I just wanted a room,' I said. He pointed around the back and then left, looking at military trucks passing on the street.

Later in the day, after racking my brains about who to try to contact with such a massive crackdown taking place, I went to the Hotel Mahkota. The ugly Indonesian government-run hotel was like a concrete and aluminium block dumped across the road from Dili Harbour in the centre of town. The interior reminded me of hotels in Eastern Europe, but behind the reception counter were pictures of Suharto and the vice-president, Try Sutrisno.

I knew from the guerrillas that one of the hotel employees worked for them and would inform them of my arrival. But I didn't know he had already been caught by the Indonesians after falling asleep and failing to collect a sensitive fax from the machine. One of his co-workers had read the fax and handed him over to the authorities.

The place was deserted. In the dining room the karaoke machine, normally a favourite of the Indonesian officers, was packed up. The Javanese waiter who brought me coffee sat down to talk but kept looking around nervously. He started talking about Dili and what was happening.

'You know they came right into Dili,' he said. I asked him if he felt safe. 'For me it is okay, I am at the hotel. But my wife, she doesn't feel safe sometimes. She hasn't left the house in the last week, since the attacks.'

He added that he didn't really think the money was worth it, although he received more than double what he received at home. 'Maybe another few months, and I will go,' he said.

An Indonesian businessman walked in and the waiter went over to serve him. The man opened his briefcase on the table, pulled a pistol out of his belt and put it in the case. I'd never seen that in Dili before.

⊱┈◉┈⊰

AT THE other major hotel in town, the Tourismo, I went to meet Tom Lyndhal, a Finnish journalist who had left Jakarta at the same time as I had, but had flown straight into Dili.

'No, the schoolteacher left today for Bali. He didn't leave any message,' the desk clerk told me. Tom later told me that the harassment he'd received from Indonesian intelligence was such that he left after a day. Like the Mahkota, the

Tourismo was empty—except for the Intel in the foyer. They followed me out the gate.

I wandered for hours until I was sure I had lost them. The few people in the street looked down when I passed, some even crossed the road. I hailed the most broken-down taxi I could find.

As it got dark, the streets emptied. Armoured trucks full of Brimob troops with their riot shields, padded vests and M-16s started driving around central Dili's grid of one-way streets.

Out in the eastern suburb of Becora, the only sign of life was the Indonesian satay and noodle stalls near the 744 military base. I asked the driver to turn into Pedro's driveway and wait, and I ran around the back.

'What the fuck are you doing here?!' was Pedro's greeting to me. 'You didn't get my letter? Don't you know what's going on? They've got Ximenes [leader of the clandestine movement], John [Malanno, our previous contact with the guerillas] has disappeared, everybody else has gone. Since the attacks they've been shooting around here every night. We don't know if they're coming for us or not.

'Are you all right? Did they see you come? Jesus, what are you doing here, John?' It all spilled out in Pedro's rapid-fire English. Then he stopped and told one of his daughters to see who was driving the car that had brought me.

They had the house boarded up so no light showed in the street. Needless to say, there were no 'tourists' staying at Pedro's guesthouse at that time.

Pedro calmed down a little when his daughter returned and told him who was driving. He was Timorese and they thought he was okay.

'Look, John, they called me in three times after you left,' he continued. 'They showed me the photos of you and David Alex. I just told them I didn't know. But you really can't stay here now. Not now. They have been arresting people around here every night since that attack in Bairo Pite, and now that John has disappeared, we think they might know about everything.'

Since January, Pedro had continued to provide accommodation to activists and journalists. A group of Melbourne University students and a team from the ABC's *Foreign Correspondent* program had stayed there and gone to meet David Alex. He was worried the Indonesian intelligence would torture John and link him to Pedro. He was worried for his wife, three daughters and his small son. I left feeling terrible, hoping that no-one had seen the visit and that the cab driver could be trusted. 'Of all the bloody people to turn up now,' Pedro said and finally laughed. He added that he would try to send someone to the hotel, but that it would be difficult.

AT THE Hotel Dili, one man sat in the run-down and overgrown courtyard the original Australian owners had intended to be a beer garden. He was an Indonesian doctor based in Ermera. On 29 May—the day of the Indonesian national elections—guerrillas had attacked the polling stations in the highlands town. An Indonesian officer had been killed in the attack and, because of that, another crackdown was going on there.

The doctor was drinking beer alone and invited me to join him. 'I have good relations with the people,' he said. 'I am the only doctor, but I am worried about my safety at the moment—the people they are angry. Any Indonesian, no matter what his or her attitude, is in danger—especially at night,' he said.

He continued to tell me how the people had become

incensed and defiant after the attack. When they saw the guerrillas shoot the officer, they shouted abuse at the Indonesian soldiers as they ran away. 'It scared me. I know these people. I've worked with them every day for over a year,' he said, adding that he would wait in Dili until things had calmed down.

We sat drinking the warm beer in silence broken only by the roar of a three-truck military convoy as it drove around and around the centre of Dili. It eventually passed on the foreshore road in front of the hotel, and we heard it, the only traffic, travel straight down the road and out to the western suburbs.

It wasn't yet nine o'clock, but everything was quiet. Nothing moved on the street and the waiter had closed the bar and disappeared. The doctor wished me good night and we went to our rooms in separate wings of the hotel—the only two guests.

Later that night I was woken by the sound of gunfire, continuous volleys of three to four rounds for over an hour. It sounded like it was coming from within a few streets away. I moved the mattress onto the floor away from the windows and went back to sleep.

▷┈◆┈◦┈◆┈◁

AMNESTY INTERNATIONAL in London was issuing urgent action reports for East Timor that week that stated over 100 individuals had been arrested by the Indonesian authorities and at least 42 people—civilians, Indonesian military and police, and Falintil guerrillas—had been killed in the attacks and their aftermath. At the end of the report was the paragraph attached to all their East Timor appeals: 'Torture or ill-treatment of political detainees in East Timor in both police or military custody is routine . . .' The blurb always ended with the statement that restrictions were placed by Indonesian authorities on access to East Timor for independent human rights monitors.

As for reporting these arrests and killings as they happened, the problem was that the only people who could or would tell a foreign journalist about them were inevitably next on the list.

But hiding on the floor in an empty hotel was not the way to get information. I'd done this before in East Timor in 1995, waiting for a contact from the guerrillas to come to see me and Daniel Pedersen, another Australian journalist.

We had waited for a week in the Hotel Dili, attracting so much attention from Indonesian intelligence and getting so used to them, we began to give those assigned to watch us stupid names and invite them in for drinks. By the time the contact eventually turned up, we were extremely wary and didn't believe his claimed identity for several days.

In the end we didn't get the interview with the guerrillas because by the time we were confident of the contact it was too late and they had been forced to move by Indonesian troop activity.

The next morning I got up early and went to the polytechnic in Hera, four kilometres out of town. I thought: screw it, if that guy on the bus in Atambua was a spy, I'll get arrested and deported. If not, I'll get information on what's going on. I didn't want to risk seeing Pedro again and I wasn't sure how long I could wander around Dili before I'd get hauled in for questioning.

The Indonesian administration liked to point to the brand new, well-equipped technical college they had built outside of Dili as a symbol of their positive presence in East Timor. They also knew the place was a hotbed of independence activity. But they'd left it alone to keep the myth of their benign development alive. (Two years later, the militia and military laid siege to the place and destroyed it—a good four months before they destroyed the rest of the country.)

I found Eduardo who the stranger on the bus had sent me to speak to, easily enough. He was in what looked like a woodwork class, and just walked out when he was told I was there to see him.

In his room in the student quarters there was enough evidence lying on the desk to have him jailed for sedition. He showed me photos of Indonesian soldiers torturing East Timorese people. 'Here, take them, they're copies,' he said, throwing some across to me. I had seen some of them before on the Foreign Editor's desk at the *Sydney Morning Herald*.

I had already vouched for their authenticity in Australia, but I had to ask Eduardo where he got them from. 'We bought them from the Indonesians,' he said. 'It's not very expensive—they take them anyway, and they want us to know what they are doing. That's the point.'

There had been some argument in Australia as to whether the photos were authentic or staged by pro-independence activists. Although one set did look like it had been set up, there was no doubt about the others. The ones showing a metal pipe being shoved down a Timorese man's throat could not have been faked. In Eduardo's room in East Timor, the photos scared the hell out of me. It occurred to me that Eduardo and his colleagues could easily be the next subjects of photos like these—later that day or the next if my visit were to be discovered. I wondered if the Indonesians would do the same to me. I didn't take any of the photos with me.

Video cameras, photos of guerrillas and bits and pieces of military equipment were scattered around the room. Three other young men arrived and squeezed in. 'Who are you?

What do you want?' they demanded. When I told them my name, they asked me how to spell it and wanted to see my passport. I showed them. 'So you're John Martinkus. How the hell did they let you in?'

'They always asked us about three of you—Max Stahl, Matthew Jardine and you,' said Eduardo. At first I felt honoured, then stupid—I realised I was the only journalist on their list who was using his real name. It was something Eduardo noticed, too. 'Get another passport,' he said disdainfully. He seemed to be used to giving orders.

When I asked about the attack on the police station, they all burst in to give their story: 'He was there—he saw it start with the machete.' 'No, I was in the other street, where were you? . . .'

The story that came out went something like this: the attack had been carried out by student activists working with guerrillas who had come down with weapons from the hills. The rest were armed only with machetes, and the attack started when two of them simply walked up to the guard post, hacked into the two guards with their machetes and ran away. Those were two of the police who were wounded. After that, all hell broke loose and the Falintil guerrillas opened up with their weapons, killing two police and wounding another two. What followed was a long, drawn-out chase and shoot-out in the streets around the police headquarters. As the police reacted, the activists and guerrillas tried to get away. According to reports at the time, four were killed.

What happened during the nights following the attack was predictable enough. The Indonesian police, military and SGI operatives went from house to house in Dili making arrests. David Dias Ximenes, leader of the clandes-tine movement in Dili, was picked up by the Indonesians on 31 May. The arrests continued throughout the next week. Eduardo and his friends gave me the details of a few other arrests they knew about. They had all taken place around 4 am in the predominantly East Timorese suburb of Becora on the eastern side of Dili. The suburb where Pedro lived.

Four fresh graves had appeared overnight in the Hera cemetery near the polytechnic. They bore no names or markings, and no-one saw who had been buried. Nobody went out at night except the military, and the students thought they knew who was in the graves—four of their number who had disappeared after the attack. The students wanted to dig up the graves, but there was a military post nearby. It would have been suicidal.

Eduardo told me I had to go to Baucau—130 kilometres east—the next day. They would try to get me information from David Alex or, if possible, arrange another meeting.

<hr>

As I slept back in Dili that night someone burned down the central market; shots were fired and more Timorese arrested. The Indonesians blamed the guerrillas, who denied involvement. Either way, in the morning there was a feeling of tension in town, and if the desired effect of the fire had been designed to terrorise the population, it had worked.

The cab driver wanted to take me past the debris. I redirected him, thinking he was trying to rip me off, but he was just trying to show me what was going on.

<hr>

On the bus to Baucau, I saw the guy who had sent me to Eduardo at the polytechnic. He was trying to be inconspicuous and held the front door open for me. When I jumped in beside him, all he said was, 'Don't look at me or speak to anyone. Just look out the window.'

Almost three hours later as we passed the military airport on the outskirts of Baucau he spoke for the first time. 'Those two stones over there is where they shot him last Friday,' he said. This man's name turned out to be Alphonse and he quickly ran through the details of the killing, giving me the name and age of the victim and the time at which it had happened. It was just another Kopassus operation. They had been killing and arresting people known to have connections with the resistance since the attack on the truck, which Alphonse told me was carried out by David Alex.

Outside Baucau at a place called Fatumaca, there is a statue of the Virgin Mary where people have claimed to have had visions. Alphonse said that if anybody asked me where I was going, I should say the statue. Then he left me at the dusty and almost deserted bus terminal in Baucau.

Off to one side there were two dilapidated *warungs* or stalls serving cold chicken, rice and leaves. I waited inside and watched for the bus.

Two young East Timorese walked in and watched me eat. They were bored and hot, and wanted to know what I was doing there. I asked them where they were going. Viqueque, they said. But they didn't seem to care whether the bus came or not. They looked across the empty bus terminal as another military truck pulled out of the base across the road. 'We are the ones they are killing,' said one of them, motioning towards the truck. 'They are trying to kill us every night in Baucau, so we go there, Viqueque, every night.' He shrugged and leaned back, putting his feet up. Neither looked more than 20, but they talked and acted as though they were a lot older. We sat in silence staring out at the hot and dusty terminal until the bus arrived.

THE BUS driver let me off at a side road and pointed to where the statue was. I'd been here before in January with one of David Alex's men.

It was a long walk to the statue. The flat road was parallel to the mountains, which were covered in bush. There was no-one else on the road; it was the middle of the day and the sun was blindingly hot. At a fork in the road beside a small hut, a child ran out to greet me. He ran up to me and put something in my hand. I looked up—there was still no-one else in sight. The child giggled and ran away. It was a note: 'Congratulations Mr John, you have all the information you need in Dili.' I stood there sweating, thinking it was a cruel joke after the long, hot walk and Eduardo would come out of the house. But there was no-one there and the child had disappeared.

SOME INDONESIANS driving a Coca-Cola truck gave me a lift back to Baucau and told me to be off the road before dark.

Back in Eduardo's room at the polytechnic the next day, he laughed. 'We have to be careful,' he said, and produced letters from Jose Belo and a short one from David Alex. We started to translate them. The commander and Jose both wrote about the increasing instability of their position with a large Indonesian military offensive underway called *Operasi Gerakan Tuntas* (Operation Extermination). It involved Battalions 744 and 312, Kopassus special forces and the locally raised Rajawahli and Team Saka units near Baucau and the town of Quelicai—near where their attack of 31 May had taken place.

The guerrillas were suffering badly in this response to their attack. They wanted me to organise a return visit by the doctor, as several men had been wounded in recent fighting.

Jose Belo, who rather dramatically signed off, 'from the jungles of East Timor', wrote: 'The situation here is very hard right now. Everywhere there are so many Indonesian soldiers and police. But our chief commandante of Falintil [Konis Santana] has stated that we should keep fighting because on 19 June there will be a new round of negotiations between Portugal and Indonesia under the auspices of the UN Secretary-General.'

They couldn't meet me—they were running and hiding for their lives near where I'd been yesterday. They had wanted to check my identity; no doubt someone on that hill had vouched for me.

▻—◅▻—◦—◅▻—◅

THAT NIGHT my nerve cracked as I tried to send a fax from the government-run Telkom centre. It was the only place in Dili with an international fax line, and as I stood in the queue a group of Indonesian and East Timorese soldiers walked in. They wore black fatigues with no identifying badges or insignia and carried automatic rifles. They were sweating heavily and appeared agitated. The Indonesian staff looked worried and even the other military personnel, who always hung around the building at night to call home to other parts of Indonesia, looked uncomfortable.

The troops, who were the Kopassus-trained hit squads known as ninjas, yelled at the staff and one of them pushed his way into a booth and made a call. It was as if frontline troops on patrol had walked straight into a peaceful government office. The East Timorese among the troops—easy to spot—would later form the nucleus of the militias. But at that time they were still in their covert stage, getting plenty of practice carrying out the kind of killing the world would find so abhorrent more than two years later.

Those guys scared the shit out of me. So I decided the fax in my pocket—which detailed some of their work—could wait until I got to Kupang the next day.

TWO WEEKS later, I was back in Kupang. I had been waiting in Bali for Chris, the English doctor, to arrive. We had planned to go back to East Timor following David Alex's request for more medical assistance. But at the last minute Chris had been denied entry into Indonesia and had flown back to Singapore. I returned to Kupang to keep a meeting in Dili with the resistance people, to tell them the bad news.

But there was more bad news—worse in fact than that. I heard about it in a seedy Kupang waterside bar, Teddy's. Two loud, drunken yachtsmen were saying David Alex had been captured and killed the previous day. I left immediately in search of a newspaper. There it was, the *Jakarta Post*'s version of his death. The military were claiming he had died as a result of wounds received when he was captured. But wire-service reports claimed he had died during torture, and other reports were quoted as saying he died in a helicopter ride from Baucau to Dili following his capture.

I left on the night bus to Dili, hoping the people I was to meet would still be there.

EDUARDO WASN'T at the house; he had left for Kupang. His two colleagues were scared stiff. I had arrived on their doorstep at first light. They had been up all night, waiting, with an old weapon, three rounds of ammunition and a video camera. They had anticipated being picked up by the military trucks still circling the area. They were sure David Alex's arrest would bring the military to them. I knew straight away I shouldn't have come.

They told me to get out, pushing me to the back of the house and outside to a drainage ditch. I waited there with one of them while the other went off to find some transport or instructions on what to do with me.

Watching nervously from the top of the ditch, the guy who stayed told me what they knew to have happened. It wasn't David Alex's body that had been buried. An ICRC representative had told the resistance that, after insisting on seeing the body of the Falintil leader, the one he was shown did not look like David Alex.

Then, when the Indonesians were burying the supposed Falintil leader, the ICRC had tried to have the coffin opened. But the military commander in Dili, the Danrem (Lieutenant Colonel Slamet Sidabatur) had refused them permission and the box was buried without being opened. The grave had been guarded since, they said.

⊱⊱⊷⊶⊙⊷⊶⊰

I WAITED all morning until a truck eventually arrived. The Indonesians were watching the bus terminal at Tacitolu, so I was driven further out of town towards Liquiça. I waited there in a hut.

The other passengers on the bus had all seen me board outside Dili, but no-one said a word to the Indonesian troops who ordered them off the bus at the border. The small kid who came around asking for the identification cards stopped and stared at me. Instead of my passport, I gave him 100,000 rupiah (about Aus$40), as I'd been told to do. That was for the guards. I sank lower in the back seat behind cases of beer and sacks of rice, praying they wouldn't inspect the bus. One by one, the passengers got back on. They had been searched and questioned. It was happening everywhere in East Timor and often, the soldiers would make them undress, look for bullet wounds or other marks. But thankfully that night, the soldiers weren't interested, weren't doing their job as thoroughly as they had been ordered to. The bus was allowed to pass, without my presence—which could have been used as an excuse to interrogate and detain everybody—being noticed.

━━◦━━

EDUARDO WAS waiting outside the Telkom centre in Kupang the next day. He arranged to meet me later. He was very nervous and, by this stage his paranoia was infectious.

I moved to an obscure hotel in the suburbs and waited until later that day when I met up with him again at Teddy's bar. He was reading a newspaper with studied indifference, and didn't glance up when I came in. I had a beer at the bar, chatting about nothing with the untrustworthy, drunken Australian yachting crowd. When I'd finished the drink, he walked out and I followed at a distance.

At the beach he brought me up to date with everything he knew. He even provided me with the name of the Indonesian intelligence officer who had spoken to David Alex after his capture, and said the Falintil leader was only lightly wounded. His account was precise and included times and the names of units and individuals involved. Eduardo's people believed the Indonesians had declared David Alex dead and rushed through a bogus funeral so they could hold him and interrogate him at will.

━━◦━━

UP TO 1,000 Indonesian troops from six different battalions had been involved in the operation in which Alex was captured in a cave four kilometres from Baucau. Jose Belo was one of the five who had been captured with him, and the last information Eduardo had had about him was that he had been beaten badly; his limp body was last seen dumped in a small cell at the Kopassus headquarters at Kota Baru in Baucau. Similar treatment was reported to have been meted out by Kopassus to the other four captured with them, and a further 14 Falintil fighters who had been brought in the previous day as part of the same operation.

Eduardo gave me a copy of the last letter they had received from Alex. It described the worsening situation. Troops had begun burning down houses of suspected resistance sympathisers in Baucau, Laga (20 kilometres east of Baucau) and Quelicai. Five civilians had been executed outside the military cemetery in Baucau on 17 June. Alex wrote how the dead had to be exhumed from their shallow graves because dogs were digging up the corpses and eating them. Women were raped after being forced to strip at road blocks in the area. The letter was dated 22 June—three days before his capture.

Australia's new ambassador to Indonesia, John McCarthy, happened to be in East Timor for his first visit when Alex was captured. He described the mood in the territory at the time as one of 'unease and discomfort'. The Australian Embassy in Jakarta reported that it was understood Alex had died and had subsequently been buried.

><><><><

I SAW Eduardo the next morning. He couldn't pay his hotel bill in Kupang and was under orders to return to Dili.

I offered to pay for a few extra days of accommodation for him, thinking it would be too dangerous for him to go back at that time. But he had work to do. I had seen him at the Telkom centre faxing something—probably information to the various overseas support networks and human rights groups. Because no other information was getting out at the time there was a huge responsibility on Eduardo's shoulders.

He told me he would send all the details he could about the continuing crackdown to where I was staying in Jakarta, and gave me some East Timorese contacts there. But he said to be careful, as these people were often watched by the Indonesian military intelligence.

He asked me for my spare tape recorder, which I gave him, and we said goodbye, promising we'd work together again in the future.

The next day, some of the permanent Australian residents I'd met in the two bars in Kupang let me know the local authorities had been asking a lot of questions about what I'd been doing. These same residents didn't like to stir up trouble in their little corner of Indonesia, and advised me to leave. 'Accidents happen in this town, son,' said one old Australian, going on to remind me of a young Australian who was killed in Kupang for promoting a rival bar to the one with military links in which we were drinking.

<hr/>

IN JAKARTA, I got out of the taxi on a nearby corner, too tired to give the driver exact directions to the place I was staying. It had been a frustrating day. I hadn't yet received the promised information from Eduardo with details of David Alex's capture and the wave of arrests of resistance members taking place and the contacts he'd given me in Jakarta weren't answering my calls.

Realising I had no cigarettes, I turned to walk to the market. And from the corner of my eye I saw five figures pull away from the fence of a nearby house they'd been leaning against.

The jagged football-sized piece of concrete caught me squarely in the centre of my back. Just as I turned, another piece hit me in the temple. Blood flowed into my eyes as the first of the men kicked me hard in the stomach, followed by blows from all directions.

My legs were kicked out from under me and I fell heavily to the ground. As they continued to kick me, I lost consciousness. Judging by the bruises that came out the next day, they must have continued the assault for some time. There were bruises along my forearms. I'd tried to block the blows to my head; the broken nose, black eyes and deep cuts to my face made it obvious I hadn't been very successful. My ribs and back ached, and I knew I was concussed—the nausea and head spins were a sure sign of that.

I remembered regaining consciousness with the police hauling me to my feet. They propped me against their car and demanded to see my passport. The five men in plain clothes who carried out the attack were still there— standing around smoking Kretek clove cigarettes and joking with the police. I started yelling at a police officer, demanding to know what the fuck was going on. One of them silenced me, his forearm clamped across my throat, pinning me to the car. After checking the passport and writing my name in a notebook, he handed the passport back to me, said something that raised a laugh from the others, and punched me in the stomach, causing me to vomit.

The same guys who had just beaten me up carried me to a car and drove the short distance to where they'd been waiting for me, in front of the house I'd arranged to stay at. As I fumbled to open the lock on the gate, the policeman smiled and said something that amused everybody. Something like, 'Now you just go fuck off.'

CHAPTER THREE

9 August 1998
Dili, East Timor

FOURTEEN MONTHS LATER, I walked into the Tourismo not even sure whether to ask at the desk for Andrew McNaughtan, the Australian doctor. I was still too paranoid to let the Indonesians know I was back in Dili. I'd bring attention to myself if I met with him, and I was sure he'd be followed. A neat young man wearing glasses, an ironed white shirt, trousers and slip-on shoes walked up to me and introduced himself as Felize. He was handling press relations for the student solidarity council. 'I presume you are with the press or an activist,' he said in perfect English, 'Here is a copy of our program.' I was stunned. 'Do you know someone called Andrew?' I asked.

'Yes, of course. He's in the garden,' Felize replied and excused himself to make a call on his mobile.

Andrew was wolfing down a meal in the hotel's garden which, for once, seemed almost half-full of East Timorese.

Waiters were serving beer and food, and people were talking loudly in groups around tables. Previously, I'd only ever seen the place deserted or full of Indonesians. I'd never noticed how pleasant it was. Tables with red Bintang Beer umbrellas were scattered throughout the well-established tropical garden. The luxury wing of the hotel with its wide balcony ran along two sides of the garden, providing plenty of shade in the afternoon.

Sitting at a table and surrounded by mostly male students from East Timor's Student Solidarity Council, Andrew was sunburnt and his hair unkempt. He'd spent the day riding around in the back of a truck filming the latest of the students' free speech dialogues—a reaction to the apparent unprecedented tolerance to free speech of the new Habibie government in Jakarta. They had begun travelling around East Timor waving pro-independence banners, shouting slogans and singing pro-independence songs. In the past, such behaviour would have brought an instant brutal response from the Indonesians. But things had changed over the past year and the turmoil surrounding the fall of Suharto during the Jakarta riots in May seemed to have temporarily stunned the military and intelligence operatives in Dili into inaction.

A series of huge demonstrations led by the Student Solidarity Council in Dili throughout June and July had challenged Indonesian authority—successfully, it seemed. Thousands had marched in support of a referendum after the new Indonesian president, Dr B.J. Habibie, offered a vague form of special autonomy to East Timor. For Habibie, it was as a way of confirming his reform credentials to the international community after taking over from Suharto. He wanted to be seen to be addressing what was a major international problem for Indonesia—East Timor. The offer basically handed the East Timorese control of everything except defence, foreign affairs and finance. No more specific details had been given.

So early in August 1998, the students' campaign had been taken to the countryside. They organised themselves into councils and mini-councils, and installed themselves in the Tourismo Hotel foyer and garden. Indonesian intelligence operatives still made regular appearances there, but the students just ignored them and went about making sure that any journalist staying at the hotel knew their program. Other students just hung out at the hotel, enjoying the act of flaunting what had been previously forbidden—contact with foreigners.

The presence of the students in the Tourismo showed who had the upper hand in the latest wave of power shifts that would form East Timor's future. In the short reform period that accompanied Habibie's offer of autonomy in mid-1998, it was the Dili-based students of the Solidarity Council, led by Antero Bendito Da Silva, who were driving change (and it was exactly this readiness to be publicly identified as supporters of independence that would make the students a prime target for militia and military violence later on.)

The students' open and noisy support for independence led the way for the rest of the population, including some influential people who had previously supported the Indonesians. Within two months, political parties and prominent East Timorese citizens would all be declaring their support for independence at rallies and meetings all over East Timor. The fear of reprisal had been pushed into the background.

<hr/>

DR ANDREW McNaughtan had been involved in the East Timor situation for at least four years. He'd already been

thrown out of East Timor three times by the Indonesians
after being identified as a political activist. Like me, he'd
waited for changes in Jakarta to usher in less repressive
times so that he could return. He was involved simply
because he was disgusted by the level of killing that had
gone on. He blamed the Australian government, in part, for
its policy of supporting Indonesia. He was an activist, not
a journalist, but thought the distinction irrelevant in the
circumstances. Andrew had better contacts in East Timor
than any other foreigner at that time.

He was filming the East Timorese student movement for
the Catholic relief agency Caritas in Norway.

'You missed the show yesterday,' he laughed. 'Indonesian
troops waving from the dock getting on board landing
craft. Everybody was there—the governor, Suratman,
Kopassus in red berets marching out of East Timor. It was
all happening. You've missed it all now.'

Another 400 Indonesian troops had taken part in the
highly publicised withdrawal of 1,300 Indonesian troops
from East Timor in late July and on 8 August. Most of the
journalists who had covered it flew straight back to Jakarta
on an aircraft provided by the Indonesian military. The
Indonesians had proclaimed there were no special forces
troops left in East Timor. In fact, they claimed there were
no combat troops left at all, just those engaged in development and humanitarian projects.

The students sitting with Andrew thought the withdrawal was a sham and said as much. 'They will just bring
them in across the border again. It is just for the cameras
and for Habibie,' said Jacinto, who was then working for
the Student Council but would later work full-time translating for journalists.

Andrew, meanwhile, insisted that the withdrawal,
however small, would still be a good thing for the East

Timorese who had lived with the military among them for long enough. Ironically, it was Andrew who later got hold of the pay records of all the Indonesian military forces in East Timor that proved, once and for all, that no withdrawal had taken place and that the Indonesian military was building up its forces. Those records also proved that paramilitary East Timorese groups were on the payroll as well.

They almost had us fooled at the time, though. Dili seemed so relaxed. Just the fact that we were sitting in the Tourismo's garden and conversing with students was an extraordinary change. And that the students were not immediately beaten up on departure.

Of course, the formation of the militias as proxies for the Indonesians in their fight against the pro-independence Timorese was already taking place at that deceptively positive time. The students kept referring to a visit to East Timor by the notorious Kopassus commander Lieutenant General Prabowo Subianto. Suharto's son-in-law, Prabowo had been responsible for the formation of East Timorese units with Indonesian commanders in the early 1990s. Those units, Team Saka, Team Sera and Team Alpha, had virtually become regular troops. They were uniformed, trained and equipped, received regular pay and lived in barracks. Often they were used in brutal reprisal operations in areas where guerrilla activity had been reported.

In mid-May, Prabowo had visited the southern towns of Suai, Ainaro and Same, as well as Lospalos in the far east and Maliana in the west. The students said he had distributed money and weapons, and laid plans for what they then called paramilitaries to be set up.

I remember thinking initially that the students' stories about Prabowo and his units were all a bit far-fetched. Prabowo had by then been relieved of his command and fled Indonesia after being implicated in moves to prop up

Suharto during the May riots. He was reported to be in Jordan where he was safe from any corruption investigations to do with his father-in-law thanks to his cosy relationship with the Jordanian royal family.

Over the next few days I heard the Prabowo story many times in relation to the new groups being formed. The National Council of Timorese Resistance—the CNRT— was then preparing itself to function as an above-ground political party to push for a referendum on independence. David Ximenes, who had been released from jail in May because of a lack of evidence to prove he was involved in the attack on Brimob the year before, told me about Prabowo as well.

Aniceto Guterres, at the time the only East Timorese lawyer working in his home country, also repeated the story and linked it to the formation of the paramilitary organisations. His organisation, Yayasan Hak (Organisation of Rights), was one of the few attempting to monitor human rights abuses in East Timor. At that time they were functioning as a legal aid service, trying to keep track of the abuses being carried out against the population by the military and police.

His office was crowded. It was mostly students and volunteers who interviewed and logged the complaints of the people who came in after their family or friends had been arrested or shot by the military. A woman wearing black or an old man would come in and wait patiently to tell someone about what had happened to someone they knew, and occasionally Aniceto or one of the workers would try to follow it up with the military.

Even though superficially the situation in Dili had eased, there were still young men posted outside Yayasan Hak watching for signs of approaching Indonesian military or intelligence. The office was always guarded at night. Across the road was an Indonesian military barracks, and the human rights workers and the military often sat in the same restaurants at lunchtime.

━━◆━○━◆━━

INSPIRED BY the recent success of the students in Jakarta forcing Suharto out of office, some volunteers had gone to East Timor. Fi—a long-haired student from Jakarta—was one of them. He had the bored resignation of those Indonesians who didn't make any excuses for their government's actions and actively worked to stop it.

Fi offered to translate when I wanted to speak to Aniceto. During one of these sessions, I asked Aniceto via Fi what he thought of the recent withdrawal. Fi laughed, and began answering the question himself: 'It's ridiculous, they are just going around the island and landing again.' Aniceto agreed it was a farce and told me there were more troops coming over the western border and reports of landings in the east near Lospalos.

Aniceto thought the threat posed by the paramilitary groups was much higher than that from the seemingly dispirited Indonesian military. 'Those people [in the paramilitary] have no concept of human rights,' he said. 'They misinterpret the orders of their commanders. It gets complicated. They combine political and personal conflicts to get what they want. The military knows about this and uses it to control them.'

He told me about the three-month paramilitary training programs he knew of in areas east of Dili, and about how the paramilitary was using these groups. 'It is because the military are frustrated they cannot win the war,' he said. 'They say they have no military operations going on but they use these groups to do it for them.' Aniceto also had a list of a series of recent unsolved murders in the western region for which he thought the paramilitary, or members of the military, were directly responsible.

‹–•–•–○–•–•–›

BACK IN the Tourismo Hotel, the students from the Solidarity Council jeered as footage from the recent Indonesian military 'withdrawal' was again shown on Indonesian television. For three days it had featured in every bulletin.

Daniel Pedersen and I decided to go to Lospalos.

‹–•–•–○–•–•–›

LOSPALOS IS in cattle country. High on a plateau at the eastern end of the island, the large, flat settlement felt like an Australian country town, surrounded by open space. The wide main street had a row of shops with deep verandas. The locals liked to dress in black and wore wide-brimmed black hats. At that time of year, the land was dry and open, and the glaring midday sun forced people to take cover in the shade.

The night before, my travelling companion, Daniel Pedersen, and I had been told about the first of the Indonesian military landings at a beach called Com. Rather than completely withdrawing, as had been reported, it looked like the Indonesians had in fact just taken their landing craft offshore for a few days and brought them back in further east. Bruno Soares, a civil servant in Baucau, had confirmed details of the landings for us. (Word travelled fast in East Timor—people were so mistrustful of official sources they kept an eye on what the army was doing for the sake of their own safety.)

The Indonesians were starting what would turn out to be the biggest offensive against the guerrillas since the fall of Suharto, and it would last until October. Here in Lospalos, it wasn't hard to see what was happening. Military with flak jackets and full military kit got into trucks in the main street.

Dan struck up a conversation with a tall, bespectacled Javanese lieutenant in one of the Chinese-run shops on the main street that sold everything from tinned fish to motorcycle parts. The guy had done some army training in Queensland and he and Dan, who had been working there as a reporter for the *Proserpine Guardian*, swapped stories. The lieutenant was extremely open about the Indonesian activity. The main problem, he said, was the heat and the amount of equipment they had to carry. Yes, the East Timorese were good soldiers, but you had to keep an eye on them. Yes, of course it was hard work, but that's why he'd joined the army, and it was a good chance to use some of his training, particularly what he'd learnt in Australia. He knew he would be there for another six months but his 'tour' would then be finished and he could go back to Jakarta.

What was he doing there? 'Having an operation against the communists,' he said, as if it was a stupid question to ask someone wearing a flak jacket and carrying an M-16 and enough ammunition, water and food to last for a week.

'Are they still around?' Dan asked.

'Yes, they are everywhere,' the lieutenant answered. 'That is why we have to be armed whenever we are off the base. But this time they don't know how many men we have here. This operation will finish them.'

Dan was almost laughing at this stage. The conversation was giving us all we needed to write about the offensive and the military operations. The lieutenant went on chatting freely about the operation and the problems with the heat. Finally, he made a great show of ordering his East Timorese corporal to give Dan some strips of sticking plaster for a blister on his foot—our reason for being in the shop.

'The Australian boots are better,' said the lieutenant sentimentally, 'the leather is softer.'

The East Timorese soldier glared at Dan while the lieutenant told him to fasten his flak jacket. Then they walked across the street, jumped onto the nearest of three trucks, pointed their weapons towards the few East Timorese dozing in the shade, and roared off to resume their operation.

After taking photographs of the soldiers in the market, we were summoned to the police headquarters to register our arrival in Lospalos. Previously, foreigners in East Timor had to do this everywhere, but the practice had lapsed and you'd avoid it if possible as it usually involved answering a lot of questions. This time, someone had alerted the police to our presence.

The guesthouse in Lospalos was run by an ex *Liurai*, or local king, called Vincente. His proudest possessions were two framed photos: one showed him holding a Portuguese-era G-3 rifle and wearing a Falintil uniform, the other showed him shaking the hand of President Suharto. It demonstrated his advancement in the community. He was good friends with the local *Bupati* (mayor), Edmundo Da Silva, who had recently declared in the local press: 'You can have your referendum in the other 12 regions, but here in Lospalos—never.'

Da Silva had been a supporter of Prabowo and had been involved in killing local independence figures in the 1980s. He impressed Prabowo so much with his loyalty, the commander made him an honorary Kopassus member and gave him his own automatic weapon and a red beret. Also, as a *Bupati* he was the highest ranking East Timorese administrator in the region and had (like most mayors there) profited nicely from his position. There was no way he was going to allow noisy students from Dili threaten the status quo, and he cancelled the student meetings. His friend Vincente told the police as soon as we arrived that journalists were in town; we'd been there in 1995, and he'd recognised us instantly.

The police grilled us for an hour. We told them we were tourists. They didn't believe us but they let us go. At 5 am the following day, the police arrived at the guesthouse with the local bus to Dili and told us to get on board. We were not welcome to come back to Lospalos again.

It didn't matter to us, we thought we had our story. The Indonesians were not withdrawing as they claimed. They were in fact running a large operation in the east that would later involve as many as 5,000 troops. The Kopassus hadn't left the island, as the Indonesians had claimed, they had simply sailed up the north coast and landed again, and they were still carrying out abuses against the locals. We had the details of beatings, rapes and one death from the people in Lospalos we had managed to speak to, and the lieutenant from Jakarta had happily confirmed the operation was taking place.

But nobody would run the story. As far as Australian newspaper editors were concerned, it didn't fit the picture. Others were saying that the situation in East Timor was easing, that there was a higher level of freedom than had ever existed before under the Indonesians. And in many ways they were right.

In Dili the meetings, what the students called the 'dialogue process', continued. Almost every day, students were setting off to another town where they arranged another dialogue. Truckloads of young men shouting '*Viva*

Independencia! Viva Xanana Gusmão! Viva Timor Leste!'
became commonplace in Dili. The students had the full
blessing of Bishop Carlos Belo and jailed leader Xanana
Gusmão. In their program of mobilising support for independence, not autonomy, they were trying to maintain
momentum by physically reaching as many people as
possible.

The local press increased the exposure by covering the
dialogues and publishing the lists of demands made by the
students and the local village representatives.

Suara Timor Timur (Voice of East Timor) began to
report, fairly, what was going on. (The Indonesian-backed
elite responded by starting another newspaper, *Novas,* to
run their views.) Unheard of liberties were taken by local
journalists, such as the publishing of an interview in *Suara
Timor Timur* with Falintil guerrilla commander-in-chief in
East Timor, Taur Matan Ruak. They featured his photo on
the front page. It was the first time many East Timorese had
seen the leader who was still fighting in the mountains.

There was still huge tension between the authorities and
the students, but it seemed to be localised. In Maliana, the
students were frustrated for weeks as the hardline *Bupati*—
the gold-toothed and volatile Guilherme Dos Santos, who
later organised and attended all the militia rallies in his
nearby province of Bobonaro—kept creating excuses why
the students could not.

Local military commander Lieutenant Colonel
Burharnudin Siagian (later named as responsible for the
deaths of many students in Maliana by the Indonesian
Commission for Human Rights) just toyed with the
students. He would allow them to arrange and prepare for
the meetings, then he would abruptly cancel them, no
doubt taking down the names of those involved for future
reference.

After many weeks of refusing to allow the students to hold a dialogue, Edmundo Da Silva organised one of his own in Lospalos. Andrew Perrin, a friend of mine who was freelancing for the *Australian*, told me how the *Bupati* had organised for the students to be seated in the centre of the hall while soldiers occupied the space around them. Outside, heavily armed East Timorese soldiers from the notorious Team Saka and Team Alpha surrounded the place, scaring away the locals who would otherwise have attended. Andrew himself chose to leave when the military demanded that he, as the only foreign journalist present, should be ejected. The students were prepared for a confrontation over this, but Andrew wisely decided to leave. He didn't want to be the catalyst for more violence, and that was obviously what the military wanted by attending in such huge numbers.

In Manatuto, east of Dili, police and military had allowed a dialogue to go ahead but had blocked roads running into the town on the day and turned back villagers trying to attend.

The dialogues and public meetings were highly emotionally charged affairs, and the Manatuto dialogue on 19 August was fairly typical. The students from Dili would start the meeting and chair it, but it would be up to the local people to express their feelings. People would be nominated by their village to stand up and speak.

At Manatuto, the first village representative stood, shaking with nervousness as he addressed a public gathering for the first time and shaking with fear of the consequences for what he was about to say. 'I represent the village of Laclubar,' he said. 'We think a referendum is the best way to solve the problem. Release Xanana Gusmão. Get the military out of East Timor. Take responsibility for the killing. Stop the violence and arrests. All the people from

Laclubar agree with me that a referendum has to happen here in East Timor.'

The crowd of several hundred crammed into the hot council office applauded and the next speaker got up. The demands were usually similar, but certain villages would add complaints or demands of a more local and direct nature. 'I am the uncle of Manuel Marcos. I demand to know who shot my nephew,' burst out one man. 'Only two weeks ago he was shot in Manatuto by soldiers. Until now I don't know who did this.' The man had to be calmed down by those near him. He knew there would be spies in the meeting, and that the soldiers responsible for Manuel's death were probably among those outside, but it was his turn to speak publicly.

'I demand the Indonesian people give back the bones of the dead to the families to be buried,' the next speaker said. 'It is also the responsibility of the Indonesian soldiers who rape Timor women for the children. Who will compensate and provide for these children?' The crowd murmured their approval—the issue of rape is difficult to deal with in East Timor's devout Catholic environment, but the people have been forced to acknowledge it.

Other speakers proved to be remarkably prescient. Jose de Fatima, a young man from Soibada, told the crowd: 'We hope the international community should come to East Timor but the Indonesians have to pull out the military. The military are killing East Timorese people. We must find out who is responsible and judge them according to international law. The Indonesians must stop sending troops across the border.'

The talking, demands, accusations and complaints went on for about three hours. When a break was called, everyone left the sweltering building exhausted.

The military in Manatuto couldn't decide whether to

stop the dialogue or just see what it was all about, so they stood around outside the council offices and listened on the loudspeakers provided for the absent crowds they themselves had turned away.

————◦————

WHEN IT was all over, some students offered us a lift back to Dili in the back of a pick-up truck. After the heat and intensity of the meeting, and the tension of never knowing whether the soldiers would break up the meeting or provoke some kind of an incident, it was good to drive along the coast road in the open.

We pulled over at a small unnamed village along the beach. At a stall that was nothing more than a thatched roof with a rough series of benches, the students helped themselves to some smoked fish covered in chilli that was hanging from the roof. Some women came out of a nearby hut and passed around jugs of milky white palm wine. The students were ecstatic. They'd been worried about Manatuto—the military had shot a few young people there in the preceding weeks—but it had been a good day with no such incidents.

We talked about the future. Alipio just laughed and said he would work for independence. 'What will you do, though?' I asked.

'I will work for independence.'

'How will you do that?'

'I will work for independence.'

It became a joke on the way back to Dili—every question was answered by the same phrase and lots of laughter, and I started to see that the question itself was quite stupid. Nobody knew what was going to happen. These guys had gone so far in support of independence, they could soon be dead, or hiding in the mountains or, if you really stretched your imagination, they could be the inheritors of a new country. But that possibility seemed so far away.

Quintão, who had been translating for me all morning, refused to take any money when they dropped us off. 'I just want to have a look at your story. I'll come around tomorrow,' he said. But I knew already that the story about that meeting would never sell in Australia.

⊢⊣⬦⬦⭘⭘⬦⊢⊣

TWO DAYS later there was a meeting of Dili's pro-independence elite at the GMT basketball stadium in the centre of town. A crowd of more than 1,000 came to listen to speakers including Indonesian pro-democracy activists Rosa Damonyanti, Father Mangunniwijaya and the PRD activist Wilson, who had just been released from prison in Jakarta after being jailed for attempting to overthrow the Suharto regime. He had been the victim of an absurd charge against the tiny left-wing PRD in another attempt by the authorities of the time to resurrect the communist bogy of Indonesian politics.

I had attended his farcical trial in Jakarta in May 1997, at which he refused to recognise the court's authority and tried to call jailed East Timorese leader Xanana Gusmão as a witness in his defence. As the police dragged him away he yelled out about the injustice of what was happening to him. BBC correspondent Jonathon Head had said at the time: 'There goes a very brave man.' And I had thought to myself: 'There goes a man who is going to be in jail for a very long time.'

But I had been wrong; with Habibie's amnesty, he was out. And where else would he be but in Dili exhorting the

East Timorese to push for their independence. When he told the crowd that the Islamic people of Indonesia were not their enemy, 'the real enemy is the Indonesian military', the people cheered and banged on their seats.

The response to the other two Indonesian speakers was the same. Father Mangunniwijaya told the people not to accept Habibie's offer of autonomy, that it was meaningless. He told them not to wait for the United Nations to organise a referendum. The crowd cheered more loudly. He told them they were already independent. My translator, Quintão, jumped to his feet and began applauding, as did the whole crowd.

The other speakers, Manuel Carrascalão (an independence leader), Domingos De Sousa (a former rector of the university of East Timor) and Aniceto Guterres (from Yayasan Hak) were all well known to the crowd and people calmed down. But they still yelled '*Viva!*' at the appropriate moments and the echo bounced loudly straight back to the crowd from the bare concrete walls and floor of the basketball courts.

The *Bupati* of Dili, Domingos Soares, took the stand. He was the only pro-autonomy representative who had accepted the invitation to speak, and said he would speak for the governor who was unable to attend.

Soares spoke of reconciliation. And about the need for unity among East Timorese—how the people shouldn't fight with each other, because that would only lead to civil war. 'Only we have the ability to solve our problems,' he said, 'not the United Nations, or the Indonesians. A referendum will only lead to civil war.'

That was the line being used by the Indonesian authorities back then: that the Timorese weren't ready for a ballot. The crowd became restless as it became obvious he was just toeing the line taken by all loyal government officials, in a more subtle way. He talked of peace while, in a way, he also threatened war.

When Domingos Soares had finished, the floor was opened for questions.

Olandina—a member of the local Indonesian government assembly, the sister-in-law of Xanana Gusmão and a well-known pro-independence supporter—was the first to stand up and directed her comment to the last speaker, the *Bupati*: 'You say independence will bring suffering because you are afraid of losing your position. Just say we don't have to be afraid to suffer.'

The crowd cheered. Domingos slumped down in his chair.

'You say there are other people in this issue,' Olandina continued, referring to the claim made by Domingos that many East Timorese supported Indonesia. 'Didn't you see on the 27th and 28th of July just what the people want? One thousand trucks, 700 motorcycles on the streets of Dili in support of a referendum.'

As Olandina sat down, the crowd cheered, and Domingos Soares appeared to shrink further.

An older man who described himself as a labourer took the microphone: 'The GPK [the guerrillas] are you who fought for your positions,' he said, pointing towards the leaders. Some of them now supported a referendum, but all enjoyed high positions in the Indonesian administration. The crowd laughed and clapped. The people liked the analogy, implying that the leaders were to blame, that they were the ones disturbing the peace because of their collaboration with the Indonesians, not the guerrillas.

'And you, Domingos,' the man continued. 'Why did you say nothing when they killed your nephew?'

Domingos Soares put his head in his hands. The man was referring to Herman Soares, one of the youths who had recently been killed near Manatuto. He had been shot dead by the army while collecting wood.

Domingos Soares began to cry. It was true he had done nothing; he hadn't even attended the demonstration after the shooting.

'Please conduct this referendum as soon as possible, because we want to take a rest,' the labourer said, putting down the microphone.

DAN WAS pissed off. His time in Dili was up and he had to return to his job at a regional Queensland newspaper. We looked at what we had: troop movement stories from Lospalos and the border that nobody seemed to believe or thought were important; endless transcripts of meetings, rallies, declarations, all saying the same thing. The East Timorese wanted independence through a referendum. There was no real news in that.

He thought that we could at least sell a story about the Australian, Gino Favarro, who had come back to claim and run his father's hotel. He had just managed to get the Hotel Dili back from the governor's sister, who had been running the place for years and taking all the profits.

Pedro laughed at us. 'Look at you two. No bloody people getting killed. No bloody shooting. No bloody story.' He thought it was funny.

We had moved back to Pedro's house in Becora mainly because, not having sold any stories, we were running out of money. This time he'd been glad to see me since things were a lot more relaxed. He told me how the Indonesian intelligence officer who had interrogated him over the photos of me had died in a helicopter crash in June 1998. Nine high ranking Indonesian officers had been killed in the crash, which they blamed on bad weather. Falintil never confirmed or denied responsibility, which made me think that even though the crash had happened in a Falintil area, it really had been an accident.

I found out later from Australian journalist Jill Jolliffe that the crash was far from an accident. The helicopter had actually been brought down by concentrated automatic weapons fire from Falintil stationed specifically for that purpose around the Indonesian military camp in Liaruca in the central Viqueque region.

On board were the Bali-based commander of eastern Indonesia, Major General Yudomo, the Indonesian military commander of East Timor, Colonel Slamet Sidabatur and seven other high ranking officials. Falintil and the Indonesians both denied it had been shot down for political reasons but it was, as Jill pointed out, the highest level political assassination in Indonesia since 1965. (To my knowledge Falintil has never admitted responsibility to what many consider a major victory in their guerrilla struggle.)

'But there is one guy you should look out for,' Pedro said to me. 'He knows you. A big skinny guy, East Timorese. Remember, he used to come around here with the Intel, checking who was here. His name is Carlos.'

I did remember. And it didn't take long in Dili, being the small town it was, before I saw him. When I did, Carlos recognised me instantly, but just nodded his head and gave me the smallest smile. I told Pedro about it. 'Maybe they're not getting paid any more,' he said.

<hr>

IT ALSO wasn't long before Jose Belo came around to Pedro's place. He'd been released from prison in late July along with another batch of East Timorese prisoners. Jose and the five others who had been arrested when David Alex was captured had been given better than normal treatment, he believed, because of the international campaign that had been run by solidarity groups and Amnesty International.

Jose had a lot of friends outside of East Timor. During his imprisonment, he was called in to see the prison commander, who slammed a pile of faxes and letters on the desk and demanded to know who was responsible for all these enquiries about Jose's safety and whereabouts and demands for his release.

'They are my friends,' he had said. 'I have many friends everywhere,' he went on, smiling to himself and knowing how Amnesty worked.

Jose had got off lightly, but his stories of prison were chilling nonetheless. They included the time he had been told to take food to an isolation cell. The man in the cell he barely recognised as John Maulano—stick thin, covered in his own filth, his skin covered in sores. And he couldn't speak.

They had told John Maulano's family he was dead back in May of 1997. When Jose saw him, it was December. For seven months they had kept him in the SGI prison, barely alive, alone in a dark room.

What had they wanted from him? There wasn't much he could tell them. The clandestine resistance movement worked in cells; each group only knew about the contacts to a certain group or level. Once a group was fractured, for instance when David Alex and Jose had been captured, the structure was reorganised. At least that was the theory.

Jose shook when he told the story. They had heard in the prison that John Maulano had died shortly afterwards. 'At night they would take the bodies out by boat into the harbour,' he said. 'That is what happened to him.'

The other stories of what happened to David Alex were less clear. Jose insisted he'd overheard some Indonesians talking about his commander as though he were still alive, as though they still had him. He talked about how the prisoners had seen the guards preparing the special food that Alex, with his stomach ulcer, needed to eat.

'I want to tell the story, but I don't want to disappear like John,' Jose said when I asked him if I could write about his time in the prison.

I wondered at the time whether Jose's captors, the Indonesian military, had not charged him or transferred him out of the military prison because they had been playing psychological games with him. He believed the Indonesians were keeping his leader alive, and it was driving him crazy with guilt.

That image of John Maulano, abandoned, isolated and dying alone, stuck in my mind. It was so incongruous with the way things were relaxing in Dili, and it had happened so recently, and quite nearby.

Things still weren't relaxed for Jose either. He was still regularly being called in for questioning, and because of that, some people thought he was an informant of the Indonesians. It wasn't very safe for him to go to the Tourismo, but he did occasionally. He was never very comfortable there and always spoke in hushed tones, not like the other students who would laugh and talk loudly and not hesitate to join us for drinks or food.

Once, when I was talking to him in the street outside the Bishop's house, Belo came out and glared at us. 'We'd better go, the Bishop will be angry with me for getting in trouble again,' he said, laughing like a schoolboy.

The Bishop had intervened with the Indonesian authorities on Jose's behalf on a number of occasions, and had told him to keep out of trouble. Talking to me in the street was still seen as a not very wise thing to be doing for someone so recently out of jail.

━┝━┥━♦━┿━O━┿━♦━┤━┥━

BISHOP BELO was more influential in Dili back then than he had ever been. In the vacuum created by the mass condemnation of and disobedience against the Indonesian authorities, people occasionally took things into their own hands and the church would step in to sort it out. As an example, one night out in Becora, local youths had grabbed some East Timorese accused of spying for the Indonesians. They had roughed them up, but decided not to take it any further. The unfortunate 'spies' were dumped, bleeding, with the Bishop, and he was left to deal with the Indonesian authorities.

Another day as I travelled through Hera, just outside of Dili, I saw a crowd in action against two suspected informants. They were chasing two young men who were running extremely fast. As the two ran across the road, the crowd followed, ignoring the traffic. Pigs and chickens ran and flew out of the way as the two were trapped near some wooden huts. The crowd encircled them, everybody yelling and screaming. 'They must be spies,' said Quintão, laughing. Dust was being kicked up in the centre of the circle, fists were being raised, women, children and old people were shouting. The whole village, small as it was, was involved.

It had started happening after the big demonstrations. People had simply become sick of the attempts to intimidate them and were starting to do something about it. Students like Quintão, who had always been prime targets for informants and spies, didn't think it was a bad thing, just part of the changes taking place.

uintão had started working with me, translating. He s proud to be from Manatuto—the hometown of Xanana. He was short, stocky, tough and unashamedly pro-independence. Privately he would eschew the reconciliation approach of the student and church leaders, but he would, of course, still obey them. With Quintão, there was none of the formality that sometimes crept into Timorese relations with foreigners, through unfamiliarity or their strict 'respect your elders' upbringing. When he was hungry, he'd ask for food. When he needed something, he'd ask for it. One time, through politeness, he let me have his seat on a minibus travelling to Baucau. Two hours later I asked him if he was comfortable. He'd been hanging out the door, holding on by the same arm the whole time without moving. 'No, I am very uncomfortable, and have been ever since I gave you my seat,' was his smiling reply.

━━◆━○━◆━━

EAST TIMOR'S two bishops, Carlos Belo and the Bishop of Baucau, Basilio Dos Nascimiento, called a meeting of the 50 prominent leaders who represented all the pre-existing political parties in East Timor and representatives from the Students Solidarity Council. Their aim was to come up with a joint statement to present at the upcoming UN talks on East Timor's future, and to establish a way forward with the approval of the Indonesian authorities.

Out of the 50 who attended the meeting, held at the seminary in Dare in the hills above Dili on 10 and 11 September, only three were openly in favour of accepting Habibie's offer of autonomy. Those three—Basilio Araujo, Domingos Policarpo and Armindo Soares Marianno— would later rise to prominence as the so-called political wing of the militia, the FPDK. It was a clear reflection of the level of support for the autonomy plan, or integration with Indonesia, among people in Dili at the time. The minority of three pro-Indonesian representatives maintained spoiling tactics whenever they could to hold up the agreement on the joint statement.

Several times these three threatened to storm out of the meeting. It was only with reluctance that they agreed that Falintil leaders in the mountains or in jail (an obvious reference to Xanana), could participate in future talks. But what most angered student leaders like Antero Bendito Da Silva, with whom I spoke afterwards, was the point-blank refusal to call for the Indonesian military's withdrawal. The other leaders, mostly ex-senior civil servants, from the originally pro-Indonesian Apodeti party all called for the Indonesian military to withdraw. They had welcomed the Indonesians and worked with them but as the killing continued, they changed their positions. There were also UDT and Fretilin delegates, who had fought each other in the brief August 1975 civil war preceding the Indonesian invasion. The small Kota and Trabalhista parties were also represented.

The majority agreed that the Indonesian troops must withdraw. 'The troops are the barrier against forward movement here in East Timor, all the parties agree on that,' said Fretilin delegate Abel Belo at the time. The relaxed, chummy atmosphere of the day before, when all the delegates had sat in the garden under the trees overlooking Dili laughing at the dirty jokes of one of the delegates, had gone. With midnight approaching and restless students outside the gates, the agreement still hadn't been signed. Shouting could be heard coming from inside the meeting room.

In the end, a revised agreement which only conceded to include the resistance leaders in future talks and, basically, to talk again, was signed. Antero was fuming. He had watched three men hold up the process from which he had expected so much, and the other leaders had let them. 'There has been no movement in concrete matters,' he said. 'The leaders are not listening to what people are saying in the towns and the villages. In four months, if there is no action, we will be out on the streets again. People will really get angry if this goes on.'

Outside the seminary on the narrow road leading back down to Dili it was pitch black under the stately old banyan trees. In the darkness, students pressed all around the four journalists leaving to send our stories. The Indonesian journalist who was walking with us was terrified. I told her not to worry, that the students were not violent, but when I looked at the mass of sullen faces staring at her out of the darkness and parting quietly as we made our way through, I didn't recognise anyone, and her nervousness became contagious. There was definitely a threatening feeling that night. The students must have realised then that their dream run in forcing change was about to end.

<hr />

A WEEK later I joined the students on a trip to Lacluta in the remote south-east of the island. The trip down there felt like a day off—sitting in an open-backed truck, surrounded by singing students, travelling through the cool hills of the centre of the island. The group that sat on the roof of the truck would sing the solo verse, and the others would join in the chorus. The singing entertained the stunned villagers along the way. But the low-hanging trees made it a dangerous game, and the best solo singer was eventually killed by one on another trip.

The students left me, the photographer John Beale and Quintão in Viqueque for the night. The local priest there told us how a man called Filomeno Da Cruz had just been attacked in his home in Lacluta by an Intel operative, to prevent the following day's dialogue from going ahead. There had been trouble in the area, and a build-up of troops. A new Indonesian military unit called Garuda Hitam (Black Eagle) had moved in and began setting up posts. That night in Lacluta, several houses were burnt down by the military in an attempt to provoke a reaction from the students who had just arrived.

When we arrived for the dialogue, the military were everywhere and the people gathered on the soccer field seemed withdrawn and nervous. There had been threats to deter participation and, unlike in neighbouring Viqueque where the previous month's dialogue had gone for two days and been attended by thousands, this gathering seemed dominated by students from Dili and old people, no more than a few hundred. One old woman kept screaming obscenities against the Indonesians as the young local representatives tried to carry on with their speeches. The students only just tolerated her, though one of them danced with her for a while when the music started in order to calm her down.

Horrible things had happened in this area, which explained the strange atmosphere and limited attendance. It wasn't long before one of the students approached me, saying someone wanted to talk.

On 8 August, 1983 at 8 am, Indonesian soldiers from Battalion 501 (who later trained in Australia) had entered the town of Kraras and began rounding up the men. They killed them all in a group and threw their bodies in a swamp. They killed the children by swinging them by their feet and slamming them against walls, or stabbing them with knives. There had been 3,000 people living in that village; only about 1,300 escaped.

The woman telling me the story said she was among 300 women who returned to the village, because she had nowhere else to go. The killings in the area went on until September of that year. The woman, who was 32 at the time of the killings, said it had all begun when some Indonesian soldiers killed seven people. When the Falintil heard about the killings, they attacked the Indonesians, killing all except one, who raised the alarm. Then the reprisals started. This was her first opportunity to tell a foreigner about it. It was the first time she had spoken to a Westerner.

THE DIALOGUE ended with the usual list of demands for an Indonesian withdrawal and the calling of a referendum. Many of the people had already left and the priest we'd come with was eager to drive back to Viqueque. He asked me if I wanted to speak to someone who had witnessed the killing of the Australian journalists in Balibo, in 1975. I immediately said yes, as the whole issue of precisely who was responsible was still unresolved. It was obvious the five Australia-based journalists had been murdered by Indonesian troops—a mountain of evidence had been accumulated as journalists and the relatives of those killed tried to disprove the Australian government's position that the five had been killed in crossfire and not executed by the Indonesian military despite a series of witnesses who had come forth. The whole issue became symbolic of Australia's position regarding East Timor and the unwillingness of the Australian government to tell the truth about what was happening there.

The witness was in Uatolari, a small town on the other side of Viqueque. Although a distance on the map of only 30 kilometres, on this never-developed south coast of the island, the road was more like a washed-out creek bed, with large ruts and ditches across its sandy surface. A lot of people use horses to get around in this area, and we had to drive slowly to avoid them. At night it was like driving in a tunnel with walls formed by thick, high grasses and the air in front of the car was thick with insects. It took us hours to get there.

There had never been any power in that area, but the sight of a whole village lit up only by oil lamps and candles was new to me. The witness, Manuel, would not agree to talk in his home because of informers, so he returned with us to Viqueque, where he was only too happy to tell all in the living room of a friend's house. He was one of the last Fretilin soldiers to leave from the old Portuguese fort on the hill as the Indonesians attacked, and he saw them shoot the journalists, then enter the house. He described in detail how it had happened. It was late, after midnight, when we finally stopped talking.

Manuel had actually relayed his whole account through José Ramos Horta to journalist Roger East when he got back to Dili after the killings. East was killed in Dili when the Indonesians swept into the capital and Horta fled the country, but his account had always been dismissed. As for Manuel, well, he'd been fighting in the mountains pretty much ever since.

I went out to relieve myself. In the moonlight, through a hole in the back fence, I saw more than 100 East Timorese in training. Silently they drilled on the parade ground of the local military barracks. Back inside, I asked the owner of the house what was going on. He said they had been gathering there every night for the last few weeks. So far they had only trained, he said, but the people were worried. It was the local militia in training.

>—+—◦—+—<

BACK IN Dili, things were still quiet. We had started spending the evenings at one of the fish restaurants out on the beach. There seemed to be an understanding that foreigners and students were welcome at the down-market restaurant closer to the Tourismo, whereas Indonesian military, businessmen and officials drove their four-wheel drives out to the other more opulent one. (Of course, the militia eventually burnt them all down, but ours was the first to go.)

There were only three foreign journalists and a photographer in Dili then, and one night we were all at the restaurant drinking beer and eating barbecued fish with some students. When we got back to the Tourismo, there were messages for us all. It was the closest thing we'd ever had to a media frenzy. Manuel Carrascalão had made a statement to the Portuguese press that 30,000 Indonesian troops had landed in East Timor and were preparing for an offensive. The comments, which had a fair amount of truth in them in terms of the troop movements, were essentially the same as those we tried to report more than a month earlier.

The next day Quintão the translator, John Beale and myself went around to see Manuel Carrascalão, who belonged to one of the so-called seven grand old families of East Timor. With his long beard and dignified yet imperious air, he looked like the landowner he was, with extensive property in the Liquiça and Maubara areas to the west of Dili. Among his family had been prominent UDT leaders. One brother, Mario, had ended up governor under the Indonesians from 1987 to 1996, and the other, João, had fled to Australia. Manuel had formed the GRPTT (Movement for Reconciliation and Unity of the People of East Timor) in late 1997; it was a political party of established, previously pro-Indonesian leaders who had begun to call for a referendum. Death threats followed, and a few attempts on his life, but he stood his ground and refused to leave Dili, although he'd had ample opportunity.

His house on the main street behind the waterfront was well barricaded and comfortable by Timorese standards. In the front room stood a large-screen television with a satellite link. It was almost always on, usually tuned to a Portuguese channel. Chris, one of his daughters, had been educated in Darwin and spoke English with an Australian accent. She usually translated for him.

After serving us coffee in his front room in the Timorese manner, we asked him about the numbers he'd given in his statement to the media. He admitted he hadn't known the exact figures; he'd heard many stories, and figures weren't the specialty of an old man like himself. He smiled and I saw a flash in his eye—he knew I knew what his game was. Sly old dog, I thought. He knew full well that those figures were massively inflated, but at least he'd gotten some attention.

I was finally able to put together a story on the Indonesians' phony withdrawal and their activities along the border, and in the east. Bishop Belo had since complained about the Indonesian activity in the local press, but the landings had continued.

In the end, the figures I quoted were lower than the true number. The truth was eventually found out by Andrew McNaughtan when he got hold of the Indonesian military pay records. I didn't ask how he got them, but I had a fair idea. They added up to more than 21,000 including militia that were already on the payroll. This figure included 18,000 regular troops. This was at a time when the Indonesians were saying they had anywhere between 10,000 and 15,000 troops depending on which spokesman was lying.

Exact numbers aside, there were all the signs of a military build-up, and you could sense it wasn't going to be long before the situation boiled over.

CHAPTER FOUR

1 November 1998
Dili, East Timor

IT WAS ANDREW Perrin who had thrown me the copy of the local Suara Timor Timur newspaper after I arrived back in Dili on the overnight bus from Kupang early on a Sunday morning. He pointed out a small article detailing the deaths of three Indonesians in the southern village of Weberek. According to the report, two Indonesian military personnel and one civilian, an engineer, were killed by Falintil when they attended a dialogue held in the village that involved Falintil members.

'If that's true, it could turn into something,' he said. 'It might be worth going down there.' He wasn't interested himself, because he was leaving. After freelancing for the *Australian* for three months, Andrew had had enough. His newspaper had begun using copy about Timor from the Jakarta correspondent, and he was feeling redundant. The situation wasn't attracting much interest anyway. Even two days of massive demonstrations in Dili in October that had nearly turned violent—when the governor tried to sack all pro-independence public servants—hadn't gone very far as a story. The call to sack the civil servants, mostly those involved in the 700-member pro-referendum group Forcarepetil, had come from Basilio Araujo, head of the 15-member pro-autonomy group. The governor had heeded that call, being pro-autonomy himself, to retain his position.

What had happened in Weberek wasn't covered in detail in the newspaper. Local journalists were coming under a lot of pressure from the military and the local government, and it was becoming necessary to read between the lines again. I finally got a version of the story from a witness a few days later. Larende, from Alas, told me how the local Falintil commander, Tere Mau Bulak, had a meeting—like a dialogue—with the youths of the town on 29 October. One intelligence operative was present and reported it to his commander as soon as the meeting began. Four Kopassus returned from the *Koramil* (military headquarters) in Alas. The young people stopped them and challenged them. The four men claimed they were civilians, but they were searched and their Kopassus identity cards, pistols and a knife were found. Falintil arrested the men and Tere Mau Bulak checked their identities against his records. He declared they had been responsible for East Timorese deaths.

The men were last seen by a villager being escorted by Falintil, who said they were taking them to 'the commander'. The villager said he didn't know which commander they meant—Indonesian or Falintil. When I spoke to him he was probably too afraid to acknowledge Falintil had killed them. It was never proven irrevocably that they had. Indonesian soldiers found the bodies the following day, three of them dumped in the Klere River. They turned out to be two Indonesian sergeants and an engineer. The fourth, who was injured, fled to the Alas military base.

That night, the military returned to Weberek and tried to arrest the village chief, but local youths began pelting them with stones so they were unable to carry out the arrest.

On the same day, local leaders and military were having a meeting in the nearby village of Abelara. The *Kepala Desa* (Indonesian-appointed village head) decided the local youths had to be dealt with. Since the previous week's dialogue in Alas (on 24 October), the Indonesians felt they were becoming uncontrollable. They decided to request military assistance. According to the local priest, Father Cornelius Ceyrans, the five local leaders met again on 1 November. The leader, Jose Tavares, made everybody sign an agreement to begin an operation against the youths of Alas.

On the afternoon of 8 November, the military and local leaders met in the village of Dotik. Guns and ammunition had been stockpiled in Alas, and the operation was planned for 11 and 12 November. They would kill all the young men in Alas using the military and local paramilitary. They planned to kill close to 200. The stockpile of weapons at the military post in Alas would be distributed to arm the paramilitaries. That night, armed men wearing balaclavas and military uniforms appeared on the streets of Alas. They were the paramilitaries.

Falintil found out about this plan and gathered about 30 fighters around Alas. On 9 November at 8 am, they attacked the *Koramil* headquarters in the Alas town centre. Three Indonesian soldiers who tried to resist were shot dead. Thirteen soldiers, including two East Timorese, were captured by Falintil and the stockpiled weapons intended for the paramilitaries were seized. Thirty-six automatic rifles, 3,600 rounds of ammunition, six grenade launchers, pistols, grenades and a military radio were the guerrillas' prize. Falintil fled on foot and the town's inhabitants, knowing what would happen, gathered in the church. Some of the youths began to flee to the surrounding mountains.

Indonesian military from Same and Dili did not arrive until 5.15 pm. They shot dead the first man they saw— Andreona Fernandez, from the area of Alas known as Lurrin, was killed instantly where he stood in the street. The soldiers then proceeded to burn down all the 40 or so houses in that area. All transport in and out of the area was stopped at hastily arranged road blocks. The area was closed.

Back in Dili, we knew nothing of the attack until the following day. The Indonesians announced their soldiers' deaths in the local paper and blamed Falintil. The authorities were silent about the captured weaponry and the hostages until the following day, when they confirmed they were working with the ICRC to secure the men's release.

During the next few days, a number of people came to the Tourismo with different versions of the story. As Quintão would read out the different versions in the two local newspapers, Sebastião—another of the students— would offer comments on what he thought was really going on. A final year student at UMTIM, the university of East Timor, Sebastião did a bit of work for journalists on the side and knew a lot of people. He was charismatic, good looking and smart, and knew how to get information from people such as the military, who wouldn't even talk to a foreigner, let alone a foreign journalist. He had the natural authority that didn't come easily to many young East Timorese because they'd grown up in a repressive Indonesian military-dominated society.

For a week or so Sebastião had been talking about the trouble after the dialogue in Same and the problems in Alas. He was convinced these flare-ups were the start of the Indonesians wanting to show the people outside of Dili that to support the city-based independence movement wasn't wise.

'That's why it's starting down there, man,' he said. 'They wouldn't get away with it here in Dili—the people would stop it. There would be too much attention.'

I remember asking Sebastião what he thought the new armed groups would do.

'They'll kill the young people. What else?' he'd answered.

The Students Solidarity Council had an office in a house on a side street near the Santa Cruz cemetery by then. They had some donated computers, but rarely kept them in the office as they were always expecting a military raid. More importantly, they had a phone, so they could contact students out in the regional areas and monitor the situation outside of Dili.

Normally, you would just sit on the floor or lean against the wall as Antero or the secretary, João Sarmento, recounted information. They didn't have many chairs.

When some students came in from Same and Alas, they described the attack and gave the names of those who had been arrested or gone missing. What they described was the systematic burning down of one part of the town, then the military shot young men as they tried to flee. Some of the descriptions became political statements.

While some of the student witnesses would calmly produce lists of names and give precise times of events, others were more emotional and gave apocalyptic descriptions: 'They have all been killed. They are killing everybody.'

How many have died?

'Hundreds,' they would reply.

Did you see the killings?

'No, I fled. That is why I am still alive,' they would say, looking at you as if you were an idiot.

João, who was always calm and always spoke in a quiet and even tone, would write down the details and translate them for me. Most of the information came from those who had fled immediately following the attack, but evidence of the beginnings of a major reprisal operation was starting to emerge.

Similar stories were being told at another formerly empty house in Dili—at the office for the new East Timorese branch of Kontras, an organisation investigating political disappearances and human rights abuses. Having just opened the office, Isabel da Costa Ferreira, a lawyer, and Rui Lourenco, a university graduate, were thrown in at the deep end. As their organisation's aim was to follow up disappearances with the military and the police, they were immediately inundated with people who had fled from Alas. At the time, they didn't even have a typewriter in the office and had to borrow one. All they could do was write down the statements and attempt to collate a report.

The CNRT were the same—under-resourced and performing a vital role. They now had an office on Jalan Balide, across the road from a military base near the hills behind the city. They had declared themselves to be an open political party on 14 September, and no longer were restricting themselves to underground and exile activities. They had become the united representatives of all the political parties for independence, and as such they were seen by the East Timorese as the society's natural leaders.

People from Alas and the surrounding areas travelled to the CNRT office to tell their stories. They appealed for calm in Dili and relayed a message from the leader, Xanana

Gusmão, in Jakarta, that a demonstration planned for 12 November to commemorate the Santa Cruz massacre would be scaled back. It was not to be a demonstration about the Alas killings; it was going to be a church service and an emotional re-enactment of the massacre by students, many of whom had survived the massacre themselves.

AT THE cemetery on 12 November thousands of people turned up to publicly commemorate the massacre for the first time since it had occurred. Thousands showed up at the 6.30 am mass at the nearby Balide church. The priest there—unaware that a memorial was being celebrated—carried on with his normal service after apologising for being unprepared.

That was one of the problems the CNRT was experiencing—it was difficult to organise things when their leader was 2,000 kilometres away and in jail.

The previous night, some at CNRT had said that Xanana didn't want the event to go ahead because it might provoke the Indonesians; others had been saying Xanana wanted a peaceful ceremony to go ahead. The leadership structure had only recently emerged from hiding, and there were many in the CNRT claiming to speak with the direct authority of Xanana, but no-one knew who was actually in charge in Dili. So things like telling a priest that thousands of people were going to turn up to his mass just didn't happen.

Outside the gate to the cemetery where the 1991 massacre occurred, a group of students threw themselves to the ground, accompanied by a tape recording of loud gunfire, recreating the massacre. One read a prayer over a loudspeaker, and others wailed. Those who took part were mostly survivors of the massacre. Many cried when they stood to hold hands and form a circle.

Several people spoke to the assembled group after the re-enactment. Mau Hudu, a well-known former guerrilla leader (who was to be murdered by the militia in West Timor nine months later), addressed the young crowd.

'If he says we have to demonstrate today, we will. If he says we have to stay at home today, it is a symbol of our unity. We must do it,' he told them, speaking of the need to follow the leadership of Xanana Gusmão.

Many of the students had been pushing for a large political demonstration to protest the situation in Alas and the accompanying killings. Xanana ordered that the killings were not to be mentioned, so as not to provoke the Indonesians. Not one of the speakers mentioned Alas specifically, but there were many guarded references. Alecio Goncalves, a UDT representative, told the students: 'I want to apologise to the youth who have become sacrificial, because we are the ones who started the war.' He was talking about the students who died in the cemetery in 1991, but everybody interpreted it as a reference to the present and themselves. People hugged each other and many cried. It was as if they were saying goodbye and steeling themselves for a young and honorable death.

By 11 am the crowd had quietly dispersed. Xanana had said from prison that they should stay at home and avoid trouble. No shops were open until after dark, everyone was indoors and the whole city was quiet. In the afternoon came the first heavy downpour of the wet season, those big, fat monsoonal drops that come straight down in the hot, still air. On the streets outside, rubbish clogged the drains and roads flooded quickly. But it didn't matter, there was no traffic anyway.

After the sun went down and the rain stopped, the people came out of their houses. Xanana's second recommendation was that candles were to be lit in memory of the dead and all over the city, candles appeared—in gardens, on windowsills, on verandas, along roads and all over the walls of the cemetery. Standing in the street in the dark, you could see candles lining the paths and roads that led up to the steep green hills that surround Dili. The rain had cleared the normal dust and smoke that had been hanging over Dili for months, and the air became fresh and cool. As the candles glowed in the cool night air all was very beautiful and calm.

><-<>-O-<>-<

EVERY NOW and then in East Timor, you'd meet someone you'd swear had stepped straight out of Europe. After more than 400 ruling years Portuguese genes were well and truly in the East Timorese pool. Unlike English colonisers, the Portuguese never carried with them the squeamish racist prudery that prevented intermarriage. But even so, an East Timorese face with distinctly European features could still take you by surprise, especially when there were so few white people in East Timor.

I had been banging on the rear door of the office of a bus company. All my attempts to get a bus south to Same had been unsuccessful so far. The man who answered the door was white and I'd obviously just woken him up. He asked me in Indonesian what I wanted. I replied in English, presuming—wrongly—that he would understand. I asked him if the company had buses going to Same. His eyes narrowed and he told me there was no point going to Same—the roads east to Viqueque and west to Suai were blocked. I didn't ask why, since we both knew: the military had blocked them and I certainly wasn't going to discuss that, not with this bloke, anyway. I asked him again if the bus company went to Same and if the buses going there were still operating.

'Okay, come here at 2 am and wait across the road,' he said.

I asked him whether there was a day bus.

'Not for you,' he spat out, looking at my camera bag.

I tried to make conversation. I wanted to know where he was from, what he was doing in Dili. I asked him in my bad Indonesian whether he was a foreigner, using the slightly derogatory Tetum word for foreigner, *Malae*. '*Saya Timorense,*' he barked emphatically—he was Timorese, and obviously pretty touchy about the subject, so I left him alone and promised to come back at 2 am.

I made it back to the bus company after very little sleep, and the bus was waiting there. Same is directly south from Dili, over the mountains across the widest part of the island. As the bus climbed the hills out of Dili, it began to get cooler. Further up, after lots of turns and doubling back as the road climbed higher, it got colder. Soon, I was freezing. The window next to me was jammed open and there was nothing I could do about it. The bus was full— all the seats were taken. I was freezing until dawn when the bus stopped in the hill town of Maubisse.

The road had not been maintained for a long time; the Indonesians seemed to have abandoned their efforts at least a year beforehand, all over the country. The early wet had already caused some big landslides. The bus stopped on the edge of a great slash in the bitumen, about 10 metres across. The road had fallen away down the side of the mountain and left a gap. The local people had thrown rocks into the hole to make the soft clay solid.

Everybody got out of the bus in the half-light and the

bus slowly moved down into the hole where the remains of the road were. It snailed through the rocks and mud, the driver revving the engine high in first gear to lurch through. When it seemed to be stuck, some boys ran down into the hole and started pushing, ignoring the large rocks and mud that were being flung out by the spinning rear wheels.

Going up the other side of the crevice, the bus looked as if it would slide back down and crush the people pushing it. But it made the climb and we all walked through the mud and got back on board. This happened again at three other landslides, and we didn't arrive in Same until after 10 am.

Before Same there was a military checkpoint. The soldiers were stationed in a small hut on a hill above the road. There was a pole across the road to stop traffic and a small sand-bagged hut next to it. Soldiers, with their hands on their guns, checked the passengers' ID cards. Other soldiers kept their guns trained on the bus from the observation post, which had a view over all the open country around. You could see all the way to the south coast, and in the moun-tains there were no trees, just the occasional clump of bushes or pile of rocks. It looked like beautiful farming country, but the hills seemed uninhabited except for a few huts along the road. I couldn't help but think how the guerrillas would stand out if they'd had to move across this area.

The thick jungle reappeared as the road descended into Same, and the sticky heat returned.

▷─◁▷─◁─○─▷◁─▷◁

I'D HOPED to get to Alas the same day to investigate the killings. I still hadn't been able to publish a story on the attack, and thought if I got first-hand evidence from the site of the killings, a newspaper would *have* to run it.

Alas was only 30 or so kilometres away on the map. But there were no buses or *bemos* (minibuses) at the markets. It was a Sunday, 15 November, and everything seemed to be closed. I was told I could only hire a small *bemo* the following morning, early.

There was only one *losmen* (guesthouse) I knew of in the town, and I walked there. It was full of big, fierce-looking Melanesian soldiers from Indonesian Battalion 602, who had just moved into the area. They were from Irian Jaya and the Indonesian who ran the *losmen* was scared of them. They were all huge and aggressive, and towered over the smaller Indonesians.

After they left I drank tea with the owner, who told me that soldiers from Battalion 744 in Dili and 745 in Lospalos had also passed through the town in the previous week. He also told me that all the villages to the east and north of Same had been visited by the military in the past week.

Eleven of the Indonesian soldiers captured in Alas by the guerrillas had been released, but things were far from quiet. In Same, almost all normal activity had stopped and the people were staying at home. Many had been arrested and harassed by the soldiers.

He directed me to a guesthouse up the hill above the town. but what he didn't tell me was that it was behind the military base. Armed soldiers were everywhere, some covered in mud. They wore a huge variety of uniforms from many different units. Trucks loaded with men were driving in and out, orders were being shouted.

When I arrived at the guesthouse, it was empty but the door was open. I walked in, but the rooms were locked. I was exhausted, so I sat on the couch in the front room and promptly fell asleep.

A machine gun was pointing in my face when I woke up.

'All right I'm leaving,' I said, after my request for a room was answered by shouts to get out of there. They had commandeered the guesthouse for their operation. Two young soldiers who looked Javanese walked me back through the military base, which was spread out over the top of a hill. The other soldiers turned instantly hostile as soon as they saw I was being escorted by armed men.

I was taken to the Brimob police commander, but he wasn't particularly interested in why I was there; the last thing he needed was a stray white person in the middle of his reprisal operation. He told me to go back to town.

I finally found a room behind a shop near the market and washed up. The priest who was in the residence attached to the church greeted me as exactly what I was— an unwanted guest. He detailed what little he had heard from nearby Alas, which was not much. He had had no contact with the priests there, as there were no phones in the town at all and the only contact was via radio, which was controlled by the military.

Not all of East Timor's Catholic priests were pro-independence, and this one seemed to think the people of Alas somehow deserved what they were getting.

'I told them there would be trouble after the dialogues,' he said.

His assistant followed me out of the building into the garden and surreptitiously gave me a list of names of people arrested around Same. He asked me to deliver the names to Manuel Abrantes in Dili at the Peace and Justice Commission—established by Bishop Belo after he won the Nobel Peace Prize in 1996, to monitor human rights abuses. He also told me that he'd just heard the village head in Alas had been killed the day before by troops in the town.

As I'd slept in Same, the church in Alas was being

surrounded by soldiers. 'They came in and broke chairs, and shot at the walls and in the air. They beat anybody within reach,' said a villager who saw it happen.

The *bemo* I'd hired at 6 am to get to Alas drove south out of town. The two guys in the front seat seemed fine. But then we took a sharp turn left and I was back in the military headquarters. It was Monday morning and there was a parade in progress. Soldiers in camouflage, black fatigues, dull green fatigues and a group of East Timorese in half-military, half-civilian dress holding very old rifles were being yelled at by an officer. His face was red and I couldn't catch what he was saying.

The same Brimob commander I'd seen the day before came out: 'Look, I will let you go to Suai, Viqueque or Dili, but you cannot go to Alas. And if you don't leave, I will have to arrest you.' He was exasperated, and the yelling of the military commander was unsettling him. He ordered the drivers to take me back to town and make sure I returned to Dili.

><>-0-<><

IT WAS only when the bus reached Maubisse in the central highlands on the way back to Dili, that the passengers began talking. They told me why they were fleeing. They reeled off a whole list of incidents of burnings, stabbings, beatings, arrests and killings perpetrated by the army. They talked about the new Timorese paramilitary units they called Gadapaksi and Milsus. They were not operating just in Alas, but in the towns of Turiscai and Fataberliu to the north and in many smaller villages in the area.

There was a lot I didn't put in the story I wrote about Alas; a lot that I'd heard about but had no way of checking. I wrote about the eleven people killed we had names for, including the village head, and the conditions in the town—no water and no food—and the plight of those sheltering in the church, and the fact that over 30 houses had been burnt down. I covered the military operations I'd seen in the area; the road blocks, the searches, the fact that the area had been effectively sealed off. I only gave the names of the people who'd been arrested if the witness could provide the details of the arrest. I knew the story would be denied by the authorities. Even though what was going on down in Alas was common knowledge in Dili, it still hadn't been reported internationally.

I didn't report the pregnant women shot and bayoneted in the stomach; or the headless corpse floating in the sea at nearby Betano; or the man with his genitals cut off with a bayonet while he was still alive in the village of Fataberliu; or the women stripped, raped and thrown in the lake at Betano to drown. None of this made it into the article, even though I'd heard the stories over and over again in Dili. All I really knew for sure was that there was a major military operation going on down there, and it was spread out over a large area, and people—civilians—were getting killed.

The story languished on the desks of several foreign editors. They didn't run it that week—there were no other reports to confirm it, no other journalist had been down there. The newspapers didn't believe it—or didn't care. It was a frustrating situation. People were putting their lives at risk to give me details of what was happening and that news was still not getting any further than me. I wondered what I was doing wrong or if it was just that nobody really gave a shit about what happened in a small, isolated village in the south of East Timor.

MANUEL ABRANTES was the head of Belo's Peace and Justice Commission. I went over the information we had with him. Piece by piece we ran through every incident we had heard about separately, trying to match them up. Basically, it looked like the military was moving through the area to the north, pursuing Falintil who were fleeing. A trail of incidents leading north from Alas showed their progress. Abrantes had information that the death toll was around 50, but he was waiting for Belo to allow him to go on the record with that information.

Minka Nijhuis, a Dutch journalist who ended up spending a long time in Timor, was there with me. After we left the Peace and Justice Commission, I asked her if she would report that figure. She would, but not attribute it to Manuel. I had heard figures of anything from 50 to 100 people dead, so I decided to report the lower figure based on what Abrantes had told us, attributing it to villagers who had fled the area, who had told me as much anyway.

Minka, Tjitska Lingsma and Irene Slegt, all Dutch, were the only other foreign print journalists in Dili. They tried to get down to Alas the next day but only got as far as Dotik, about 10 kilometres from Alas, when their driver refused to go on. The military at the Dotik checkpoint had been mentioned in many accounts of those who fled; they had arrested people who had subsequently disappeared.

The Dutch journalists were able to get more information from the checkpoint and some local people about what had been happening, and they came back and wrote graphic accounts of the violence which were published in Europe.

In response, there was a statement from United Nations Secretary-General Kofi Annan, who demanded that the Indonesian government cease its military activity around Alas.

Finally, my own account was published in Australia two weeks after we'd first become aware of the violence.

THE STUDENTS had been champing at the bit to protest about the killings in the Alas region, and now with international pressure on Indonesia, they were determined to demand an investigation into what was going on. It was the first time the students and the newly established organisations such as Kontras and CNRT in Dili had openly challenged the administration. It was a test of power between the Indonesian administration and the new groups in Dili, and was led, again, by the students.

After marching around Dili, past the military commander's office, the law courts and the governor's office, roughly 2,000 students occupied the local legislative assembly, the DPR. The building—a hexagonal two-storey structure—stands alone in spacious grounds, home to the 40-member assembly that governed East Timor in the name of Indonesia. The students set up their banners all over the outside of the building and stood on top of the concrete veranda and demanded an inquiry into the Alas killings. Riot police kept a distance of 500 metres as a series of students and independence leaders made speeches. They were angry and they were letting it out over a loudspeaker, reading out all the stories of the atrocities that had been attributed to the Indonesian military since the operation began on 9 November. Students who had fled from Same and Weberek, Turiscai and Alas told about what had happened and why they had fled for their lives. One of them screamed into the microphone, 'There are spies among us. I have information 20 paramilitary have been sent from Same to kill us. Let them try!' The crowd applauded.

That morning, Monday 23 November, the Indonesian commander, Lieutenant Colonel Tono Suratman, had declared in the *Suara Timor Timur* that he had ordered the troops in Alas to return to their bases. Bishop Belo also appealed for calm. But for once nobody listened to the Bishop, and nobody believed Suratman was telling the truth.

Manuel Carrascalão rose to speak, and said the new Indonesian government of Habibie had changed nothing: 'The military will still kill us.'

Antonio Cardoso, a senior intellectual, said, 'The governor and the military commander won't come in front of us today because they have no respect for us as human beings. Of course they don't respect our opinions.'

It went on like that all afternoon, with the list of speakers getting longer and more varied. There was a lot of time to fill, and the students had vowed not to move until they got some sort of result. Four of their leaders were involved in talks with Armindo Marianno Soares, the chairman of the DPR, but he had no real power anyway, and the talks were going nowhere. The students spent the night occupying the building.

After a long night and a hot, listless morning of more speeches, the students picked up their banners and marched to the governor's office on the foreshore. Everybody was tired and angry about the refusal of the authorities to bend to any of the demands. The governor agreed to meet with two students, Manuel Carrascalão and David Ximenes, and the military commander Tono Suratman. While the meeting happened, outside the Brimob riot police took up positions on the balcony of the building with their guns pointed at the students who continued with their speeches and songs.

About 5 pm, the meeting broke up. In the corridor

outside the room there was a crowd of soldiers, police, students and some journalists. The journalists were told to wait in a side room. The military commander and the governor were ushered into the next room. We waited for what we expected to be an announcement. Ten minutes later somebody looked into that next office—the back door opened onto the rear balcony and the room was empty. The governor and the commander had run away rather than face the students.

Downstairs the crowd listened to the announcement of the agreement. An independent investigation team to find out exactly what was happening in Alas would be formed from students, the CNRT, Kontras, Yayasan Hak, the governor's office and the military. The commander had agreed to cease all military action in the territory and to disband the paramilitaries. He claimed he would fly directly to Lospalos personally to deliver the order. He also said he would release all those in military custody from the recent operations.

'They admit they have captured many young people,' said Francisco Da Costa, one of the student negotiators, who then went on to list the paramilitary organisations Suratman had vowed to disband. It was an interesting list, including the three units—Teams Saka, Sera and Makikit—set up by Kopassus in the early 1990s. But the assurance turned out ultimately to be meaningless.

The students were furious. The commander had run away; he hadn't accepted responsibility for anything; he had just repeated assurances that in the past had meant nothing. There was yelling and scuffling among those who wanted the microphone.

'We have lost so many people, we don't care about this decision. We don't believe the troops will withdraw,' said one young man before he was pushed out of the way.

There was more scuffling in the crowd as a group of students tried to push their way to the flagpole directly in front of the building. It was a symbolic spot, the site of endless pro-Indonesian ceremonies and Fretilin's declaration of the brief nine days of independence from the Portuguese, before the Indonesians invaded. The Brimob aimed their automatic weapons at the students, who were struggling with other students trying to stop them from reaching the flagpole.

Everybody believed that if the flag was pulled down, the troops would begin shooting, but there were some in the crowd who just seemed to no longer care. Sebastião grabbed the microphone and began screaming: 'Don't touch the flag! We should be fighting for peace and calm. Do you just want to give them an excuse to kill us? For what? Nothing. We will never win if we keep fighting each other.'

He kept it up until he was hoarse and the students had stopped pushing each other, but they still refused to leave. They felt betrayed by their own leaders and lied to once again by a military that wouldn't even come to speak with them. An old Catholic nun, Sister Margarida, was given the microphone. She spoke of peace and calmed everybody down, and they began to disperse. In East Timorese society, it would be unthinkable to scream in protest against an ageing nun. The students went home.

▷─◁▶─◦─◀◁─◁

LATER, BACK at the Tourismo, Sebastião was furious. He had been told the whole flagpole incident was suggested by the two members of a Swiss film crew, Pascal and Olivier.

'They fuckin' offered to pay someone to rip the flag down. I don't believe it. What assholes,' he said, adding that they also wanted the students to raise the Portuguese flag—they were trying to sell footage to Portuguese networks.

A few beers later our talk had gone to beating them up. But of course we didn't.

When I saw Pascal and Olivier at breakfast the following day, they asked me if I knew where to hire a car. They wanted to go to Alas. I arranged it, and we left early the next day. Suratman had told the local newspaper there was now free movement to and from Alas. He had said the operation was over and the troops had returned to their barracks, and once again had refused to confirm details of any violence in the area. I didn't know whether I could trust the Swiss guys or not. A few people warned me against travelling with them, but they were the only ones prepared to try and get into the area.

WE STARTED walking at about 7 am and it began to rain almost immediately. At first, the road ran flat through the tall elephant grass and I cursed the driver who had refused to go down there, claiming the road was too bad. But it soon became muddy and full of holes, and it was very hard to stay upright.

At the first river crossing it was obvious why the driver had refused to go. We could barely climb down the eroded mud banks ourselves, and crossing the flooded river was a matter of jumping from rock to rock and then wading through the shallow bits.

It was not the main route into the town; we had tried that one the day before, but it was blocked by a flooded river. That first time, as we had waded out into the river to see if we could get the car across, three truckloads of Brimob soldiers appeared out of the scrub on the other side and started driving across. As the troops on the back of the trucks were yelling and posing with their guns—they had seen our cameras—the lead truck lurched into what was probably the original creek bed. The water came up over the windscreen and the driver revved the engine as the water flowed over the men in the back. They were dripping wet when the truck pulled out of the river next to us. The soldiers just wanted cigarettes, but pointed to Alas making 'knife across the throat' gestures. One guy even drew his bayonet, waved it in our faces, and told us not to go to Alas.

But it was obvious from the state of the river we weren't going anywhere, so they weren't too concerned about stopping us.

Later that day, as we tried to get back to Dili, the road was blocked by one of the same Brimob trucks. The weight of their passage had caused a landslide underneath the middle truck in the convoy, and it was balanced on a precipice, leaning as if about to fall down the valley. The bravado the same guys had shown earlier had gone. It was getting dark and they had nervously deployed a perimeter guard around the trucks, which were full of stolen livestock—chickens and goats—and other villagers' possessions.

———◦———

PAST THE river, we came to a small village that seemed deserted, although smoke still came from several of the grass-roofed huts. The people were hiding from us. We walked all morning through some more small villages and crossed four more rivers and began to climb upwards. I was falling behind. I'd contracted giardia a few days before and had to constantly stop to relieve myself. We were out of water and all of us were being eaten alive by mosquitoes.

Around 1 pm we finally reached one last hill and the guide pointed out some white buildings at the bottom of the valley. That was Alas.

The town was in a green valley with a river running down one side and a small wooden bridge. I went up to what looked like a standard Timorese kiosk—a small wooden shack with a hinged shutter on the front that, when lowered, became a counter. I was trying to buy water but the three men inside were just selling alcohol. Warm beer, Indonesian whisky and the clear East Timorese spirit *Dwasabo*, was all they had.

They didn't look like soldiers. Two of them had long hair and looked out of shape, and they were sloppily dressed. The other was an incredibly thin Javanese man with insect bites all over him; I presumed he was one of the many trans-migrants the Indonesians had settled on the south coast. They were all armed with the heavy old wooden-stocked automatic rifles I'd seen on the East Timorese soldiers in Same. Men like these were everywhere, walking along the street, or sitting under the shade of a veranda or a tree. They watched us walk through the town, to the church.

Father Cornelius Ceyrans looked shocked to see us. We were covered in mud and insect bites, and he immediately ordered coffee for us and began to tell what had been going on. It was true most of the people had come to shelter in the church after the Falintil attack, when the Indonesian military and the paramilitary began reprisals. After the 15th, when the paramilitary came into the church, they started leaving, as ordered. Those who had lived in Lurrin, which was the area of town burnt to the ground, were ordered to stay in the school.

Father Cornelius himself had only seen one man killed, on the first day, but he had seen another man, Antonio Policarpo, bayoneted in the neck by soldiers. Since then, he had stayed in the church and the people had relayed stories of what was happening to him. Most of the killing was happening outside of town, as the military tracked down those who had fled. He thought more than 50 people had died, because the operation was being conducted in the mountains and that was where the majority of the young people had fled to.

The operation continued, he said, and they were still getting reports of individual killings. He sat down and wrote a list of those who he knew had been arrested and not seen again from a nearby village called Labelara.

Pascal began filming Father Cornelius as he wrote. I put my hand in front of the camera. He hadn't asked permission, and if that footage was seen by Indonesian security forces—a priest giving journalists that kind of information—Cornelius would be a dead man. I was relieved when both Pascal and Olivier left to shoot some footage outside. There were 17 names on Father Cornelius's list, taken by the military and by the paramilitary. Only three of those arrested by the military he knew had been taken to Same, he said; he didn't know where the others had been taken and presumed they were dead.

Several other local people gathered around and began telling their stories. They were angry but also had the wide-eyed look of fear when they spoke of the military and the paramilitary that still controlled the town.

Waving his hand towards the main street, one man said: 'The Indonesians have made no provision to control the rifles they have handed out. There is no order, no control, no law here. Just look.'

Others spoke of their missing relatives or friends. After the attack, the entire population of the town had either fled to the church or hidden in the forest. They had no way of knowing what was going on and who was alive, but there were constant stories of atrocities. One man said a para-military soldier told him of 10 people executed and dumped in a river. Others spoke of women raped in the school and of people who tried to get to Same who never made it and disappeared.

The community was thoroughly isolated and terrorised. I told them about the demonstrations in Dili and the assur-ances by Tono Suratman four days earlier that operations in the area would cease. They hadn't noticed any difference.

Father Cornelius was the only one who had heard about the demonstrations, during a visit by the ICRC. I was inter-ested in what he had told the ICRC, because they had issued a report from Jakarta stating only nine people had died in the area as a result of the violence, and that was including the three Indonesian soldiers who died in the attack. The report had caused a lot of anger in Dili, with the leader of Falintil, Taur Matan Ruak, declaring in the local newspaper: 'We don't have confidence in the current leadership of the ICRC in Dili.'

Months later, when I finally made it to the Falintil camp which was home to those involved in the attack, Commander Falur Rate Laek told me he had continually called the ICRC in Dili from his satellite phone through-out this period offering details of the reprisals. He had detailed accounts of 42 deaths at the hands of the Indonesian and paramilitary forces, but they had never asked him for the information. I asked Father Cornelius what he'd told them, and he said it was exactly what he had been telling me.

It was time to leave. Father Cornelius had told me there would probably be questions asked about our visit and we had better go. He said it would be dangerous for us to be walking after dark. If they wanted to kill us, that was when they would do it. The military would then claim Falintil was responsible; that was normally how things were done.

I went with the guide to find the others. We went along the river to Lurrin, which was totally gutted. I counted more than 30 buildings burnt down and took some photos. I found Pascal and Olivier back in the main street outside the school. It was then that all hell broke loose among the paramilitaries.

Half-dressed soldiers streamed out of every building in the main street of Alas. Guns were pointed in our faces, and loaded and aimed at the head of our Timorese guide. A crowd of more than 50 men, some dressed in shorts and T-shirts, others in full camouflage, all carrying an assortment of automatic weapons, yelled in three different languages at us, at each other, and at our hapless guide, as they tried to drag him out of our grasp and into the police station.

We had stayed too long, and all it took was one half-drunk paramilitary soldier to come tearing out of one of the buildings on the main street for the situation to become suddenly unpredictable and terrifying. All the small shops and public buildings had been commandeered, and soldiers stood in the doorways and lounged on balconies. The man who had started the commotion was screaming in a mixture of Indonesian and Tetum. Pascal was screaming back in Indonesian and Olivier just kept filming.

I watched the man, shirtless, sweating and yelling, raise a gun to his shoulder and pull back the bolt. It was aimed directly at our unfortunate East Timorese guide, who had been the only one prepared to accompany us to this town. I could smell the alcohol on the armed man's breath, he was so close, and see his bloodshot eyes aiming squarely down the barrel of his outdated automatic rifle—straight at the head of the guide who was standing next to me.

Shaking with fear, the guide agreed to go with us to the police station where an Indonesian teenager with an ancient

SKS automatic rifle questioned us all, watched over by an Indonesian officer who said nothing. Outside, the crowd of shabby paramilitaries continued to yell at each other.

Minutes before, I'd been urging the others to stop filming and leave. Although the Indonesian commander in Dili had said Alas was open, the violence was definitely not over and the priest had known that the apparent calm that had allowed us to walk into town unhindered was only temporary. The paramilitary was running the town and the military showed no sign of restoring order. The people in Alas were in the hands of these very dangerous men.

Pascal and Olivier had been trying to interview the 'refugees' in the school on the main street. They weren't really refugees, they were captives. The irregular soldiers who guarded them had sat around listlessly in the hot early-afternoon sun. They were the same soldiers who had burnt down the houses two weeks earlier, and whom the people at the church had accused of rape.

After we argued with the police and showed them our passports we were allowed to leave, with a warning that if we were out after dark we would be mistaken for Falintil. A dirty finger was drawn across a throat. They had told the guide they were going to kill him and had forced him to give up his ID card, but they let him go. As we walked out, the drunken paramilitary soldiers followed us to the bridge and kept shouting. It was a show of force to the town, but we didn't know how far it would go. On the hill above the town, with the shouts of the paramilitary fading behind us, the Timorese guide collapsed to his knees. Tears ran down his face and his hands were clasped in prayer.

We walked like maniacs to get as far away as possible before it got dark. Just as I felt ready to collapse and with the light fading, some Timorese people with an earthmover appeared around a bend in the road. It was possibly the only nonmilitary vehicle that could have moved on that sodden road, and they gave us a lift all the way back to the car.

The guide was still with us, and after stopping at his house to tell his family what had happened, he joined us on the trip to Dili. The soldiers in Alas had his ID and his address. It would not be safe for him to stay at home any longer.

Heading back along the winding road across the mountains, ours was the only vehicle moving. Fog had settled over the mountains, and people walking along the road kept trying to flag us down.

We stopped for a group of them. They were young men from Turiscai, a village north of Same. They were fleeing to Maubisse to get away from the military operation. They weren't any more or less pro-independence than any other young people in the area, they just wanted to get away from the soldiers and this operation. About five of them piled into the car and we continued driving, painfully slowly in the fog along the badly damaged road.

At the next landslide, they leapt out of the car and began piling stones in the gap in the road to allow the car to get across, and then they pushed to get us through. One of them told me how, the day before, two men from his village near Turiscai were shot dead by soldiers. One was shot outside his house and the other, Martinho, was captured and tortured in his house before the soldiers told him to run, then shot him down.

The road was a mess and we didn't get back to Dili until well after midnight. All the way between Same and Maubisse, frightened faces glanced back at our headlights. Hundreds of people were moving at night to avoid the violence, heading north towards the capital.

>―+◆>―0―◆+―<

AFTER THAT trip, I became very ill. It was a measure of how far the Indonesians had neglected the health system in Timor that the simple antibiotics to treat giardia couldn't be bought in Dili. Many Indonesian doctors had left to go to other parts of the country, and the main hospital was closed in Dili, except for a handful of patients who couldn't be moved. An American doctor, Dan Murphy, had arrived in the territory and, without waiting for permission from the authorities—which probably never would have come— simply started working at the Motael clinic behind the church on the foreshore in Dili.

Dan's clinic became an important feature of Dili as the violence spiralled out of control. It was always the first place to check to see what had been happening, and the only place where people could be treated for serious injuries. The only other option in town for treatment of serious wounds was the Wirahusada military hospital which, for obvious reasons, people were reluctant to use.

Dan gave me some outdated Indonesian pills that didn't really do the job, and for a few days I was out of action and had to decline an offer to join the investigation team's trip to Alas—the investigation that was going ahead despite the nonparticipation of the Indonesian military and local government officials.

Thirty-two representatives from the Students Council, CNRT, Kontras and the Peace and Justice Commission got as far as Same, where soldiers stopped them at a makeshift road block. The soldiers surrounded the convoy and started shooting into the air.

'When they established we were the team to investigate the killings in Alas,' said João Alves 'they just began yelling and emptying their weapons in the air and began to search each vehicle.'

The team was escorted back to Dili by the military.

The incident was explained away by Tono Suratman the next day as 'a mistake'. He implied to the press that the investigation team had somehow provoked the soldiers with weapons of their own. It was an absurd argument, and it just made all those involved in the investigation realise how cynical the military really were, and how far they would go to discredit any reports of the brutal tactics they were employing. They had agreed to an investigation, then they shot at the team to prevent them from doing their job. Then, back in the capital at a press conference, they blamed the investigators for initiating the violence.

>-+»-0-«+-<

THE AUSTRALIAN army attaché had been due to visit East Timor, to introduce his successor to Indonesian military counterparts in Dili. Facing domestic pressure, Australian Foreign Minister Alexander Downer began referring to the visit as an investigation of the human rights situation in Alas.

I saw the Australian attaché and his successor in the dining room of the Tourismo. They were drinking beer and asked me to join them. Even though they wore civilian clothes, there was no doubt they were military. The hair cuts, the raw shaved faces, even the shorts and running shoes. It was a look we were going to see a lot more of in Timor.

They wanted to talk about Alas. I pointed to Sebastião and some other students sitting at a table in the garden, and said they should talk to them. After all, that was where a lot of my information came from, and it was no secret what the students were doing. The elder man, the outgoing attaché Colonel Brian Millen, said he didn't think that would be appropriate. I wondered why not, since he was going to be reporting back to Downer on the situation, he should have the whole story.

We began talking about the general situation. There had been a wave of killings of prominent people in small villages. The latest had been a schoolteacher in Uatolari. It had been reported in the local newspaper that a schoolteacher had been shot down in a classroom on 2 December. The man, Francisco Carvalho, had been shot seven times by two men who burst in wearing ski masks. They carried M-16s and Suratman had claimed they were Falintil; the Falintil were saying they were either Indonesian military or paramilitary. Millen cited the incident in conversation as an example that Falintil were not angels.

As far as I could see, it was a classic counter-insurgency tactic. Masked gunmen burst in and kill a schoolteacher, and they blame Falintil and use it as a pretext for an operation in the area. In Nicaragua in the early 1980s the Contra rebels had a little handbook written by the Americans that detailed this kind of operation as a way to terrorise villagers into not supporting the Sandinista government. The protocol was simple enough and dated back to the covert 'Phoenix' operations used in Vietnam by the Americans (something that should have been familiar to the Australians): as an example to the rest, kill the prominent people preferably those with standing in the community such as teachers or healthworkers, then blame the killings on the other side. It served to keep the people in check, created a reason to carry out reprisals and eliminated those educated people in a community that might otherwise support independence and provide an example to the others.

There had been similar shootings in the previous few weeks in Baucau, Venilale, Ossu and Becoli, all towns in the east, and all were blamed on Falintil. They often took place in towns where it would not have been difficult for Falintil to access. It was all bullshit. The military was behind the killings and everybody knew that, but here was the Australian army giving me the line trotted out by the Indonesian military.

⊳─┤◆├─O─┤◆├─◄

THE REPORT issued in Australia regarding the Alas killings following the visit played down the level of violence. It said a maximum of nine people had died and three of those were the Indonesian soldiers. At the end of the day, a soldier is under orders and the Australian government was seeking to minimise the situation. John Howard's position was that the East Timorese should accept the autonomy deal being offered and leave it at that. Downer used the report that played down the killings to deflect domestic criticism of the Howard government's support for autonomy. Australia's so-called 'special relationship' with Jakarta was to be maintained.

⊳─┤◆├─O─┤◆├─◄

MANUEL CARRASCALÃO had seen it all before. When I asked him if he knew if the military attaché had attempted to contact anyone in the CNRT regarding the situation in Alas or the failed investigation, he just laughed and said, 'The Australians will just speak to people who have been trained to give the right story.'

I went around to check if they had followed up on any of the suggestions I made to them when they had asked me what I knew about Alas. They had not tried Kontras or Yayasan Hak. The students tried to talk to them—Sebastião had approached them in the Tourismo but they had shooed him away. They had, to their credit, called Abrantes at the

Peace and Justice Commission, but that was about it.

They made a visit to Alas and Antonio Da Conçeição, a friend who was working for Care Indonesia at the time, was there delivering rice to the school the day they came. He told me how they arrived by Indonesian military helicopter at 7.30 am on 4 December and went to put a wreath on the graves of the three Indonesian soldiers who died in the 9 November attack, and then met briefly with the local military commander, in the company of regional military commander, and then left at 8.00 am. It was this visit that was the basis of their report on the situation.

Antonio and some other Timorese had attempted to talk to them, but they were prevented by the Indonesian soldiers in the town from getting anywhere near the Australians, and that was it.

⊳⊷⊶○⊷⊷⊲

As MID-DECEMBER came, the reports of killings in Turiscai in the central mountains continued. Among East Timorese human rights workers, an air of hopelessness gradually crept in. Reports and refugees started coming in from Maliana, Atabae and Bobonaro. Horrible stories of a new group of militia called Halilintar in the western regions started going around. Ears cut off, tongues cut out, throats slashed and bodies dumped in the sea. That was what Rui would tell me when I went around to the still-unfurnished Kontras office where he laboured over his typed reports. The name of João Tavares, the ex-*Bupati* of the Bobonaro region that runs along the northern end of the western border, started cropping up in the accounts. There was no doubt he was linked to Halilintar.

⊳⊷⊶○⊷⊷⊲

I TRIED to file some stories on Turiscai, but the demand for news dried up after the Australian government statement on Alas came out saying reports of violence were exaggerated. It wasn't until early January that a videotape smuggled out by José Ramos Horta's mother containing the testimonies of refugees from Alas revived the story. All the foreign journalists except for myself and Dutch journalist Irene Slegt left after mid-December. I stayed on for a while, still too sick to travel and waiting for a cheque to pay the hotel bill.

Quintão came out to the bus station at Tacitolu when I finally did leave. He was smiling and telling me to buy him some shoes in Darwin. He wanted some Nikes. I asked him if he was planning to do a lot of running in the New Year. He just laughed and said, 'Of course,' and told me to watch my stuff—some of the guys on the bus looked Sulawesi and he joked that they couldn't be trusted.

CHAPTER FIVE

27 January 1999
Suai, East Timor

AS THE SUN went down, the more than 4,000 people crammed into the church compound in Suai settled in for the evening. Small fires were lit. There were family groups: dirty kids with matted hair, mothers holding babies, uninterested fathers sitting off to one side smoking, squatting and talking quietly. People claimed their space on the ground as trucks arrived with more, who assembled at the platform that resembled a bandstand in the middle of the church grounds.

Adrianno do Nascimiento stood above the crowd of new arrivals, shouting above the noise, asking them to give him their names and where they had come from. He was writing it all down, trying to create a register of the refugees. Other helpers handed out packets of instant noodles which people, mostly kids, ripped open and ate raw. In one corner, women queued at the water source—a single tap.

These were all people who had arrived from the east where some horrible killings had thrown thousands into panic. The villages were emptying rapidly. By then, only two days since people had started arriving, the smell of human faeces and vomit was everywhere in the area and people just sat amongst it. There was nowhere else. The classrooms that formed a square around the compound were already full, mostly with women and children. Every spot of floor space was occupied by someone trying to sleep or just sit there. One wing was occupied entirely by farmers, transmigrants from Bali and Java, their skinny arms and legs an indicator of the poverty of their life on the malarial south coast of Timor where they had been sent by the Indonesian government.

Outside, the half-built, roofless cathedral on the hill behind the compound dominated the town. Its triangular walls could be seen from all around. It was also full of people. Young men climbed to the top of the unfinished façade for something to do, and to look out at the town they were now too scared to spend the night in.

From up there in the unfinished walls of the cathedral, the compound, covered in smoke and clouds of dust in the fading light, looked benign. The voices of thousands of people quietly talking amongst themselves was just a constant hum; the details couldn't be heard, just odd words and phrases—militia and scalping, knives and machetes, and when would they arrive.

Suddenly, people were running. A girl had raced into the compound, crying and screaming. Men grabbed iron bars, knives, stones—anything. They ran towards the gate in the wall that surrounded the school and church area. Women were screaming and grabbing their children. A crowd gathered around the girl who had run as far as the church and Father Hilario came out to see what the hell was going on. She was sobbing, out of breath and could barely talk, but Father Hilario persisted. When she finally spoke, some of the men ran off towards the gate.

'She says four trucks of militia have just arrived from Cassa, they will be here soon. They are outside the police station now,' Father Hilario translated for my benefit. The police station was just up the road past the market, a couple of hundred metres away.

Adrianno pulled me aside and led me into the priest's house, away from the excited crowd gathered around the girl. He had finished his refugee registration for the day and as we sat in the priest's house, I wondered if it was worth trying to call anybody. Adrianno was a student from Suai who worked with CNRT. That day he was referring to himself as the co-ordinator of refugees. It was a job that had only existed in Suai for the previous two days—since the killings in the village of Galitas on Monday 25 January.

The latest round of trouble that caused this flight of people started on the Sunday with the arrival in Zumalai of the militia from Cassa. They called themselves Ratih—a people's unit trained by the Indonesian army—and began to shoot their weapons and generally harass the people before returning east to Cassa. Later that day, they came back and bailed up two brothers on a motorbike. They shot one, Fernando Cardoso, in the head, killing him, and took the other back to Cassa where they tortured him. The militia returned twice that day to beat some people up. Everybody started fleeing.

The next day, an investigation team was sent by the local government in Suai. The militia in Cassa, led by Cançio Lopes De Carvalho, detained one of the team and sent the rest back. Cançio and his men then went to the town of Galitas, together with some members of the local military, and surrounded the house of a well-known pro-independence family. They went on a shooting spree through the village that lasted for about an hour, killing three people in the house and wounding two who tried to escape. But it was what they did next that really caused the panic.

'They slashed the skin and peeled off the scalp of one of them,' said Adrianno, who had seen the corpse the day before when he travelled to the village with the other local priest, Father Francisco Soares, to pick up the bodies. He made a peeling gesture with his hands as he said it. Then they disembowelled the dead pregnant woman and removed her baby. That was apparently done by the leader, Cançio. Adrianno gave me a roll of film he'd taken of the bodies, because he wouldn't be able to get it developed. His shot of the bodies in the back of a truck was later used by a Sydney newspaper.

The road that connects this south-west corner of East Timor to the rest of the country runs up through Cassa, where the mountains start, over through Ainaro, and then back to Dili. It is about 200 kilometres from Suai to Dili as the crow flies, but the state of the road across the mountains makes it a whole day's travel. With the militia in Cassa, people could not go north-east back to Dili.

The villages visited by the militia rapidly emptied and everybody fled west to Suai on the only available road. The militia had vowed that night—27 January—to attack the villages of Kuloan in Zumalai, Assumatun along the road to Suai, and Dais, only 20 kilometres from where we were. That was why the arrival of the trucks had caused such a panic. The people had no way of knowing whether the militia would come to the church grounds and, aside from their hands or whatever they could find, such as rocks, they were defenceless. All the rules of normal behaviour and punishment in that remote corner of the country had just been turned upside-down. It had always been a lot more peaceful than other parts of East Timor, which made what was happening just that much worse for the people.

Outside there was another commotion. A woman was screaming and howling hysterically, and people were trying to calm her down. She clutched a baby to her chest. Someone took it from her. The baby, four months old, was dead. She had held it tight against her chest as she ran from the militia. She had just run almost the entire 20 kilometres to the church from her village in the east only to see, when she arrived, that she had killed her baby in her fear.

IN DILI that morning, I had been sceptical of the figures being given to me by Lansell regarding the refugees in the church at Suai. Lansell Taudevin ran the only Australian government-aid project in East Timor, a clean water project; it had an office and local staff in Suai. He had come round to ask me if I had heard about the killings in Galitas on Monday. I had, but had not thought to report it, thinking that just three dead was not enough to sustain a report that probably wouldn't be published anyway. Lansell had been told by his Timorese staff of the brutal nature of the killings and the number of people who had begun pouring into Suai. He had become good friends with Father Hilario while working down there and was very worried about the situation.

At the time, I was the only foreign reporter in Dili, and Lansell couldn't believe my ambivalence towards the story. He was sending an Ausaid car down there and asked me if I would like a ride. I said of course I would, but wanted to file a quick report first.

We drove straight down the coast road to the West

Timorese border, crossed over and drove south along the road on the West Timor side, then crossed back over at the southern end to Suai. It was the only way to avoid the militia-controlled area.

The conditions in the church compound shocked me. I was astounded by the number of people and the immensity of their fear. In the time it had taken us to drive down, almost 2,000 more people had arrived, and Hilario and Francisco were wondering how the hell they were going to cope. It was an unprecedented situation. They had no stockpiles of food and no way to make shelter for the people. Those who had fled the violence were just sitting around in the open, and the two priests were worried that disease would start to spread.

Late in the evening, I sat smoking with Adrianno and a Caritas worker, Gil Da Costa, who had also just arrived from Dili. We were talking generalities about the situation and where it would go. They were both profoundly negative about what had happened in December and January. Gil had been working with refugees in Dili and said there were now more and more people coming in from Maubara and Liquiça. A new militia group called Besih Merah Putih (Red and White Iron) had begun operating in those towns west of Dili, and people were getting killed, while others were fleeing. Similar things were happening in Atabae and Maliana where it was Halilintar militia commanded by João Tavares. Then, in Ainaro, Cassa and Zumalai, this other group had caused this exodus. They talked about how people could not rely on any help from outside East Timor, as Indonesia would prevent it.

We were still out in the church compound, surrounded by sleeping people, when Father Hilario came out and told us what he'd heard on the radio: the Indonesian Information Minister, Yunus Yosfiah, and the Foreign

Minister, Ali Alatas, had just announced that if East Timor rejected the autonomy proposal, independence could possibly be granted. It was the first time since they invaded in 1975 that the Indonesians had admitted the possibility of independence for East Timor; and it was a major turn-around.

Adrianno responded angrily: 'Look what they will leave us with. This mess . . .' he said. We were sitting in the middle of a makeshift refugee camp and I could see his point. There was no elation or joy among us.

Father Hilario excused himself, he said it was time for bed. Gil didn't say much and Adrianno talked for a while about what a mess the situation had become before falling silent. We sat out there in the open for awhile in silence, and then went to bed.

I slept in the nuns' house, and the sisters were up at the crack of dawn and served a big breakfast with unfailing cheer. It would be fine, the killing was over and the people would go home in a few days said Sister Elsa as she served me another fried egg—she managed to escape the massacre at the same church in September, but Fathers Hilario and Francisco and more than 200 of the refugees were killed.

Gil arrived in a good mood and eager for me to hurry; he had someone for me to meet.

A militia who had run away had just come to the church seeking protection. The boy I was introduced to didn't look much older than 15, but swore he was 18 and, at first, I was disappointed. I was expecting someone a little more senior. He talked about how he had been recruited, while Gil translated for me. An Indonesian policeman had offered him a job three weeks earlier. The monthly wage, 250,000 rupiah (Aus$50), was good—more than he could hope to make anywhere else. He joined with 34 other people from

Suai. They were told they were joining a group called Ratih and were sent to Dili, where they were taken to the Indonesian military headquarters, Korem. There they received two weeks' training—mostly drilling and weapons training with M-16s—and slept in the barracks. They had not been allowed to go out in Dili.

When he returned to Suai, he was supposed to receive a weapon, but when he heard about what had happened in Galitas, he got scared and ran away, returning home. He was worried that he would be arrested or targeted by the militia and wanted to stay at the church with everybody else.

I wrote the boy's story up on one of the Ausaid computers in the Suai office, feeling sure that in this instance Lansell wouldn't mind this misuse of property. He had urged me to go down there; it was his staff members who had been threatened by the militia for working with foreigners.

Then, of course, I had to send the story. There was no email and the fax only went to Lansell's office in Dili. I called him and the line was so bad, I had to shout to make myself understood. He said he would fax the story on to the newspaper for me. But as soon as I'd sent it, I wasn't sure whether it had been a good idea. The information would go straight to the Australian Embassy in Jakarta, and probably Canberra, before it got into the newspaper.

Lansell's status as the only Australian government employee in Dili meant he had been asked to write regular reports on the situation for the Embassy and for Canberra. I was always wary of him because of that, but then, after a while, I just accepted that as part of his job and dealt with him anyway. Often there were no other Australians in town, and we both had a vested interest in knowing what the latest developments were.

But things would change very quickly for Lansell. After years in Dili maintaining cordial relations with all sides, he was suddenly—because he used Ausaid emergency tarpaulins for the refugees in Suai and set up a sanitary system at the church—identified as pro-independence. He was then targeted by the militia and forced to leave East Timor.

◄►◄►◄—○—◄►◄►◄

IT WAS 11 am on 29 January, a busy Friday morning in the centre of Dili. Outside the Hotel Mahkota—the most prestigious in town—where pro-integrationists were meeting to formulate a response to Habibie's suggestion of independence for East Timor, the street was about as busy as it ever got. An inter-island ferry, the Awu, had just docked across the road at the harbour, and the road was clogged with cars, trucks and taxis.

A group of men walked out onto the steps of the hotel. They were wearing an assortment of quasi-military gear—army pants, combat vests covered in pockets over black T-shirts—and they carried guns, pistols, M-16s and a few old Portuguese-era G3 automatics. They started blasting away with their weapons putting over 100 rounds into the air. People scattered. You could hear the racket all over town and then it stopped abruptly.

Dili now had its own militia, and their leader, Eurico Guterres, who wore his hair long at the back and had a penchant for extreme statements, was laughing—they had just announced the formation of the Forum for Unity, Democracy and Justice, the FPDK.

The core of this group had belonged to Basilio Araujo's 15-member 'East Timorese Intellectuals for Autonomy' back in October 1998. They had pressured the governor to try to sack the 700 or so East Timorese members of the public service who had called for a referendum by joining Forçarepetil, the East Timorese Intellectuals for a Referendum. The numbers involved accurately reflected the levels of support enjoyed by the two groups in the community, but that was irrelevant. The FPDK had money to burn from the coffers of the Indonesian military and civil service budgets and, more importantly, the full support of the Indonesian military for their violent activities. Everyone in Dili was to be treated to the spontaneous expression of their violent desire for East Timor to remain a part of Indonesia.

▻—◆—0—◆—◅

EURICO GUTERRES shook our hands stiffly at the beginning of the interview. It was the first time he had been introduced to the foreign press. Basilio Araujo, because of his fondness for the city where he went to university—Manchester, England—he had granted an interview with the *Guardian*'s correspondent, John Aglionby. Habibie's announcement of the possibility of independence for East Timor had brought the first of many journalists to Dili, including Dennis Schulz from the *Bulletin*, and Denis and I tagged along.

Basilio was slick. He spoke rapid and articulate English, and his tone had a pleading quality. He was always trying to present himself and the FPDK as the victims in this conflict. He introduced Eurico as 'our militia commander, the head of our armed wing' and explained away Friday's shooting outburst: 'Eurico here, he cannot take risks—there are a lot of leaders inside. A few people outside started shouting that we are dogs and we are selling this land. One of them started pulling something out of his pocket. I think it was a hand grenade.'

Eurico nodded gravely in agreement. A hand grenade, yes.

'So that's why you all stood out the front of the hotel and shot over 100 rounds in the air?'

'Yes. The military commander Suratman had already left an hour before. There was no military there, we had to protect ourselves,' said Eurico, looking at Basilio, who nodded. Okay, that was that matter dealt with.

John and I knew this was rubbish. We'd arrived there minutes after it had happened. But there would always be an element of truth in the little scenarios presented by Basilio and Eurico to explain away violent activities of the militia. It was highly likely that people were on the street outside calling them dogs.

As leader of the armed militia for the FPDK, Eurico claimed to have 818 armed men under his command in Dili alone. His group would work with all the other groups in East Timor who had the same aims—the other militia groups. The names of these groups had been constantly changing, but it was at about this time that they finally settled down into definable units, each with a public East Timorese leader.

The 2,000 guns Eurico claimed he had were from the Portuguese era. They had kept them hidden from the Indonesian military, he said. John pointed out that some of them were M-16s, which the Portuguese didn't have.

'They had to replace some,' said Eurico.

Who did?

'The military, they replaced some of the weapons. They dumped some in the sea.'

But you didn't get the guns from the Indonesian military . . .

'No, we get no support from them at all,' said Eurico.

We asked Eurico about the recent militia activity near Suai.

'What the people are saying is rubbish, lies spread by the

other side. There are acts of terror being committed against the pro-integrationists. Members of Fretilin or CNRT are responsible for the atrocities.' He stared us down as he spoke. His voice was raised and he was lifting one hand in the air, index finger extended to make his point. He continued. He feared for his safety. Fretilin and CNRT were terrorising the pro-integrationists. 'If Fretilin cannot guarantee my safety, we will begin a war!' Then he added: 'We are trying to find the most peaceful way forward for all groups.'

Eurico said he was shocked and surprised by Habibie's suggestion of the possibility of independence for East Timor. 'I have to tell you, East Timor will be total chaos. We are not educated. If we have different opinions, we tend to see people as enemies,' he said.

'In the period of the Suharto regime, there were lots of human rights violations. Now things start to get better. You cannot expect us to build democracy quickly. What the other side is pushing for is the wrong thing. I hate war. I don't want war. It all depends on Fretilin.'

The interview went on for a long time. We asked about his background. He said he'd been a leader of the pro-integrationists since 1995. He was only 28, he said at the time, but believed someone had to defend the people against the atrocities of CNRT.

He didn't talk about his real background—as a member of the Gadapaksi groups established by the Indonesians. He didn't mention their tactics of kidnapping pro-independence Timorese from their houses at night. Or the fact that it was only after he'd been soundly beaten by Kopassus in 1988 and then again in prison for participating at Santa Cruz on 12 November 1991 that he was recruited as a Gadapaksi leader. He didn't discuss the fact that the method of recruitment was a combination of offers of large sums of money, the clearing of his gambling debts and a promise that the beatings would continue if he was not 'smart' enough to accept their offer. Other issues he failed to mention included the amount of time he'd been spending in Jakarta recently, and the fact that the militia he now claimed to head was just the reactivated Gadapaksi network—Kopassus-trained, formed and paid for—that had been linked to the torture and killing of East Timorese people for years.

He'd been presented to us as a legitimate leader, and we were supposed to take him seriously—or else we were being biased.

After Eurico and Basilio had left, we stayed sitting in the Hotel Dili beer garden and ordered another beer. Hmm, well, he's pretty good. He gives the right answers. He's good looking in a thuggish, Indian screen-idol kind of way, with that long hair and intense expression. And he gives great quotes. He's constantly declaring war, claiming that he is the victim and he is East Timorese. And the guns? Well, they're only to protect the people, we said to each other over our drinks. We all had our story for the next day.

It was a bit like discovering a second-rate celebrity for the first time. We all knew he was going to be a big hit with the media. He was the bad guy to counter spokesman Basilio's supposedly reasonable arguments. The sickening thing was, he did have guns and his men did kill people, but only when they were told to by the real bosses—the Indonesian military.

'He'll be great when television arrives,' John Aglionby said.

In the following week, a lot of media did come down to East Timor from Jakarta. They did the story of the refugees in Suai, the refugees in Carrascalão's house in Dili from Maubara and Liquiça, and the reaction to Habibie's change of position. And, of course, Basilio and Eurico started to appear prominently as representatives of the pro-integration East Timorese. And they revelled in the attention. They were accessible, you could call them on their mobile phones and arrange interviews.

That was not something you could easily have done with the CNRT leaders in Dili. David Ximenes was often in hiding and couldn't be contacted. Manuel Carrascalão and Leandro Isaac, a prominent CNRT leader in Dili, were available, but they didn't speak English, so they were no good for Australian television. And security was far too important for the guerrillas in the mountains to let anybody come on short notice—and you had to walk a long way to get to them.

The CNRT's reaction to Habibie's announcement was summed up by João Alves who, as he gave me a lift across town, just shook his head and said: 'Independence by January 2000, it is insane. We are not ready, we have so much to do before then,' and thumped the steering wheel of his car.

But, unfortunately, Eurico and Basilio were not only bad hair and bluster. They were receiving weapons and had begun to openly threaten people.

Manuel Carrascalão was worried about the distribution of weapons. 'Now the pro-integration people are becoming very secretive,' he said. 'They were never like that in the past. The military has a lot of weapons and they are eager to share them out with the pro-integrationists. I hear between 10,000 and 12,000 weapons. In Ainaro they gave out 300 in the last two weeks.'

Manuel said the military had two motives for this. Revenge being one; if they pulled out, the country would be in chaos. 'They have been so arrogant about the situation in the past,' he said, 'they are not concerned about repercussions now.'

The second reason was to try to terrorise the people into supporting autonomy. With the militias breaking up pro-independence networks outside of Dili, it would give the appearance of civil war, he said. 'Whatever happens, the situation is going to get worse. The only way to get out of it now is to have peacekeepers.'

His 21-year-old daughter, Chris, was translating for him. I liked Chris, she was refreshingly normal, even as she was helping to look after the 400 or so refugees from Maubara and Liquiça who were camping in the garden of her family home.

What her father had said had upset her, but she had gone on translating, and mentioned that she thought he was tired. But Manuel was right. The militia under Eurico had virtually moved in next door to their home; they had made the Hotel Tropical, just a few doors down, their base. It used to be a Gadapaksi office anyway, but now, with the heightened activity and the influx of more weapons, the presence of hundreds of refugees—who'd fled from militia violence—in the garden of Manuel's house had brought more threats.

The old Carrascalão family home was surrounded by a high steel and wire fence, and someone was usually at the gate to unlock and relock it when you entered. But that was about all the protection they had. The refugees had come to Carrascalão because many had family connections or had worked his land in the Maubara and Liquiça areas. Manuel felt responsible when the people started arriving at the CNRT office and they had to move them out since they had no facilities for them.

I could just imagine the old man standing up and declaring in a grandiose gesture that they could all stay at his house. 'If CNRT won't look after them, I will.' Or words to that effect. Either way, the refugees stayed at his house until they were attacked months later, in April.

>-+-+-0-+-+-<

I HAD met former guerilla leader Mau Hudu at a picnic at a beautiful beach east of Dili back in mid-January. He had turned up to talk with a group of students from the Solidarity Council. It had been Antero's idea that every-body should relax and do something normal, like going to the beach. So we all sat under trees on the grass and listened to Antero and Mau Hudu's ideas on what was about to happen. It was the last time the students would do this for a long time and many of them would shortly have to flee to the hills, or abroad. Others would be killed.

Mau Hudu had asked to meet with me at his house. He wanted to talk about the militia. He said the divide and rule tactics of the Indonesian military were nothing new. Since 1982, they had been arming around 2,000 East Timorese. They were taken to Bandung (Kopassus officer college) in Java for training. The Indonesians then used them in oper-ations. In September and October 1998, they used them in the attack on the camp of Taur Matan Ruak. They had wanted to capture him, but couldn't.

Mau Hudu told me about the Indonesians using money from the International Monetary Fund to pay for the resumed training and the camps in Atapupu and Atambua, just across the West Timor border. He quoted a report in the Indonesian magazine *Detik* that said in September 1998 officers loyal to Prabowo started disappearing from their positions at Magalang training college in Java and had been turning up in Kupang.

He even told me where these officers were staying in Kefamenanu, a West Timorese town with training camps nearby. Mau Hudu explained the power struggle in the Indonesian military and identified armed forces chief General Wiranto, Major-General Adam Damiri (in charge of the Udayana command based in Bali that took in East Timor) and the chief of staff, Brigadier-General Mahidin

Simbolon as all involved in the militia's command structure.

'The paramilitary were formed many years ago. Disarmed, then rearmed. Now they have 12,000 arms ready to be distributed,' he said, mentioning the groups Gadapaksi in Alas, Mahidi in Ainaro and Halilintar in Maliana. We ran through all the small incidents that had been happening near Maubara and Liquiça throughout January.

At the time, I focused on the minor details of each incident, and the importance of what Mau Hudu had told me about the build-up of the militia escaped me. Afterwards I had raced off to Suai to report on the refugees and hadn't thought much more about the rest of the conversation. Now after speaking with Eurico, I remembered it all.

The Indonesian military commander in Dili, Tono Suratman, denied everything almost as a matter of course. According to him, the militia were just spontaneously bursting into violence all over the country, bristling with weapons from another era. It was absurd, but the Australian government and then the United Nations both maintained throughout this period there was no link between the Indonesian military and the militia. It was convenient and gave all sides a diplomatic sidestep—they did not have to address the source of the violence in East Timor, at least for the time being.

⊳−◆−○−◆−◁

Mau Hudu's assistant, Jose, turned up at the hotel to take me to see the guerillas. He was suspicious of Quintão and was not sure whether he should be allowed to come. But it turned out Quintão was somehow related to him—as often happens in East Timor—so there was no problem.

We headed off in a battered Kijang utility—a slow and uncomfortable vehicle made of pressed metal and powered by a three-cylinder engine. The vehicle's only advantage was that it was light and easy to push when it got stuck in mud, and it was relatively inconspicuous.

East of Dili behind Manatuto we turned straight up to the mountains and southward. In the previous three months the guerrillas involved in the attack on Alas had walked across the island's central mountains, away from the military and militia operations that continued further south. They had gone to the steep and rugged hills behind the picturesque traditional village of Laclubar, where the people still lived in wooden huts with tall cone-shaped thatched roofs as they had for centuries.

We hid the car behind a hut and waited until night fell, then started a long and difficult descent by foot into a valley. Rain started to fall before we got to the camp of the Falintil chief of staff, Lu-Olo, who'd been in the mountains since 1975. He told me that the guerrillas had no problem with a guarantee of safety for the militia leaders—in fact, they were observing a self-imposed ceasefire ordered by Xanana, who had recently been moved from Cipinang jail to house arrest in Jakarta.

'We are trying our best to have contact with them [the militia] to avoid the reopening of old wounds that Indonesia is trying to do,' he said. 'All through the years, we have been the ones who have always wanted a ceasefire. If Indonesia wants a ceasefire as well, then okay, we will. Then work for independence in other ways.'

We climbed back up and out of the valley in the morning, still wet and cold from a long night spent sleeping in rough shelters of bamboo and thatch. Radio contact was made from the top of the hill with the camp of the regional commander, Falur Rate Laek, and we were allowed to proceed. This involved another drive past an Indonesian military post to a small group of huts.

The people inside gave us lunch and the guides insisted on eating it, even though the Indonesian military had walked right past on the road outside, oblivious to us as we watched through the cracks in the walls of the hut. The young Indonesian soldiers seemed bored. Their guns were slung across their backs, and they were just strolling down the road. It looked like they had no idea that a few valleys away, only about an hour's walk, there were about 100 heavily armed Falintil fighters.

It started to rain heavily as we walked—the type of rain that made it difficult to see. It got into your eyes and soaked you to the bone. The path turned into a stream as water poured down the mountains, and everybody had trouble staying upright. Jose stopped, cut down some big banana leaves and handed them out. The shape of the leaf fits a human head, and even though everybody looked silly, it was a relief not to have to wipe the water off your face to see where you were stepping.

We climbed another hill, crossed a river and came to a small grass-roofed platform built on stilts among the trees. It was raining so hard, I didn't stop to see if anybody was inside.

After we'd passed some trees and came to a clearing, my first reaction was that we had made a terrible mistake: there were about 30 men wearing Indonesian camouflage uniforms. A lot of the uniforms were new and some had unit and rank badges. But these were Falintil, they were Falur's men.

This was a real camp, a far cry from the concealed hole in the ground near Baucau where I visited David Alex in 1997. Here they had built huts in rows, like a barracks. There was a large central building that looked like a meeting area. It had a thatched grass roof and some crude wooden furniture inside.

Falur invited us in out of the rain to sit down. Lying around on the dirt floor were boxes of ammunition, and rifles were stacked in the corner. A large Falintil flag hung from the rafters. Falur sat down in front of it and began talking.

He was a tall, strong, well-built man with a rapid and aggressive way of talking that could quickly dissolve into good-natured laughter. The boxes of ammunition were from Alas; they had lugged them more than 100 kilometres across the mountains, along with the rifles. Some young people who had fled their homes near Alas in November had helped. It was not safe for them to return, so they had joined the guerrillas. That explained the women around the camp, dressed in oversized camouflage shirts and pants.

Coffee was served and Falur told me about the flight from the south and the Indonesian reprisals. His men were now well armed and he said he could afford to support more people in the mountains, which was why he had allowed more young people into the camp.

It was easy to tell the veterans from the newcomers; they were well muscled and had long hair, some had long beards. Their brown skin was burnt darker by years of outdoor living. Falur himself had been in the mountains since 1983, when he deserted back to the guerrillas after a three-year stint in the Indonesian army—after he was forced to take part in the massacres around the village of Kraras.

We talked about the militia and he said that, in his experience, the Indonesians had always treated their Timorese troops so badly he couldn't see the militia being very loyal. Two East Timorese soldiers they had captured in Alas were still in his camp. One of them, Mateus Santos, stood next to me and still wore his Indonesian uniform with its insignia and battalion numbers. I sensed a good story, but his answers were short and to the point.

'I want to stay here because I feel safe,' he said. 'I am always hit and beaten by the Indonesian soldiers. They always suspect me of cooperating with the guerrillas. Years ago, they killed my wife and my children. They suspect me all the time. They are always beating me. With the guerrillas, they are East Timorese, they are brothers. We want to stay here and work together for independence.'

Regarding the Alas attack in November, Falur, who had directed it but didn't take an active part, said Falintil had no choice. The plans were in place to have the same kind of reprisal operation in place anyway. He also complained about the ICRC and the Australian government's response.

'After we conducted that operation in Alas, the military responded against the local civilian population in Alas and then Turiscai, where they have tortured and beaten many more of our people,' he said. 'There is mass killing in that area and many people were violated by the Indonesian military.

'If people still doubt that, it is because they don't understand about the military situation here and the Indonesian military.'

He said operations were still being conducted against the guerrillas. Patrols were still being sent out to find them, and they remained on high alert, but they felt reasonably safe where they were at that time. They had a lot more people, and they were well spread out in the thick jungle around us. There wouldn't be any surprises.

I went to take some photos around the camp. It had stopped raining and we didn't have much time because Falur had given Jose, Mau Hudu's assistant, some documents to be taken out of the country. Mau Hudu was leaving the following day to travel to Australia, so we had to depart soon.

The men and the few women in the camp were mostly resting in the small huts, but they all kept their guns beside them. I was looking intently at one guy and the others started laughing. He made a comical dash into one of the huts with his hands over his face. He was white and obviously Caucasian.

'No photos! No photos!' he said in a broad Australian accent before coming out of the hut.

He was obviously fair-haired but had dyed it black, along with his thick full-face beard. He wouldn't talk at first, except to mumble something in Tetum. He was dressed in brand new Indonesian camouflage and lace-up combat boots. When I asked him what he was doing there, he told me he was on holiday and had been there for 10 days.

'Look, I won't tell anybody you're up here. That's your business. But what are you doing here?' I asked him. He didn't come across as a military type, and he told me he was a butcher from England, but I knew from the accent that he was lying.

Falur walked up and said, 'Ha, see, now we are an international army,' as he laughed and slapped the guy on the back.

We had to leave shortly afterwards, and I told the mystery man to look me up in Dili. He never did, but I saw him a lot during the next few months whenever I visited the Falintil. He never left the guerrillas.

────◦────

ALL DAY Jose drove us like a drill-master. On the long walks in the rain he'd constantly exhorted us to move faster. He'd kept saying things like, 'So, you think this is hard? Try doing it at night carrying a gun and Indonesians trying to kill you.'

I was thoroughly sick of his macho competitiveness by the end of the day, but that was just part of him. He had lived a tough day-to-day life for too long and he valued physical endurance and strength highly. It had been drilled into him since he was a small boy as the only way to survive.

We didn't realise that the headlights of the utility weren't working until it was dark and pouring with rain again, and we were on a high mountain road with a sheer drop to one side.

One lone roadworker and his son were camped by the side of the road under a tarpaulin. Jose walked into their shelter and told them we needed to dry out. The man looked terrified. There were five of us and we were all covered in mud and soaked through. Jose told the man not to worry, pointing at me. 'He's a priest,' and then laughed maniacally. I was trying to push my way to the fire like everybody else in the tiny tent, and certainly didn't behave like any priest. I nodded to the roadworker, who still looked terrified.

It was a long, cold night on the mountain, and at the first hint of light we piled into the car and headed off again, desperate to get back to Dili, and to cigarettes and food.

CHAPTER SIX

24 February 1999
Dili, East Timor

THE INTERNATIONAL COMMITTEE for the Red Cross was already there when we arrived. They were taking the fatally wounded Joaquim De Jesus, a 21-year-old student, to the hospital. His chest was a mess of thick blood and his brown face was already turning grey as a group of Timorese and the ICRC worker put him in the car. Our taxi driver refused to go any further into the shouting mass of people, mostly young men, who were standing around the old Becora bus terminal, pointing and telling us to go up a small side street.

Jacinto had heard the shooting and came to get me from the hotel moments before, and Johan, a Dutch journalist who had been in Dili less than 24 hours, also came along. We were in the middle of a group of youths who were screaming at a house. They were standing in the middle of the street, some with swords in their hands, others with rocks. Some just stood there baring their chests and hurling abuse at a house further up the street. I began asking questions.

'They are still in there—in the house, they went into the house.'

Who?

'Milisi with guns, six of them,' said Chrispin Lopes Munis, a student I knew from the university. He lived in this street, and Joaquim who had been shot in the chest about 15 minutes earlier was his friend.

Six men carrying M-16s and in military dress but with long hair had just walked down the street, asked for him by name and then shot him in the chest. Then they started shooting into the air as youths ran out of houses and from the market near the bus station. The armed men had run into a nearby house and the young people who now stood on the road were screaming and working themselves into a fury over the death of their friend.

Shots started coming out of the house. One or two at first, then a continuous volley; it sounded like the shots were being fired into the air, close to us, but not straight at us. The young men stood in the street, oblivious to the shooting, still yelling abuse at the house. Some started picking up rocks.

I was just starting to move off the street to a ditch at the side when another student, Francisco Hornai, fell to the ground suddenly. He was not more than seven metres away from me, and I could already see the blood pouring out of him. He had been shot straight through the chest, and now shots were being fired directly at the youths in the middle of the road. Some ran and some leapt into the same ditch I had made it to. A group of them ran forward and, with bullets flying at them as the noise of the shooting increased, grabbed Francisco and dragged him back to where the trees blocked the line of sight from the house. From the way his body moved when they dragged him, it was obvious he was already dead. I tried to take a photo but my hands were shaking too much and my chest was pounding; the picture was hopelessly out of focus. I'd never seen someone shot dead before.

The shooting intensified and we could hear it coming through the trees. The young men who had been crouching behind fences and trees or lying in the ditch all stood up and ran back towards the market. Jacinto grabbed my arm and we ran with Johan about 300 metres along Jalan Bedois as the shooting continued. People were jumping fences, leaping into windows and running down the gaps between houses—anything to get off the straight street that the bullets were flying down.

Jacinto pointed at a house and we jumped the side of the concrete veranda and sat behind the waist-high wall. Johan bolted up the hill behind us, and I went to follow him, but Jacinto grabbed me and said we were safer where we were.

The shots continued and got louder and louder as the six militia walked back along the street they had just cleared. Paint and bits of concrete were flying off the top of the wall we were crouching behind as the bullets hit the other side. They were walking closer and closer and the shots became louder until it sounded as if they were standing right beside where we had taken cover. I was dripping with sweat and having trouble breathing, and Jacinto just motioned me to be quiet. He was pressed up against the wall listening intently.

The volleys stopped, but then the shots started again individually. I imagined they were killing people they'd found hiding. Gradually, the sound of the shots moved further along the street towards the market. I looked over the wall and quickly squatted back down—there was a militia member walking away towards the market. His gun was pointed straight at the houses, which he was scanning as he walked slowly forward. From behind he looked like a normal soldier, except his hair was long and he was sloppily dressed in Indonesian camouflage with a photographer's vest over the top.

A few random shots broke a period of silence and then we heard someone shouting, but it was too far away to understand. What had actually happened was two Portuguese television journalists had arrived in a car in the market just as the militia entered from the side street where we were. Jose Maria Cyrne, a cameraman, and the popular presenter Jose Alberto Carvalho had been surrounded by the militia, who began to beat them. They were kicked and punched and jabbed with rifle butts. Everything they had on them was stolen: cameras, passports, mobile phones and money. The militia marched them, with guns to their heads, down through Becora's main road to the large military base of Battalion 745. There, at least, the beating stopped, but it was another two hours before they were released and escorted back to their hotel.

We were to speculate later that the reason for their ill-treatment could have been the fact they were the first Portuguese to report live from Dili via a satellite link-up. Their coverage was being watched by the militia. Of course, reporting in Portuguese, a language many East Timorese still spoke, made it easy for the militia to monitor their unflattering coverage. But, in any case, both the Indonesians and the militia hated the Portuguese, and given that the militia had just shot two people dead then shot their way out of an angry crowd, they were clearly in no mood to respect the press.

><+>-O-<+><

I HAD just gone back out into the street when my mobile phone flashed a message. It was the ABC. I called them back. They wanted a short question and answer on that morning's meeting of East Timorese leaders to establish the Commission of East Timorese People for Peace. The report was to be aired on Radio Australia.

My mind was blank. I told them I couldn't really do that and told them what had just happened. 'Okay,' they said, 'we'll just go ahead and do something on the violence.'

The shooting started again, but further away. It must have been the militia forcing people back as they marched the Portuguese TV people to the military base, but I didn't know that. I thought they might have been coming back. I ran into a small wooden shack and sat in the front room, and Jacinto followed. There was a whole family sitting inside and Jacinto told them to be quiet while I did the radio report, sweating heavily and straining to hear whether there were more shots outside. I had no idea whether the militia would come back and I had a lot of trouble concentrating on what I was saying.

After asking about the violence, Peter Meares, the presenter back in Melbourne, asked about the morning's meeting. It had been a major meeting of all the parties, similar to the meeting in Dare in September. This time there had been a UN representative, Tamrat Samuel, present. Indonesia's roving ambassador for East Timor, Francisco Lopes Da Cruz, and many other representatives were also involved, as were CNRT pro-independence leaders, the governor, Tono Suratman and one or two of the militia leaders. Eurico had been pointedly absent.

Lopes Da Cruz, now presenting himself as a moderate pro-autonomy leader, had said: 'We do not want to create a civil war, we will be an example to the Asia Pacific.'

A CNRT representative, Aporico Apolinario, read a message from Xanana, who was still under house arrest in Jakarta, that supported the foundation of the Commission for Peace. His statement urged that respect be extended to all parties in the process, no matter what their opinions or backgrounds.

After speeches from the military commander Tono Suratman and the governor Abilio Soares which both promoted peace, reconciliation and a nonviolent solution to the problem, UN envoy Tamrat Samuel had basically told the meeting a vote of some form was going to go ahead. The vote would be a choice between independence for East Timor versus autonomy within Indonesia, and would be supervised by the United Nations. He continued: 'We will have to find ways of asking whether they will accept or reject the offer of autonomy—we hope through this process launched in Dili today, East Timorese leaders will make a commitment to renounce violence.'

His speech had been met by applause from all those present in the large meeting hall of the Hotel Mahkota.

It was quite an important meeting in terms of East Timor's immediate future, and Peter Mares was right in wanting to focus on it, but at the time all I could think of were the people who had just been shot, and what was happening outside.

The shooting was just another incident in the terror campaign that everybody knew was going on, but on that day it was also the militia and military's response to the peace process—the process represented by the establishment of the commission that morning of 24 February.

After I had finished the interview, I thanked the family who had just sat there staring at me warily. I went outside. Some young people were talking to Jacinto and Johan, who had run up the hill and burst into a church to get away from the shooting. He had joined in the prayers, under the direction of a priest, of several hundred children. They prayed until the noise died down.

I asked one of the students who called himself Ilutu Rambo, if he'd seen what had started the outburst.

'Nothing happened here,' he said. 'It seems the Indonesian military try to make a condition to frighten the people because they know right now Tamrat Samuel is here, and they want to create a disturbance. It's one of the Indonesian military strategies to make Timorese kill each other and not have a dialogue.'

That was the sort of answer I should have given Peter Meares, but my mind had been too scrambled. I wrote it down.

People were just coming back out onto the street cautiously when we got back to the market, and we asked what had happened to the Portuguese TV people. Nobody knew, other than that they were taken away by the militia who were pointing guns at them and hitting them.

It was about 5.30 pm and I remember thinking that if I could get back to the hotel quickly, there would still be time to file for the following day. The newspaper had knocked back the morning's story of the meeting but I thought with these latest shootings, they would have to want something.

The street was now full of people. The shooting had attracted all the local Becora youths who were now milling around carrying knives and rocks. They said they wanted to defend their area against a possible return of the militia.

With crowds gathering on the road outside the base of Indonesian Battalion 745, soldiers with weapons in hand stayed inside the fence. As a precaution, they were stationed all along the wire. Young East Timorese men had thrown branches across the road to stop traffic, and they pressed up against the cars to see who was inside. They said they were checking for militia. They were acting threateningly but that was only because everybody was afraid and angry and defenceless. They waved us through.

Makeshift barricades were being thrown up all along the main road back to Dili. Some were 44-gallon drums, others were just branches and bits of junk, like old tyres. The young people moved them out of the way once they had checked who was in each car. Despite the yelling and waving around of old swords and machetes, the groups of young men at the barricades were behaving in a relatively orderly way. They had loosely organised themselves into groups to protect particular areas. It was a response to the now almost daily violence in Dili that had been growing throughout February.

The increased defiance of the people following the period of political freedom manifested itself in their will-ingness to get out and fight on the street when threatened by militia or military violence. In the past, they would have run, or stayed in their homes, but now they noisily took control of the streets. This response helped the militia in their goal, to create the appearance of chaos and civil war in the capital. It also made confrontations inevitable.

Back towards the Tourismo, Eurico's men had also formed barricades of old tyres. They hadn't manned them, however; they would probably have been attacked if they had. They just poured petrol on them, lit them and ran away, blocking the road outside their headquarters at the Hotel Tropical. Clouds of thick black smoke enveloped the street.

▷▶▸•○•◂◁◁

BACK AT the Tourismo I raced to my room, wrote a version of the day's events and sent it. I called the newspaper to see if they had received it. It was about 6.30 pm in Dili when I sent it; that would be 9.30 pm in Sydney. It was too late. The person on the foreign desk wasn't interested and everybody else had left for the day. Besides, they told me, they'd included a wire brief of the incident. They read it back to me. It went something like: 'Two killed in clashes between pro-independence and pro-autonomy supporters in Dili.'

I slammed down the phone. I was furious. The word 'clash' implied that both sides were armed and fighting each other. What I had seen was a clear case of unarmed people being murdered in broad daylight. Whether the militia were serving members of the TNI or not seemed irrelevant. They were wearing standard-issue uniforms, carrying standard-issue weapons and had fled straight back to a military base after the shooting. If that didn't constitute TNI involvement, I didn't know what would.

But the version of events people would read the following day would be of groups of armed Timorese clashing in Dili suburbs as they disagreed over whether to remain a part of Indonesia or not. The whole public relations program that had led to the formation of the militia by the Indonesian military seemed to be working very well. They could now blame the Timorese themselves for the violence, as they continued to coordinate and implement it; they could then use that as an excuse to block a ballot. Or if the ballot went ahead, they could make sure conditions were far from fair.

⊱⋅•⋅⊱⊰⋅•⋅⊰

EARLIER IN the day, as I left the meeting at the Hotel Mahkota, Albertino, a former political prisoner, had told me to go to the CNRT office because there were some people there who wanted to talk to a journalist. The five of them had just arrived from a small town called Guico, in the mountains behind Maubara, about 50 kilometres west of Dili. They all had untreated gunshot wounds. One, Bruno Dos Santos Cardoso, had been shot in the head. He wanted to talk, and even though he had become drowsy and his eyes didn't seem to focus, he seemed remarkably lucid.

The day before, all the villagers in Guico had been called to a meeting. The *Camat*, or district administrator, Jose Arfat, was there, along with Indonesian troops from the local garrison, Battalion 143. Also present were some of those who had joined the militia group in nearby Maubara—Besih Merah Putih.

As the villagers approached the building where the meeting was to be held, Jose Arfat opened fire with an M-16 and was quickly joined by the troops and the militia, who were also armed with automatic rifles. About 200 villagers who were on their way to the meeting all ran as the shots continued. Bruno said he thought three men had been killed and many others had been wounded. They said 500 people from the area had fled inland towards the town of Ermera after the shooting, and they told of spending the night trying to cross the rivers Lou-ilu and Morobo. They had made it to the town of Hatolia, about 20 kilometres inland, where they were able to get a car to Dili. Arriving in Dili, they had gone straight to the CNRT office to tell their story, even before seeking treatment for their wounds.

An East Timorese doctor, Nelson Martins, told me that they had not been able to take the injured people from Guico to the main hospital, because the Indonesian soldiers who were guarding the building would not have prevented the militia coming to take the wounded men away. He said he and Dan Murphy would have to try and remove the bullets at the Motael clinic. 'But we don't know if we will be able to in the case of the head wound,' he had said in a matter of fact way, standing next to Bruno.

There was nowhere else to treat the man in Dili. Most Indonesian doctors had left and the only other hospital was run by the military. Bruno died when they tried to remove the bullet from his head the following day. A BBC camera crew filmed the unsuccessful operation, but there was nothing that could be done for the man.

It was a shocking story in that it showed the local administration's active involvement in the destruction of the communities they were appointed by the Indonesians to lead. What had happened at Guico could be compared with an Australian shire councillor blowing away his constituents as they arrived at a meeting he had called.

The militia and Battalion 143 were at that time clearing the whole area behind Maubara, but it was to be a week or so before we realised the extent of what had happened. The roads in and out of the area had been blocked. The militia had destroyed the towns of Guico, Lissa Dila and Gugleur. Windows had been smashed, houses burnt down and anything of value stolen. The places became ghost towns as the people fled either to Maubara on the coast, where they lived under the control of the militia, or further inland to Sare, an area that was said to be under Falintil's control.

><+◦+◦+◦+<

THAT NIGHT, 24 February, barricades were erected in Dili and shooting was again heard in Becora and in the residential area of Bidau. Dili had come to a standstill. No businesses opened the following morning and the streets were deserted until the early afternoon. After 3 pm, a crowd of more than 2,000 people began to gather at the CNRT office in Balide, where the bodies of the two students who'd been shot were being kept.

The night before, just as we'd left Becora, local youths had killed a soldier, Mario Da Costa, as he returned to his home in the area. He was a member of the Milsus attached to Kodim and based in Dili. He was stabbed by youths after they'd accused him of being a spy, but it was really just revenge for the murder of the students that afternoon.

The military agreed with CNRT the two funerals—of the students and the soldier—should take place separately. The military cemetery in Dili is across the road from the Santa Cruz cemetery where the two students were to be buried. The two groups of mourners would inevitably come face to face if both funerals were held at the same time, so it was agreed the military would bury their man at 1 pm, well before the scheduled 3 pm start of the procession to honour the two students.

East Timorese funerals in Dili usually include a procession through the city that ends at the graveyard. If the person was well known, they involve a slow-moving parade of many vehicles full of mourners. Such processions often held up traffic in Dili in the afternoon.

Just one week before this funeral, Dili had been brought to a standstill by another one with political overtones. Thousands of people marched or rode in trucks, buses and cars in a procession that wound its way past all of the government offices and the military headquarters and then on to the cemetery in Santa Cruz. Their protest was over the Sunday afternoon shooting of Bendito Fortunato Pires in the head and chest after a confrontation between local youths and militia.

Six Mahidi militia, Cançio Carvalho's men from Ainaro and Cassa, had come down to Dili on a Sunday afternoon to kidnap some pro-independence people who had fled from their area, to take them back to kill or torture them. About 100 local young men had heard about their plans. They surrounded the militia's car and pelted it with rocks as the Mahidi men, firing shots into the air, tried to approach the house in Bairo Pite where the people they were after were staying.

The militia had fled to the local police headquarters, and the youths had gathered outside and demanded they be handed over. The police responded by shooting 25-year-old Bendito in the head and chest, killing him instantly. People who had seen it happen later told me that the killer had been a police sniper with a telescopic sight on his rifle. He had shot Bendito from behind the safety of the police compound's wall.

Another young man was dead, but what made it even sadder was that Bendito was not even part of the group screaming at the police to hand over the militia. He had been standing over to one side, just watching. The police commander, Lieutenant-Colonel Timbul Silaen, described that night as a 'clash between pro-autonomy and pro-independence elements' and told us that the police had not been involved.

━━◆━○━◆━━

I JOINED the thousands of people walking up from the governor's office on the foreshore and past the market in the direction of the cemetery. Albertino walked beside me and we talked. He had a big dent in his high forehead where a soldier had whacked him with an M-16 many years ago at a demonstration outside the university. He had since been jailed for several years and released during the July 1998 amnesties following the fall of Suharto.

The large turnout for the funeral, so soon after the last one, impressed Albertino, who smiled and said: 'When they kill the next, we will have another funeral like this and stop Dili again. And we will keep going until they stop killing, or until they kill us all.' Albertino was fond of dramatic gestures.

We walked back from the cemetery to the CNRT office

as it was getting dark. The road was full of people walking, and motorbikes, cars and vans, some with loudspeakers amplifying the crackling sound of voices reciting prayers. I found it all profoundly depressing, and after checking that nothing else had happened at the CNRT office where more than 1,000 people were still milling about, I got Albertino to give me a ride on his motorbike to the Hotel Resende so I could have a beer. The newspaper wasn't interested in another funeral story so soon after the last one . . .

The large restaurant, with its red-and-white checked tablecloths, was empty. It had been a long time since the Indonesian officers had come in to use the karaoke machine that still sat on the small stage at one end of the room. The Indonesian businessmen who had often brought their families here for dinner had either left and closed their businesses or didn't go out at night any more.

Pro-independence leaders such as Leandro Isaac, João Alves and others who worked across the road at the governor's office had started coming here in the second half of 1998. Student leaders such as Antero from the Solidarity Council came too, if someone else footed the bill. But at that time, they were all too busy. And, besides they were starting to get death threats from the militia, so going out at night was not done without good reason.

For a short while, the emerging pro-autonomy elite had come into the Resende to spend some of their newly acquired wealth. It was not unusual to see Eurico and some of his men enjoying dinner and a few beers at lunchtime. But their notoriety had increased and in those days they tended only to go out at night armed—for reasons other than enjoying a good dinner.

The other main customers—foreigners and journalists—were not present that night either. At the time, I thought it was probably to do with the beating the TV guys Jose

Maria and Jose Alberto had received the day before. It had affected a few fellow Portuguese, who had left on that day's flight, no longer feeling they could work properly. And the two Joses were trying to arrange to leave without their passports.

So I sat with the barman and chatted in my bad Indonesian. He was talking about his brother who had been forced to leave Ermera because of threats. We talked about the funeral and what had happened in Becora. Then the conversation dried up and we both stared out the window at the empty street. After my third can of beer, he asked me to leave because he wanted to pack up and get home. There was no food, anyway; the cook had not turned up because she would not have been able to get home—there was no transport.

I walked back to the Tourismo along the foreshore, avoiding the back street with Eurico's headquarters. Even the small beer carts and outdoor eating stalls that usually sold noodles and rice across the road from the military barracks were absent that night. The Indonesian owners had either returned to where they came from in other parts of Indonesia, or were too scared of the East Timorese to set up for the time being.

Further along, the Hotel Dili was deserted, but that didn't surprise me. Ever since the two Australian brothers Gino and Ernesto Favarro had returned in August of 1998 to reclaim their family's hotel, business had been slow. I knew they were going broke trying to keep the place open.

Lansell and the other full-time Ausaid employees were having a meeting in the Tourismo's garden when I got back. A fax was being passed around. It had been distributed that afternoon in Jakarta to news organisations and was signed by Eurico Guterres and Cançio Carvalho. The main gist of it was expressed in the line: 'It is better to sacrifice an

Australian diplomat or journalist to save the lives of 850,000 East Timorese.' It was a death threat.

The language suggested that it had been written in response to the change of the Australian government position in January. Canberra had moved from supporting Indonesian sovereignty in East Timor to supporting the East Timorese in being given the chance of self-determination. But the Australian government still publicly supported the continuation of Indonesian rule in East Timor when it said that the autonomy option was the preferred solution in its eyes.

That change of position—Australia had formerly been the only country internationally to recognise Indonesia's takeover of East Timor in 1976—had supposedly drawn this threatening response from the hard-line pro-Indonesian leaders. The letter also stated that 15,000 pro-Indonesian militia would be waiting for 'Australian hypocrites and deceivers' if they arrived on East Timorese soil 'day or night'. The letter went on to explain that Australia's policy shift would spark a civil war in East Timor—that was why we must be killed.

Even with the pro-Indonesian group's twisted logic, that fax was a first. They were the only group running around declaring there was going to be a civil war. They were openly saying they would be 'forced' to start one, and that was why they were arming themselves. It had become Australia's fault for interfering in East Timor. The shift in Canberra's policy was actually a step back from its previous support of the Indonesian side and, if anything, a step back from interference in the internal affairs of East Timor. The real reason for the threat was that Australian Foreign Minister Alexander Downer was in Jakarta at the time. He had met with President Habibie and visited Xanana Gusmão, still under house-arrest in Jakarta, but had refused a meeting with the militia leaders. They were annoyed. The following day, Basilio Araujo handed the letter now making the rounds of the Tourismo garden to Alexander Downer personally.

But in Dili, all we had that night was the fax from Jakarta with the stated intention to 'sacrifice' us. The fax itself became barely readable as the group of 15 Australians passed it around the table; clammy hands smudged the print on the thermal fax paper, making it barely readable.

Lansell, who was definitely the closest thing we had to an Australian diplomat, was concerned. He felt responsible for his five remaining staff and if the threat was carried out on any of the people present and he had not recommended an evacuation, he would feel he had done the wrong thing. The atmosphere at the table began to develop its own dynamic as people started justifying their reasons for leaving and attempted to convince others to join them.

There was reason for concern. Dili had not witnessed chaos like that of the previous week since May of 1997, and even then it had not led to the widespread occupation of the streets by pro-independence youths. What the militia and the military were doing in the countryside had forced about 8,000 people to leave their homes. People were being shot with alarming regularity and the Indonesian authorities were at best ambivalent, at worst directly involved. If there had been a political shift that said foreigners were fair game, we would all be sitting ducks.

The conversation went on and people began to talk about how defenceless they were. They talked about the lack of medical services if someone was injured; the lack of transport out of Dili if it really became necessary to leave in a hurry. The only airline flying into Dili, Merpati, had scaled back their flights to three times a week. The only way out of East Timor by road was to the west, and that route was through an area now controlled by militia. Road blocks were a permanent feature and there had been many reports of cars being searched and people being detained by the militia. The conversation went around in circles, and the anxiety increased. I went to bed.

The others stayed up most of the night and attempted to get on an Indonesian military helicopter that had been arranged by the new Portuguese representative in Jakarta, Ana Gomes, to fly out the two Portuguese journalists to the West Timorese capital of Kupang early in the morning. The Australians were not allowed on, and their attempts to arrange to fly out on the standard Merpati commercial flight had also been frustrated; the only flight was apparently full with the Indonesian Merpati airline staff and their families.

By the time I joined them for breakfast, they were tired and disheartened, but even more determined to leave. The difficulties they encountered had added a sense of urgency.

Lansell was organising four vehicles to drive to Kupang, and had sought and received permission from the military that guaranteed them safe passage at any road block. Several people recommended I leave with them, pointing out that I was one of only two Australian journalists there, and the letter had specified journalists as potential sacrifices.

I did seriously consider joining them, because their departure seemed so final. With the growing transport problems, it was beginning to look like it was leave then or never get another chance. But Ric Curnow, an Australian cameraman who had been running the satellite up-link for the Portuguese, was staying, and that reassured me. I couldn't really believe they would just kill us in cold blood.

Another unlikely character determined to stay was Isa Bradidge, from Ballina in New South Wales. A Christian with a slightly evangelical edge, he had come to East Timor to help the people in any way he could. He'd done this by spending money raised by his hometown church on relief supplies for refugees and delivering them himself. I couldn't help but agree when he said, 'They [the East Timorese] put their lives on the line constantly for us [by working with foreigners]; that is what they have been living with for 23 years. It is time for us to be here.'

The Sydney newspaper wanted a piece on the people leaving. Gino Favarro complained about being forced to abandon his hotel again. Preben Larsen from Ausaid said he actually felt safer with pro-independence people maintaining barricades in the street where he lived, but he would still leave because he couldn't work. Perhaps the most outspoken was an Australian businessman, Don Lang, who had only arrived the day before. 'Why should I stay? It has nothing to do with me. It's people like you who cause these sorts of problems,' he said when I asked him what he thought.

They piled into their vehicles and left about midday. When I walked back into the hotel, João, the old waiter who had been working there since before the Indonesian invasion, shook his head.

'Next they will come and kill you like they did to Roger East,' he said, continuing to shake his head as he swept the foyer. João served Roger East breakfast the day he was killed, and it was a story he often told.

Shut up, that's all I need to hear, was what I thought to myself as I went back to my room, which was at the back of the hotel. I immediately looked around and began packing. This room was too exposed. It was right at the rear of the hotel, near the back alley and the fence, and surrounded by a disused tennis court and garden. Suddenly it felt like a place from which you could easily be abducted. The hotel was almost empty, and I finally moved into an air-conditioned room at the front of the building, negotiating a special discounted rate. They expected business to be slow; the place was going to be empty for a while.

As evacuations go, this one had been minor, with 11 Australians leaving and six staying. But it sent a clear signal to the militia leaders in Jakarta that they could intimidate the foreign community and could, as a result, get the attention they wanted. It also left those of us who remained feeling particularly exposed. If anything happened to us from then on, we had been warned and we had made our choice.

BASILIO MUST have flown back from Jakarta to Dili that afternoon after handing the death threat letter to Downer. I saw him in the Hotel Mahkota and he feigned surprise. 'I thought you had left with the others,' he said, all smug and smiling. 'No, but you did have us slightly concerned,' I told him, and then asked him if there was any danger. His answer was something like, if I reported fairly on what was really happening in East Timor, there would be no problem. He then handed me a press release for the rally the following day, 27 February, in the town of Atabae. They were naming João Tavares *Pang Lima* (commander in chief) of all the militia organisations in East Timor. He said there would be no problems and he would personally drive me there, and could I tell the other journalists about it. I lied and said, of course I'd go with him. I would be glad to help, I said.

'WHAT A revolting situation to be in,' I remember telling Ric Curnow as we sat in his room at the Mahkota. Basilio,

Eurico and Cançio had basically threatened us into covering their events. Our safety was being dictated by them, and then they wanted me to be their press agent for the few foreign reporters still in Dili. Ric told me not to worry about it, to just cover the rally the next day and then do something on the other side.

Ric had been the first to organise satellite gear to be brought down to Dili. He had set himself up doing everything from filming and editing to transmitting live crosses for the first time ever from East Timor. He had been running interviews with Basilio for Singapore-based CNBC and SBS television in Australia. I had personally felt he had been giving Basilio too much coverage, but then I was glad that the two of them seemed to get along so well.

Basilio, of course, needed television, and Ric was the only television reporter who was always there. He needed me in a lesser capacity, and he treated me accordingly. Ric immediately agreed to come to Atabae with us the following day, knowing he could sell footage of militia leaders issuing death threats to Australians.

THE PRO-INTEGRATION rallies had begun one week before in Balibo, on 19 February. As we were driving down there, Sebastião had seen all the trucks and buses arriving draped in red and white Indonesian flags. He looked genuinely distressed: 'Oh my God, it is a mass mobilisation by the authorities,' he had said.

On the sports field near the old Portuguese fort, there were probably about 2,000 people. Sebastião saw a girl he knew walking past with a red and white headband on. He asked her what she was doing there. 'We were told to come here about two days ago,' she said. She lived in nearby

Maliana and worked for the civil service. Government employees had been given the day off to attend.

The banners were held at the front of the crowd, which gathered around the public address system. There were rows of chairs to one side. The banners were in English, Indonesian and Tetum. 'Alive or dead we are still with integration.' 'Once integrated always integrated.' 'Referendum causing civil war.' The best one in English read: 'Portugal shut up, you're a bloody imperialist.'

Mark Davis was filming for the ABC's *Four Corners*. He asked Sebastião to ask the people if they knew what the English banners said. The people shrugged or shook their heads and said they didn't know, they were just told to hold them.

A man called Francisco Soares told us that it was not an official ceremony; the people just wanted to show the foreign media how much they loved the red and white flag of Indonesia.

Eurico took the microphone after the dignitaries—the *Bupati*, Guilherme Dos Santos, the local military commander, João Tavares, his brother and his sons, and Cançio Carvalho—had taken their seats at the front of the crowd.

'Whether they want to listen to us or not, if the Indonesians leave, they will find a war here,' Eurico said, and the crowd applauded.

He was a forceful public speaker. He didn't talk, he shouted. He emphasised each point with a clenched fist punching the air, a finger pointing at the crowd or a raised arm. As he finished a statement, his voice went higher, as if he was expecting the cheers of the crowd to drown him out. Eurico told the crowd the militia was there to protect them, that they could safely support Indonesia. That was why the people of Maubara had risen up and supported the militia, the Besih Merah Putih.

His statement, like the rally, turned the truth on its head. The people, many of the young men at least, had been fleeing the town since early January because of the violence carried out by this very group. Everybody knew the local Indonesian military was also to blame; they knew they had worked with the militia. They had also been killing some of the students involved in the free-speech dialogues in the area.

The militia themselves were also there, a group of maybe 100 young men in khaki T-shirts with the words 'Hali Linta' stencilled on the front. Some wore red and white headbands, but otherwise they just looked like a group of ordinary young men. They stood around under the trees behind where the leaders addressed the crowd. They looked relatively harmless, but later in the day—as the rally was finishing—a few others turned up with guns. But the turnout looked nothing like the thousands of warriors each militia leader said he controlled.

The speakers' arguments were all related to the problems of independence. They spoke of how there would be civil war; how it would be the civilians who suffered as a result. There would be no food, no electricity, no hospitals. Between statements to each other, committing themselves to fight for integration, they talked about the nightmare of independence. Eurico vowed to support Tavares, Cançio vowed to support Tavares, they all declared they would fight a war if Indonesia left.

João Tavares, an old man, got up in front of the crowd. He was a big man in this area. He had fought for the Indonesians after he fled across the border from Fretilin following UDT's failed coup against the Portuguese. That had begun the civil war in August of 1975. When the Indonesian military initiated their pre-invasion strategy of cross-border raids against East Timor, they claimed it was the work of East Timorese irregulars. João Tavares was in charge of a group of these troops; in reality they merely acted in a support role to the Indonesian troops who conducted the raids. That was what the five journalists were trying to report when they were killed in Balibo in October of 1975. João Tavares was there, and it was rumoured he still had the watch of one of the dead journalists; it was alleged he kept it as a souvenir.

After fighting for the Indonesians, he was rewarded by being made the *Bupati* of Bobonaro regency, a post he vacated in 1989 after holding it for 13 years. His personal wealth was greatly enhanced by his time as *Bupati* and he accumulated a lot of land in the area.

He bellowed at the crowd: 'Do you want to eat stones? That is all you will have if Indonesia leaves.'

The crowd waved the flags and banners. Tavares, on the western border, represented money and power. They understood that and responded accordingly.

As the speeches went on into the early afternoon, most of the Indonesian television cameras left. I was getting bored, but Mark wanted to stay, and I had come down in his car. I began taking photos and I couldn't help but notice the face of one man who held a banner. He dutifully moved the banner up and down in response to the speakers like everybody else, but his expression was profoundly sad. He was dressed in traditional clothes, wore a red and white headband, but his face, with its mournful look and the deadness of his eyes, illustrated the coercion that had brought him there.

After the rally, Mark interviewed Cançio using Sebastião as an interpreter. I muscled in on the interview. Cançio was constantly glancing around, his eyes never still for a moment. He was conscious of the crowd of people around him under the shade of the trees; they were watching the interview and listening to his answers. Mark asked him why he had sliced open the pregnant woman and removed the baby. You could see Cançio's face stiffen and darken as Sebastião coolly translated the question. He fixed his gaze on Mark and his eyes started to bulge. They were going bloodshot in front of us and you could see the fury rising in him, along with his blood pressure. It looked as though he was going to kill Mark there and then. I began edging back involuntarily into the surrounding crowd as Cançio launched into a denial. He spoke rapidly and furiously. He spat out his words, along with flecks of saliva. The effort of controlling himself and not launching himself at Mark was almost too much for him.

━━━◆━○━◆━━

THE TUESDAY after the rally, 23 February, Basilio turned up at the Tourismo. It was about 9 am and I was still finishing breakfast. The Indonesian journalists had all gone down to the next big pro-autonomy rally at Cançio's hometown of Cassa, but I had declined the offer as it was a five-hour drive and I was sick of rallies. Basilio insisted I went along; he was going down by Indonesian military helicopter with Eurico and he was supposed to be taking the foreign press, but no-one had turned up. He was in a bind. It was going to look very bad if he turned up at the helicopter with no-one in tow. I agreed to go on the condition I could finish my breakfast, and enjoyed watching him make a call on his mobile to hold up the helicopter.

While he was waiting for me to finish, Basilio told me how the Indonesian Information Minister, Yunus Yosfiah, had offered him a job as a newsreader for the state television channel TVRI when he was recently in Jakarta. 'The governor wants me, the *Danrem* [Tono Suratman] wants me, and now these people want me—all because of my English,' he said.

Yunus Yosfiah was widely regarded as being being the officer who directly ordered the killing of the five Australian-based journalists in Balibo. He was a special forces captain at the time, and in charge of one of the units that attacked the town. Mark Davis had mentioned that he had seen Cançio and Eurico at Yunus's house in Jakarta when he had tried to interview him. It was obvious this same crowd was organising the latest operation in East Timor.

Minka Nijhuis was walking by and agreed to come along. She had been in nearby Ainaro recently, and had told me some of the details of what Cançio's Mahidi militia had been doing there.

Eurico and two Indonesian military officers were waiting at the military heliport at what used to be the old Portuguese airport, not far from the centre of town. I laughed, it was all too absurd. Tono Suratman was still claiming there was no link between the military and the militia, yet there we all were in the helicopter together, on our way to another 'spontaneous' expression of the people's desire to remain a part of Indonesia.

I didn't feel that comfortable flying over the central mountains of East Timor in an Indonesian army helicopter. Andy, a cameraman from Associated Press, had also turned up and was filming out of the open doors as we flew low over the mountains, beneath the clouds. I couldn't help thinking of the helicopter that came down in 1998, killing those nine high-ranking Indonesian officers. Was it shot down or was it really a mechanical failure? I made a mental note to ask Falintil again next time I saw them to see if they would finally confirm shooting it down.

Cassa is a small town with a soccer field in the middle.

On one side of the field is the main road to Suai from Ainaro. At that time there was a military base, a school, a church and some shops, and that was about it. On the other side of the football field where we landed, was Cançio's house. The majority of the crowd was gathered there. As the helicopter landed, Cançio, his brother Nemezio and the local military commander came forward to greet us. Behind the rows of young men in khaki T-shirts with 'Mahidi' stencilled on them who surrounded the soccer field, were Indonesian military trucks. They were unloading civilians from the back of the trucks. The soldiers were holding their weapons at the ready as they moved them off. That was the crowd.

The same banners we saw the previous Friday in Balibo were handed out and Indonesian flags were distributed by two Indonesian soldiers, straight from a military truck. The rally got under way with Nemezio Carvalho thanking the assorted dignitaries behind him. The line-up of 'dignitaries' seated on Cançio's veranda left little doubt about who was running the show. There was the SGI commander of East Timor in civilian dress, the regional army commander, Lieutenant-Colonel Gatot, the local police commander, Major Razali, and the head of the Ainaro subdistrict, Agostinho Sarmiento. There were also several older Indonesian men who refused to give me their names. They had a military look about them, and I presumed they were Kopassus. They were all relaxing, enjoying the spectacle.

The speeches were the same as those given in Balibo, but with a little more intensity.

'Autonomy, yes! Independence, no!' He stood face to face with me, screaming in my face. It was not a statement, it was a challenge. He screamed again. 'Autonomy, yes! Independence, no!' Spittle flew all over me. The crowd laughed. Behind him, on the veranda, Cançio, the local military commander, Basilio and the host of Indonesians in civilian clothes who refused to give me their names, laughed at the sight of Vasco screaming me down.

Vasco was a big man for a Timorese. I had gone to take a photo of him—he stood out and it was an obvious photo: the big man standing at the front of the crowd, screaming and revving them up. '*Hidup Integrasi! Hidup Otonomi!*' As his superiors seemed to be enjoying the spectacle, Vasco became more animated, and I decided it was time to forget about the photo.

'So you see,' said Nemezio, Cançio's well-spoken brother, 'our people feel very strongly. They want to remain with Indonesia. You can write that the people are brought here by the military or they are forced to come here, but I think maybe now you will understand.'

That's the thing about Nemezio, and to a lesser extent Cançio, that distinguished them from the rest of the militia leaders being presented to us at the time. Nemezio believed in what he was doing. He believed in the rightness of his cause and I really believed he actually would fight an extended war in the mountains against Fretilin—the communists—which is what they said they would do if autonomy did not win.

Their grandfather, Mateus Lopes De Carvalho, was the traditional ruler in this area. He was one of the East Timorese leaders who signed the Balibo declaration in 1976 that recognised the Indonesian takeover of East Timor and declared the territory Indonesia's 27th province. In many ways, Nemezio came across as a reasonable, well-spoken man, but as soon as you spoke of the past or Falintil, some deep hatred was triggered and his whole demeanor changed.

In Cassa, 230 kilometres by road from Dili and surrounded by rugged mountains, the Carvalho brothers

said they felt very vulnerable. 'If they want to become independent, why don't they embrace us and not kill us like in
1975?' asked Nemezia. 'The way to independence is not
through killing your own.'

He told a story of how, when he was a young boy, Fretilin
soldiers came to Cassa and stayed in his father's house.
'They had three of them sharing one woman. It was
disgusting,' he said.

His conversation was dominated by references to Fretilin
atrocities. When he claimed to be related to the schoolteacher in Uatolari who had recently been shot, I made a
note to check that detail. (Back in Dili, I did follow it up,
and Nemezio was no more related to the dead individual
than I was.) The dead were being claimed by the pro-
Indonesian groups as their own, even though they were the
victims of Indonesian military and militia violence.

The rally ran its course and we headed back to the helicopter. I stopped and took a photo—Eurico was waving
from the open door of the helicopter, behind him was
Minka, adding a touch of glamour and laughter, and
Basilio in the front seat had a broad grin on his face. Eurico
looked like he was having the time of his life. His vanity
was stroked by his Indonesian bosses and when they
allowed him occasional indulgences—such as a helicopter—he loved it. As a phony figurehead of a largely
invented political group, he was getting more than his fair
share of coverage, and his Indonesian bosses were obviously
very happy with how he'd gone so far.

Driving to the rally in Atabae on Saturday 27 February,
Basilio gave me an indication of how closely our reports
were being monitored. 'You won't see any Indonesian
military driving these people to this rally at gunpoint,' he
said to me, making a reference to the lead I had used about
the last rally in Cassa. The thing was, that article had not

been published back in Australia, so they must have intercepted my emailed reports from the hotel, or somebody had downloaded the story from my computer. It was interesting, but not unexpected.

I had half-heartedly performed my role as Basilio's contact with the foreign press and told them about the rally. A few other journalists were reluctant to go to a rally of people who had been threatening to kill us a few days before, and who had not yet retracted their statement. The night before at dinner, the BBC crew thought it was very funny to take 'the last images' of Ric and I. And in the morning, all those who had said they were coming suddenly had something else very pressing to do. So it ended up being just Ric, Basilio and I in the car going down to Atabae.

The Besih Merah Putih militia had set up road blocks and posts near Liquiça and Maubara. Groups of young men stood on the road and flagged cars down. They wore red and white headbands, and some had machetes and spears, or those long homemade spear guns which had a roughly carved stock and pistol grip, a thick piece of elastic or rubber and a nasty-looking metal-tipped spear, supposedly ready to fire.

Basilio stopped at every roadblock and handed out cartons of Gudang Garam, clove cigarettes. He didn't look very comfortable with these people, and they didn't seem to know who he was. I joined in handing out the cigarettes, thinking it couldn't do me any harm in the future.

Once again, we arrived at a football field draped in flags with a podium and public address system. They were the same banners, with a few additions, and the local military chief, *Bupati* and police chief sitting in the shade. Jorge Tavares, son of João, began: 'If you choose autonomy, you can avoid civil war. If you want to become independent, you will have to step over the pro-integrationists and militia's dead bodies.' And it went on and on: threats to begin a war, accusations levelled at independence leaders such as Manuel Carrascalão and José Ramos Horta. Jorge Tavares and then Eurico made all kinds of accusations against CNRT and Xanana. Then they began, for our benefit, to abuse the Australian government.

'We will fight Australia here under the red and white flag. The diplomats and journalists only destroy the East Timorese,' said João Tavares, who also told the villagers that he would hold a month-long party at his property for them all if they chose autonomy.

Afterwards, we interviewed João Tavares in the shade near his home. Behind him, militia carrying spears and homemade spear guns milled about, enjoying the free lunch he'd put on. The old man repeated the threats against the Australian diplomats and journalists, adding that he would kill any Australian peacekeepers that set foot in Bobonaro regency. He used the same words as the printed threat in the letter: 'Is it not right to sacrifice one Australian journalist or diplomat to save the lives of 850,000 East Timorese?'

Ric tried to draw him out and make him say he would kill the Australians: 'Sacrifice, you keep talking about sacrifice, does this mean kill?' Ric asked the same question over and over again, trying to get that one line from Tavares that he could use in his report. But Tavares did not deviate from the script. The line was sacrifice, and he repeated it over and over again.

On the way back to Dili, we passed the small wharf in Tibar. Possessions were piled high on it and being loaded onto a high-prowed Indonesian sailing ship like the ones still used throughout the islands for cargo. More Indonesians leaving for other parts of the country. The recent violence had accelerated their movement out of East Timor, as they realised there was no future for them in the half island. Many Indonesian businesses closed down during this period, and goods became harder to get hold of and more expensive as shortages developed. In the main post office in Dili, huge piles of boxes had appeared at the rear of the building as goods accumulated in the 24-year rule of Indonesia were mailed elsewhere.

Basilio looked at the pile of household goods and boxes on the wharf, and blamed the pro-independence for terrorising the people.

AT THE CNRT office in Balide, things were chaotic as usual. People rushed in and out, and others loitered in the corridors waiting to give information on the latest violence. They were trying to coordinate and organise themselves to be East Timor's future government but constantly they, like all of us, were responding to the latest killings, disappearances and shootings.

João Alves pulled me aside to give me a list of those killed in Suai where Cançio's men had been attacking again. He was always stressed. He was a big man, but you could see he had lost weight, and his English had become more fragmentary. He was one of the few leaders trying to carry on amidst all the threats.

Seven people were missing and another two had been confirmed killed. There were still over 1,000 people in the church, and a new Suai-based militia called Lak Saur had become active close to the West Timorese border. João Alves gave me a list of 11 names of those responsible for the latest violence. Four came from West Timor, one was a serving soldier, one a former Gadapaksi member, and the rest were government employees. It showed where the militia were coming from.

All the institutions of the Indonesian state in East Timor were pressuring and coercing their members to take part in the violence, and the poverty of neighbouring West Timor had helped recruit young men. Alves received another report while I was talking to him: another 800 people had fled to the church in Suai, but this time they had come from the west, fleeing another militia group.

Kontras had been trying to monitor the violence and investigate each individual report—a big job for which they were hardly prepared. They still hadn't really received any funding, and were working from handwritten and typed statements and long lists collated in their bare offices. Often, their investigators were in more danger than the people whose deaths they were investigating; they were higher on the militia's lists. Their organisation had been receiving threats, so it was often only Rui Lourenco working alone in the sparsely furnished office.

They decided to hold a press conference.

They had compiled details of a total of 97 incidents of killings and violence against East Timorese in January and February. These had involved the Indonesian military, and were just the ones that could be confirmed. Kontras had been trying to force Tono Suratman into giving a written agreement guaranteeing the security of the refugees who wanted to return to Maliana in the west. Of course, Tono agreed; he said he would personally instruct his men to protect those who returned to their homes. But he would not put it on paper; he would only agree verbally, which was worthless. Those who took him at his word were attacked when they returned to Maliana.

▻━◆━०━◆━◅

THE HEAD of Intel in Dili used to go and see Isabel da Costa Ferreira after her meetings with Tono Suratman. He told Isabel that Suratman, although he was the head of the military in East Timor, could not give a written agreement for the safety of the refugees because of the effect it would have on the prestige of the military.

Rui and Isabel sat behind the bare table trying to explain their attempts to hold the military accountable for what was going on. Their organisation was trying to use Indonesian law to make the military respect human rights, but they were mocked, ignored and lied to by the military at every turn. Watching their efforts was frustrating because it was obvious by February that East Timor was outside the rule of law, however loosely that was applied in other parts of Indonesia.

When I asked them why they continued to try and work within the system when it was so obviously responsible for what was happening, Rui replied: 'Kontras is preparing reports on human rights abuses under Suratman. They will be held responsible for this. If not now under Indonesian law, then later under international law. We will present this evidence to Wiranto because it is clear that Suratman is not the authority.'

But the reality was Wiranto was just as involved in the organisation of this terror campaign; any report to him would not affect the campaign of violence.

Rui went on to detail shootings in Suai, Ainaro, the clearing of the villages of Guico and Lissa Dila, and the creation of another large refugee population in Sare, where people had no food and were trapped by the Indonesian military and militia on one side, and flooded rivers on the other.

He talked about the continued killings in Atabae, Maubara and Maliana, and the increased problems they were facing moving around in the western parts of East Timor because the road blocks were targeting young people.

It was a depressing picture, and the truth was this wasn't even half the story. People couldn't travel freely, many were killed with no witnesses, and those who saw a murder were often too afraid to come forward. There was a lot going on that we could only guess at.

CHAPTER SEVEN

19 April 1999
Kupang, West Timor

THE CROWD ON the dock at Kupang was restless and tired of waiting. And we saw why we had been kept behind a cyclone wire fence for three hours before being allowed to board the inter-island passenger ship the *Dobonsolo*.

Indonesian military trucks had arrived and the soldiers on them had started changing out of their uniforms into civilian clothing. They were standing in the middle of the carpark by the dock, before boarding the ship headed for Dili. It was such a public place, I couldn't figure why they even bothered to make this small effort to conceal their identities.

I had been stuck in Kupang for three days trying to get to Dili. The day I arrived in West Timor from Darwin, 17 April, the militia, openly led by Eurico, had attacked Carrascalão's house in Dili and killed at least 13 people, including Manuel's 19-year-old son. The militia had also attacked the offices of the *Saura Timor Timur* newspaper, destroying all the equipment. They had then spent the afternoon randomly firing into the air as they drove around the capital. Out in Becora, they burnt cars and shops, and at least one bystander was shot dead. In Dili's centre, they surrounded journalists near the Hotel Mahkota and entered the foyer discharging their weapons.

Carmela Baranowska, a filmmaker from Australia, later showed me her footage of the rally and the behaviour of the militia outside the governor's office that had preceded the violence. Eurico clearly ordered his men to go and shoot those in favour of independence, and said he alone would take responsibility. Overseen by Indonesian military officers, Eurico and Tavares stood in a jeep as it drove slowly along the lines of shabby militia bearing their 'homemade' rifles and other 'traditional weapons'. What happened next was laughable. The line of militia with homemade guns stood to fire off a salute. The fuses on their guns were lit like firecrackers, and the Indonesian soldiers near them frantically told them to raise their guns before they discharged. Then they boomed away, all at different times. There were huge clouds of smoke billowing out of the guns—basically just bits of pipe strapped to a wooden stock. The militia was so obviously incompetent and their weapons so primitive, and the Indonesian troops were so clearly directing proceedings, that what was supposed to be a show of strength served as exactly the opposite.

But there was nothing funny about what happened next. The Aitarak militia, joined by the Besih Merah Putih— who a week earlier had perpetrated the 6 April massacre in the churchgrounds in Liquiça—left the rally and attacked the nearby house of Manuel Carrascalão. The violence went on all afternoon.

In Kupang, I sat in my hotel room listening to reports of the violence with a West Timorese friend, Ben. He was a friend of Chris Carrascalão—Manuel's daughter. Ben was worried. The confusing reports did not mention what had happened to Chris, or her father, and we both presumed they were dead.

They were in fact safe in Indonesian police custody, but many of the refugees who were still in the house when it was attacked were missing. Later I was told the number of those killed could have been as high as 60, but nobody really knew. The area was sealed off by the police immediately after the attack, and the bodies were reportedly taken by truck to a lake 50 kilometres west of Dili, near Maubara.

Geoff Thompson, the ABC reporter we were listening to on the radio, had arrived in Dili for the first time as the violence erupted. In Darwin the day before, he had asked me what I thought would happen with the militia's planned rally and their threats to attack targets in Dili. I told him that it would probably just be a noisy show of strength, like those I had seen in Balibo or Atabae. But I had been out of East Timor for the best part of a month, and had no idea how bad things had become, aside from the reports of the massacre in the church at Liquiça the week before. Geoff and his cameraman, Terry, literally landed right in the middle of it, and were confronted by the worst open organised violence yet seen in Dili. I could hear Geoff on the radio trying to get a grasp and make sense of what this was: state-organised violence.

Ben and I tried to hire a car to get to Dili. But there was no amount of money that could convince anyone to drive us there. The public buses weren't running any more and the only scheduled flight into Dili had terminated at Kupang and returned to Bali. The only alternative was to wait for the boat. I wanted to be back in Dili. I could tell what was going on from Geoff's reports. He had recorded the screaming and weeping relatives as they brought in the bodies of the dead and injured to the Motael clinic; the confused, angry shouting of people who had just seen someone shot dead before them for no reason. And all the time there was the presence of the Indonesian police or military, claiming they were trying to control the situation and then blatantly taking part themselves. At that time they were ordering journalists out of certain areas at gunpoint— just as another act of militia violence was about to begin.

As the *Dobonsolo* pulled into Dili on the morning of 20 April I stood at the rail with an East Timorese student returning from Jakarta. He didn't know whether to get off or not, but the next destination of the boat was Ambon, then Jayapura, and we laughed about the comparative danger of all three places. Hundreds of East Timorese who had been studying in other parts of Indonesia were now returning to take part in the lead-up to the ballot even though the details had not yet been finalised. They planned to go to the villages and educate the people about voting, to counter the propaganda of the autonomy campaign, and the terror created by the militias. Many of those who did do this were, in the later stages of the campaign, killed or had to hide in the mountains, themselves victims of the militia and the military.

On the wharf in Dili, a crowd of people waited to board. They were pushing and shoving to get onto the gangplank, but were held back by a row of police. Several military officers and several men with long hair, wearing the militia-style quasi-military garb were allowed through the cordon and walked unhindered up the gangplank into the first-class section. They were obviously militia leaving to enjoy a break with their military commanders.

Forcing my way down the gangplank against the tide of people pushing to get on the boat and out of East Timor,

I saw some local photographers getting the 'Thousands flee violence' shots as people crowded on board and I struggled in the opposite direction.

⊢⊣◆⊶O⊶◆⊢⊣

THE INDONESIAN armed forces chief, General Wiranto, arrived the following day. He appealed for an end to the violence and presided over the signing of a 'peace agreement' between both 'sides' that was held on the morning of 21 April in the garden of Bishop Belo's house. Belo was there, along with Wiranto, Eurico, Basilio, João Tavares and a host of other pro-autonomy officials and lesser ranks from the army and the police. Privately, the East Timorese people expressed dismay that the Bishop was taking part, but they also conceded he probably had been given little choice.

Just as the ceremony was about to begin, Manuel Carrascalão and Leandro Isaac were escorted by police to take their positions on the stage.

After speeches from Belo and Wiranto, who spoke about peace and reconciliation between all parties, the leaders stepped forward to sign a document. Then Wiranto encouraged the leaders to not only shake hands, but to hug each other. Manuel Carrascalão was almost in tears as he was forced to hug João Tavares, who only three days before had stood by Eurico Guterres as he ordered the attack on Manuel's house in which his son had been killed.

Leandro Isaac was also forced to take part in the charade. He, too, had taken refuge in the police station from the paramilitaries and was now virtually a prisoner.

'We are completely cut off from the outside world in the police station, and we cannot leave,' said Leandro after the ceremony when we managed to talk to him before he was whisked away.

Manuel was devastated and the farce of the peace ceremony was a public humiliation.

Despite being under obvious pressure to leave, he insisted on making a quick statement. Carrascalão called the ceremony 'theatre' and said that for 23 years he could not trust the police, but now his and his family's safety depended on their protection from the militia groups who had attacked his house.

It was a terrible moment: the militia leaders who had ordered a massacre to be carried out in broad daylight three days previously were signing a peace deal with those they had attacked and who were now in custody. Wiranto looked happy with himself and Belo was there lending credibility to the whole sham. Nobody mentioned that the violence was one-sided, unprovoked and carried out under the noses, and with the assistance of, the same military that were now taking credit for the 'peace'.

Maria Ressa from CNN stood off to one side and began her piece to camera: 'East Timor's warring factions signed a peace deal here today that will hopefully bring an end to clashes between pro-independence and pro-autonomy groups in the capital Dili.'

'I can't stand it, I have to say something,' said Irene Slegt, a Dutch journalist who had seen as much of Saturday's attacks as anyone, and stormed off to correct Maria.

After the signing, some journalists went out to see if there had been any more trouble. Just outside of Dili, heading east, we got to the first road block. In Hera, militia and, further down, military, stood on the road. They ordered us out of the car. Diarmid O'Sullivan, an English journalist who fortunately spoke Indonesian well, was with me and we walked over to the house of the local militia leader, Mateus Carvalho, surrounded by some very tense-looking men with machetes. Diarmid had seen what had happened in Carrascalāo's house when they attacked, and was still wary. He had seen how easy it was for the militia to kill. Mateus sat on his veranda that overlooked the road block, with his M-16 close by.

He was the village head of Hera, had become a militia leader and seemed to be enjoying his role. For the next 15 minutes he gave us the familiar arguments of the pro-autonomy groups: 'These are not people with a history of democracy. There will be fighting if they are allowed to choose.'

He directed his men to stop another vehicle, in which was a Chinese businessman. 'Just get some money from him and let him through,' Mateus said to his men.

Mateus had the road east of Dili blocked and was virtually laying siege to the students and staff at the polytechnic college down the road. He told us that the road block was to defend his own village from Falintil, and that they had recently killed two of his men, although he could not give us their names. Of course, if we went any further he could not guarantee our safety. That, with his men blocking the road, was enough to make us turn around and go back to Dili.

⊶•◦•◦•⊷

THE CNRT was now totally underground. The only leaders who remained in the public eye were those at the police station. The rest were in hiding and the office had ceased to exist.

'It is very risky for us now,' said CNRT leader David Ximenes. 'The militia post vigilantes all over Dili, they control all access to Dili. We hear they are going to start searching house-to-house soon. I can't do anything openly at the moment.' He was speaking from a temporary safe house in Dili.

Only a few weeks earlier, if I had wanted information or a comment, I would just have walked around to Carrascalão's house or gone to the CNRT office where I was always able to find somebody. But now, nothing.

The attacks in Dili had closed everything down. Antero Bendito Da Silva met me at the back of the Student Council office where he was getting his things together. He said the student leaders in the towns of Hera, Lospalos, Viqueque and Baucau had all been arrested or had fled. Those who remained in Dili slept at a different house each night to avoid the groups of paramilitary and Indonesian military who came every night to their homes and threatened their families and neighbours.

'We cannot have the large emotional demonstrations as before,' said Antero. 'We would simply be killed on the street in this new climate.'

Antero, who left Dili along with another 10 students on 24 April, told how normal life had become impossible for the students: 'We go to the university and there are no teachers. Many students have gone to the forest to join the guerrillas. There is no alternative. We are living in a country where all the legal systems have been stacked against us; the paramilitaries are civilians with guns who have been told to kill students.'

Things did quieten down in Dili after the peace agreement, but it was a false and tense calm that was characterised by stories of killings outside the town and a new arrogance on the part of the militia on the streets at night and at their posts during the day.

One area continually mentioned by East Timorese human rights workers and aid workers was Ermera, in the mountains about 40 kilometres from Dili. I made about three trips to Ermera in the two weeks following the agreement, and each time I was told more stories of killings, arrests and beatings, and of areas being sealed off by the militia and the military. It was a rolling pogrom against the pro-independence population.

This was the kind of operation where a few people were arrested or killed in one night in one area, a few more the next night somewhere else close by, and then some people would be plucked off the street during the day. Next, a few houses were burned down and some people disappeared. The effectiveness of these kinds of tactics was that there was never one big incident that could be documented and used to condemn the military. At the same time, it created an atmosphere of terror in the whole district. It was probably a more effective way to scare the population because it was ongoing and everywhere. People were scared all the time, not just during an attack. And, of course, these isolated killings in remote areas could always be blamed on Falintil.

When Ian Timberlake from Agence France Press told me the police in Ermera had exhumed 11 bodies from a grave near the town and were displaying them in the medical clinic in Gleno, I immediately thought it meant there would soon be an operation against Falintil in the area. We went up there the next morning to have a look.

We spoke to the Indonesian commander in Gleno—a low, flat town built by the Indonesians to replace Ermera in the hills as an administrative centre. After serving us coffee and telling us they had two witnesses to the killing in custody, and that it had been carried out by CNRT, he offered to take us to see the bodies.

The stench of formaldehyde was so strong, it made our eyes water and the air stick in our throats. There they were, 11 decomposed corpses laid out on a black plastic sheet in an empty room of the clinic. It was possible to see that the victims' hands had been bound behind their backs, and you could make out the congealed mess of dirt and blood that marked the stab wounds that had killed them. Shoes and bits of human hair were still easily recognisable, but two months underground had obscured the victims' faces. According to the police chief, they had been in the ground since 28 February and had been killed by Falintil in the remote village of Bauhate, where they had been found.

Outside, local militia members calling themselves Darah Merah (Red Blood) sat about wearing red and white headbands. Ian's attempts to talk to them got nothing but glares and one-word answers. They blamed Falintil for the bodies, whose stench was still powerful across the road, but they said little else. They continually glanced nervously at the police who had accompanied us. Satisfied we had seen enough, the police commander left, saying, 'We are still looking for the others connected to the killings, but we think they are in the forest with Falintil and we will get the military to assist us in an operation against them.'

The operation was already underway and there was no-one we could speak with about the other side of the story, because the local CNRT office, known as the 'reconciliation' house, had been destroyed on 17 April. The military had killed nine people, including a human rights worker and a local CNRT member, then shot prominent pro-independence businessman Antonio Lima in the street, and stabbed him to death in the ambulance they had called for him. Three of the surviving CNRT leaders in the town had been made to attend a pro-autonomy rally in the town the Monday after their office was destroyed, and they had to sign an agreement formally disbanding the organisation in the Ermera district. They were then returned to protective police custody.

Because of the coffee grown in the area, worth about US$30 million annually to the local people, the military had a lot of problems recruiting militia in the Ermera region. The responsibility for forming militia seemed to rest with the *Bupati*. He had told me on an earlier trip how he had tried to keep the militia out of his area. Ironically, the same day I spoke to him, he got a visit from Tono Suratman and some other high-ranking military officials. The next day he fled to Jakarta and the military operation in the area was launched full swing.

The priest in Ermera told us how the whole region near Hatolia was sealed by troops he couldn't identify. He reeled off a list of those who'd been killed or had disappeared, including six high school students who had been killed and then thrown into a river. Workers from his church who had gone to Hatolia—15 kilometres away in the hills—had not returned, and he heard they had been detained. He said he thought the town contained more than 6,000 refugees from the military operations in the area. Those were the worst times he had ever seen, he said.

Reporting this kind of an operation and presenting it in a way in which people would appreciate the extent of the terror was difficult. The reports and stories were all over the place and often the human rights organisations in Dili, such as Kontras, Yayasan Hak and Belo's Peace and Justice Commission knew less than we did—because it was their workers who had been killed, or threatened and they couldn't return to the area.

Rui, a worker at Yayasan Hak, gave me a note from Ular, the local Falintil commander in the area. The commander said Falintil was not responsible for the killings, even though they had detained the men. The men had been released and were killed by the Indonesians when they tried to return home. Ular then listed areas attacked by the Indonesians. They formed an arc around the town of Hatolia, and that was why the town was full of refugees. He identified six Indonesian battalions involved in the operation that he said involved around 6,000 troops.

Rui had been a civil servant in Ermera but, like everybody employed by the government, had been asked to sign an agreement pledging to support autonomy and to attend militia rallies. He refused and had to leave town before they arrested or killed him. It was a common story at the time as the authorities forced people to make such a choice.

〜〜〜

On 5 May, the UN met with representatives of Portugal and Indonesia in New York to sign the agreement that would allow the ballot to go ahead. I drove with Fairfax photographer Jason South up into the hills to try and find out what was happening in Hatolia.

On the way we passed a field of young men doing military drills. Instructed by members of the Indonesian military, the young men formed lines and paraded with sticks instead of guns.

In a bizarre twist of logic, the responsibility for security was being given to groups that were now to be called *Pam swa kasa* units. They were to include those civilians now being recruited for the Kamra and Wanra groups—previously little-known civil defence units under the command of the local administration. They wore uniforms, but were usually unarmed and were supposed to join the local militia units in providing local security. It was an attempt to somehow legalise all the armed men now running around.

Hatolia is at the end of a rugged road that climbs the hills above Ermera. The town is the last place a heavy vehicle can access before the mountains drop away to the swampy river lowlands behind Maubara. It was from where the people had been driven by the militia back in February. The camps that housed the people who fled the coast were run by Falintil, and now the military was breaking them up. We ran into the other side of the operation about a kilometre outside the town.

On the narrow road with a steep drop on one side and a cliff on the other, a truck carrying five men stopped in front of us. They were carrying the latest automatic weapons and weren't Timorese. They had long hair and the thin features of Javanese, but their hair and their dress showed they weren't regular soldiers. Dressed in jeans and T-shirts, they got out of their vehicle, aimed their guns at us and told us to go back. We got out of the car and clumsily attempted to reason with them, or bribe them. We persisted, and the whirring of Jason's motordrive as he took photos from the hip caught their attention. Immediately they all started cocking their rifles and yelling at us to move, charging straight towards the car as we backed away. They gave the car a few parting kicks, aiming their guns through the windows, and we left.

We had driven all morning to get to this town, but it had become obvious we couldn't get through. According to Stanislav Martins from Caritas—the only aid organisation that had tried to get supplies to Hatolia—his people were beaten up when they tried to get through and they had lost a truck at the same place. Nothing was going in or out of there, and details of individual killings kept coming back to Dili for the next few weeks. Inside the town, it was people such as the only local healthworker, Bonifacio Dos Reis, and two of his staff, who were tortured by the military for helping the refugees. Corpses of people who tried to leave Hatolia were later found near the road block we had encountered. Most had their hands tied behind their backs and had been stabbed to death.

THE 5 May agreement stated a ballot would be conducted by the United Nations to allow the people of East Timor to choose between autonomy within Indonesia, or independence. The date of the ballot was set for 8 August and a UN mission was to be put in place immediately to supervise it. Security was to be in the hands of the Indonesian authorities.

Reaction in Dili was slight. About 200 students staged a brief demonstration outside the university, but many were too afraid to attend and it wound up early. In the afternoon, I attended the funeral of a young man killed by the militia. There were only about 30 people there. A month before, there would have been thousands marching through the city. Now Longinos Da Silva, a 20-year-old whose body was found on the beach in Hera, was buried with only his family and an ICRC representative in attendance. He had been arrested by the militia in Hera on 2 May. He was killed and his body thrown in the sea. He was found by fishermen, a few days later, floating on the tide. The family tried to take the body to the Indonesian police for an autopsy, but the police were 'busy' and 'in a meeting' and they were told to go away. The man's brother told me he was trying to get to Dili from Metinaro, because all the young men in that village were being forced to join Aitarak. After he told me the details of his brother's death, he said he wanted to appeal to the international community for the presence of UN peacekeepers in East Timor. 'How can the Indonesians be responsible for security? The weapons they used to kill my brother are from Indonesia,' he said.

But it was too late, the agreement had been signed.

A few days later, the pro-autonomy groups rallied in Liquiça to establish the local branch of the political front for the militia—the FPDK. Jose Arfat, the official who shot his own constituents, was named as head of the branch. Eurico used the rally as an opportunity to disarm himself publicly. He ceremoniously handed over an old Portuguese G3 rifle and a carload of homemade guns to the local police chief. That was the first of three times I watched Eurico hand in that weapon at public disarming ceremonies. He preferred an M-16 anyway.

Photographers pushed each other to get the picture of the day—Eurico with his gun—and Jason almost came to blows with a Portuguese photographer. There was a horrified look on Eurico's face. This man ordered people's deaths for a living, but he seemed genuinely shocked at the behaviour of the press.

JOÃO TAVARES publicly rescinded the death threats against Australian journalists and diplomats, and pledged to give support to the UN process. He warned the UN the process had to be fair and transparent, and the pro-integrationists and the Indonesian military had to be involved in discussions regarding the process. He seemed happy with the result of the 5 May agreement and declared his intention to disarm.

The foreign population in Dili was expanding rapidly. Reporters were to be based there permanently from then on. All the major Australian and Portuguese news organisations were represented, as well as the international wire services, radio and print. Diplomats from Jakarta had become a more or less permanent feature in Dili. There were about 100 foreigners who had become permanent residents of Dili. Everybody turned up to the first party that was held on the roof of the Mahkota, thrown by Ric Curnow and Jenny Grant, who were soon to ditch their freelance journalism jobs to work for the UN.

It was a great spot, one of the highest buildings in Dili,

with a 360-degree view of the whole city, the mountains behind and the sea in front. The party was attended by diplomats and journalists, and Timorese from both political groupings. Drinking went on until late, and there was no trouble. Dili, for once, was peaceful as people made their way home.

IT WAS after lunch when I finally went down to get a coffee the next day. I had a terrible hangover. A car pulled up and Ginny Stein and Geoff Thompson from the ABC, and Karen Polglaze from AAP, all jumped out panting, red-faced and babbling rapidly into their mobile phones: 'The market, shooting, militia attacked us. Now, it's happening now.'

I didn't have to ask them what had happened, I just had to look at them and listen to their reports.

At the corner before the market, I saw Ric Curnow and Jenny Grant. Ric was trying to get into the Telkom building where he had set up his satellite link. Another carload of reporters had just driven straight the mass of militia, police and plain-clothes military. The police had jumped on their car and fired shots into the air, and taken them to the police station. There were Indonesians with pistols and submachine guns, and Timorese with rocks, and everybody was yelling. Shots were being fired occasionally, and a fire was burning in the market. Ric walked up to the corner where a Kopassus officer he knew called Bambang shouted at him to get out of there, and Eurico was also there yelling orders.

I tried to approach the corner, but an Indonesian in plain clothes with short hair, carrying a pistol, ordered an East Timorese to get rid of me. He ran forward with a rock and a chunk of wood. I ran back and he stopped, but he hurled the rock at me anyway. Masao, a Japanese photographer, got out of a car covered in blood; he had just taken a man who had been shot to the clinic. He told us that the residents of Audian, the area to the east of the market, were throwing up barricades and fighting the militia who were trying to get through. Someone had been shot dead in the market and then all hell had broken loose. But, as we could see, the place was crawling with armed Indonesians who had suddenly appeared and joined in the chaos—and helped further it.

An Indonesian reporter came to convey the message 'that all journalists must leave from here—now'.

Back at the Tourismo, everything was almost normal. Australian ambassador John McCarthy stood and watched as the seven journalists who had been taken by the police 'for their own safety' were unloaded from a police truck out the front. It was a funny sight. They were all talking on their mobile phones or interviewing and photographing each other or the police; they were a babbling, excited mass.

McCarthy laughed and said he thought it was all a bit overblown. He had been having lunch with some of the journalists when they got the call about trouble in the market, and had watched them race up there.

I went back up to the area where Masao had said there was fighting. Groups of Timorese stood on the road, some had machetes, some had rocks in their hands. A radio journalist and I walked further towards the market where a line of burning tyres marked the end of the pro-independence area. Youths crowded around and screamed into our tape recorders: '*Viva Xanana Gusmão! Viva Timor Leste!*' It was getting dark, but they were preparing for what they thought would be another attack.

Militia had come from the market earlier and shot a

man; another had been killed further towards the market, and the people had pelted the militia with rocks. They were exuberant. They had won and they danced around the burning tyres screaming insults at the police and military who were now moving into the area around the market as the militia seemed to disappear. The soldiers kept their distance.

THE NEXT morning, everybody in town knew something was going to happen. Hardly any shops were opened and barricades manned by militia with automatic weapons had been set up along the road where they had their base next to Carrascalão's destroyed house.

I watched as militia chased two youths who had sped past on a motorbike, which had then stalled further up the street. The two young guys abandoned their frantic efforts to start the machine and left it, fleeing on foot as the militia ran towards them, one with a pistol held behind his back.

Around the corner, Jason South and News Limited photographer John Feder were ducking out from behind a wall, trying to take photos of the militia with guns at the barricades who were stopping what little traffic there was. Beyond the barricades we could see trucks of militia arriving and milling around in the street outside their headquarters.

When Jason and I went to have lunch at the Resende, nothing was happening. But outside, truckloads of Brimob riot troops headed up towards the market as we waited for our food. My mobile rang. It was Ian Timberlake.

'Are you guys having lunch at the Resende?' he asked in his nasal Canadian drawl. 'Well there's about 300 militia just outside. I just thought you should know.'

We got outside just as the militia broke into a run and

began yelling, waving machetes, swords, homemade guns and automatic guns. Jason ran off in front of the mob and I ran into an open doorway in the governor's office across the road. I was suddenly in a room full of typists, all at their machines in their brown civil service uniforms. They continued to type while on the other side of the window the militia ran past yelling and waving their weapons above their heads as they jogged to the market. Across the road, employees from one of the largest banks in Dili just stood there, outside their building, and watched the parade.

The government employees directed me out the other side of the building. A taxi stopped. It was Karen Polglaze. I'd started working for AAP and she was the senior correspondent, effectively my boss. She had been trying to get to see the wife of Oscar Lima, a prominent Timorese businessman, who had been reported to be under attack in her house on the other side of the market. Now we could hear shouting and shooting coming from that area, and the surrounding streets had become deserted.

We found Ian on the steps of the Mahkota, red in the face, dripping with sweat and panting. He had just run all the way from the governor's office when the militia had started charging.

'Fuck this for $50 a day,' [which is how much a wire service stringer gets]. This is bullshit. Those guys wanted to kill me,' he said, throwing his notebook and cameras on the ground.

To get close enough to know what was going on, you were going to be at risk. But if you didn't go there, you couldn't find out with any reliability what had really happened, because everything was cloaked in so much bullshit by the authorities and the militia. They had their story figured out before the violence even began. We had to see for ourselves who was doing the killing.

From the roof of the Mahkota, we could hear the shooting and see the smoke from the fires. Some of the shooting was coming from a lot closer than the market, and three wounded people had already turned up at the Motael clinic.

After checking the wounded at the clinic, we headed back up to the market. There was still shooting going on, but the army seemed to be moving in. Along the main road to Becora, military trucks were parked and the soldiers were getting out and taking up positions.

John Feder and News Limited journalist Brian Woodley burst out of an alley and ran past, sweating and panting and saying there were still militia in the backstreets, that they were still smashing up houses and killing people. Now, as we sat in our car on the Becora road, militia trucks loaded up with televisions, motorcycles and furniture started coming out of the side streets. The Indonesian soldiers just stood and watched. The trucks were parked, and some of the militia leapt out and ran into a nearby shop, then jumped back onto the trucks, their arms full of goods. They were soon joined by more vehicles with smashed-out windscreens, obviously looted, that were also piled up with goods and driven by militia.

Next, a squad of Brimob police arrived in a truck which took the lead as the others formed up behind it. The whole convoy drove slowly out through the main business district of Dili. The few Timorese still on the street stared in disbelief as the trucks full of red and white flag-waving militia and their obviously looted booty drove straight out of town, back through the centre of the city, escorted by the police. These were the same police who had just been given the role of providing security for the ballot.

The militia headed straight back out west to Liquiça. They were Besih Merah Putih, brought into town for the day to carry out what was supposed to be a reaction to the arrival of the UN. Indonesia's Foreign Minister, Ali Alatas, had said that that day, Monday 10 May, would be the day the UN would arrive in Dili.

Joaquim from Yayasan Hak told me what the militia's plan had been. Seven trucks full of militia arrived in Dili from Liquiça, escorted by two truckloads of Brimob. At the Aitarak militia headquarters, they split into three groups.

'The first went to Dili airport to meet the UN with red and white Indonesian flags, the second left for Baucau to the east carrying Falintil flags, and the plan was to fight the UN police as soon as they landed, because they knew they would be unarmed,' said Joaquim.

The third group had charged up the main street and attacked the Audian area. The Brimob trucks we had seen going past as we waited for our lunch actually arrived in the area first and began shooting before the militia. The militia targeted specific houses, and they had photos of the people they were looking for. The militia had run in after the police, interrogating, beating and slashing the terrified inhabitants with machetes and rifle butts. Some houses were totally destroyed and the contents smashed or stolen by the militias. And the police stood by.

A FUNERAL took place at one of the targeted houses the next morning. CNRT pro-independence party member Manuel Dos Reis was burying his son, Elijier, who was shot in the head by militia as he tried to retrieve the body of his neighbour, who had been killed moments before.

In a house on the property, Marta Caitano, a government employee with no political ties, was slashed in the head with a machete by the militia as they destroyed her house. 'You take money from Indonesia and everyday you demonstrate and yell *Viva Xanana*,' they told her as they attacked her in her home. The militias destroyed one vehicle from this property and stole another. As Marta packed her things from her smashed-up house, she remarked to us, 'How can I live here like this when they come and kill us in broad daylight?'

The foreign presence in Dili had done nothing to stop the most blatant daylight violence—they just chased us away.

Joaquim said the militia violence was just a way for the Indonesians to show the people that no matter how great the foreign presence, no-one was safe, even in their own homes in the centre of Dili, in the middle of the day.

Basilio said the violence was caused by pro-independence supporters calling his men names, 'and, besides, we only killed maybe a few—in the US they kill 20 at one high school,' he said, referring to a recent high school shooting we had all seen on CNN. One of his own party members put the number of dead at 30 for the two days' violence, but we were only able to confirm six.

▷─◆─○─◆─◁

WE SAT around a table in the Tourismo garden. There were only about six journalists, and David Wimhurst, the UN spokesman who had just arrived that day. The first UN press briefing was a pretty low-key affair. There were only 10 UN staff in Dili by 13 May when the briefing took place, and Wimhurst didn't even have enough copies of the 5 May agreement to hand out. Stuck in Dili, where information from outside was hard to come by, I still hadn't read the agreement.

Wimhurst ran through the numbers in the mission and how they expected to get the ballot done. There would be 600 staff in place by mid-June and 250 international police officers, who would advise the Indonesian police regarding matters of security. The task of disarming the militia would be carried out by the Indonesian military, under the terms of the agreement. He told us how the ballots would be protected and counted by the UN, and that the UN would definitely maintain a presence for the transitional period after the ballot. 'We have barely three months to do this and the climate is extremely tense, but we will get it done,' Wimhurst said, before asking us to turn off our tape recorders.

He then asked us what we thought of the situation. Most of us had just had a pretty close look at the work of the militia and the authorities' complicity just two days before in the market attacks. The idea of the same Indonesian police, who had escorted the militia to and from their work (killing and looting), being given the role of security for the ballot was absurd.

We told him that, and listed all the other recent incidents. Wimhurst hadn't heard about some of them, but didn't look overly concerned. He was sure the UN would have a calming effect on the situation, and the Indonesian government would order cessation of the violence, as was tacitly implied in the agreement. He had just come from Angola and the pattern of violence we were explaining must have seemed like small beer compared to that conflict. East Timor is, after all, a small half island and the Tourismo garden on a warm evening is a deceptively pleasant place.

Three nights later, Wimhurst was among a party of nine diners at the seafood restaurant on the beach—the up-market one previously frequented by the military. It was a quiet East Timor Sunday, when not much happens except everybody goes to mass.

Around 10 pm, some cars stopped about 50 metres down the road and blocked the route back to Dili. Armed men got out and began shooting into the air. They went into a small community of houses set back from the road and began beating people, dragging them out of their houses and smashing up their homes. They burnt the houses down.

The inhabitants of the area, probably about 100 people, ran frantically up the steep hill behind their homes to get away. All of this could be seen clearly from the restaurant, like some kind of weird entertainment—a show put on for the new arrivals in town. And that was exactly what it was. Dili is a small place and not many people were going out at night.

The diners—UN personnel, NGO workers and a diplomat—were stuck out there for more than an hour. They didn't try to leave and run the gauntlet of armed men, who were still burning houses. They called the Indonesian police, who eventually arrived and escorted them back to Dili.

It was after midnight when they got back to the hotel. Brian Woodley and I were the only ones still awake and drinking in the garden, so we got the whole story.

First thing in the morning, we headed out to the village of Metio, now just a smoking ruin. The inhabitants were picking through their destroyed houses. They didn't know why this had happened. They just ran when the militia arrived and now their houses had either been burnt to the ground or smashed up.

Wimhurst was back at the Mahkota. He was furious as he relayed the details of the incident to us. He hadn't spoken to anyone else about it, and he seemed genuinely angry, glad to make a statement.

'The militia are still active. We saw it ourselves,' he said. 'The security authorities here must take the necessary steps to stop these militia attacking civilians, burning down homes and intimidating the civilian population. It is incumbent on the Indonesians to disarm these groups according to the terms of the 5 May agreement.'

He asked us if there had been any other disturbances, and we told him about an attack by militia we had heard about in a village called Atara, in the hills behind Hatolia; we couldn't get up there. The reports we were getting said that maybe 20 people had been killed by militia in a coffee plantation in the remote area. He was now interested and wanted to know all the details.

If the militia had organised the evening shooting to intimidate the UN, it had had the opposite effect. Now Wimhurst, with only 10 UN staff in the country, was going to try to create a situation where he could beat the Indonesian authorities over the head with the UN's moral authority. Like a dog pissing out his new territory—his own words—Wimhurst organised a trip to Atara.

It wasn't until two days later that we assembled at the Mahkota to board a bus provided by the police to take Wimhurst and his entourage to where the latest violence had taken place. The Indonesians had provided security in the form of five police armed with AK-47s. It was to be a common sight, Indonesian police providing escorts to UN officials. It was their way of saying they were providing security for the ballot. But, often, all they were doing was shepherding around the officials, and the result was that often the officials saw or heard less about what was going on than if they had been unaccompanied. Creating a disturbance to intimidate or kill the local population, then sending in the police to 'protect' the foreigners—and thereby getting them out of the way—was something the Indonesian authorities mastered during the coming months.

WE TRAVELLED to Gleno where the local police chief, after much discussion and relating his version of events in Atara, finally allowed Wimhurst and some reporters to proceed. They changed to four-wheel drive vehicles, and I lost my seat and returned to Dili.

Then Wimhurst got the runaround. After travelling for hours, they were prevented from entering the area. The police escort gave them all sorts of excuses; the car wouldn't make it; the road was too rough; it was dangerous because night was approaching; the militia they had seen earlier in the day would attack them. Finally, after protesting, Wimhurst agreed to turn around, but not until he had talked to a local priest and barged into what was a militia training session in the town of Atsabe. Uniformed soldiers were instructing a room full of Timorese men, who were sitting on the floor. Having witnessed one of the countryside training sessions, Wimhurst had enough evidence to make a statement.

'We saw a group of men being trained in a classroom situation,' said Wimhurst the following day. 'The militia are not only still active, they are training. These militia are involved in preparation for acts of violence. This is totally against the accord.

'Anything that happens now is in breach of the accord, and is the responsibility of the Indonesian authorities as laid out in the terms of the 5 May agreement.'

Wimhurst was trying to lay the ground rules, and to an extent it had worked. He had brought the attention of his superiors in the UN to conditions on the ground and had confronted the Indonesian authorities over the violence. He met with Tono Suratman, who gave him assurances that the activities of the militia would be stopped, but we were to hear assurances from the military and police on an almost daily basis from now on; and the training, recruiting and violent activities of the militia continued regardless.

While we were preoccupied with the violence in Dili, the entire staff and students of the polytechnic in Hera were still besieged by Mateus Carvalho and his militia. On Saturday 8 May he had walked into the campus of the technical college with some armed men and started shooting. They wounded one student. The next day he returned and told all the non-Timorese staff at the university to leave or they would be killed along with the others. There were more than 400 students and staff there, and they hid again as Mateus and his men started shooting into the campus after giving them the warning. Soldiers from Battalion 744 had then arrived and started looting the houses across the road. They stole pigs and chickens, rice—anything they could find. Finally, the police from Dili arrived and loaded the majority of the students and staff onto trucks and drove them over the hills, back to Dili.

Twenty-one students from the technical college were unaccounted for, and a member of the militia who worked with Mateus said they had been killed and buried behind his house on the night of 10 May.

Four girls among them had been repeatedly raped before being killed.

Ten days later, a group of eight students tried to return to the campus to get their belongings. The place had been thoroughly looted and destroyed, there wasn't much left. Everything in the college—computers, books and furniture—had been stolen by the militia and the military. The eight students were arrested by the military and two of them were beaten and handed over to Mateus. They disappeared.

The road blocks outside the college stayed in place, manned by militia and military, and nobody said anything about one of the largest tertiary institutions in East Timor just ceasing to exist.

⊱⊱⊰⊰

THE UN started flying huge Ilyushin transport planes into Baucau airport late in May. They were also visiting outlying areas for the first time, and some reporters used that excuse to get out of Dili and find out what was happening.

Life took on a frantic, exhausting pace because everywhere outside of Dili there was violence, and everywhere there were soldiers, recent dead and militia.

One morning we arrived in Baucau and a guy on a motorbike rode up alongside the car. '*Orang mati di rumah sakit*,' he shouted. Dead person in the hospital.

The body of the boy with the bullet-smashed skull still lay bleeding on the white tiles in the hospital. The family was there, wailing and demanding answers. They told us what had happened. He was shot dead the day before by the military as soldiers surrounded the religious procession in which he was taking part. Two others were wounded, but were too afraid to come to the hospital. There was blood everywhere, all over the old woman who held the dead boy's head—which was in pieces. There was no trace of any authority or doctor, just the dead boy with his head blown in half and his wailing family. A few terrified people stood around outside, gaping.

Soldiers arrived, levelled their guns and ordered the family away from the body. They were from the same unit that had killed the boy the day before. The mother was still clutching the body, sobbing quietly. The soldiers were yelling. Everybody froze, afraid to move. The soldiers were tense; they cocked their weapons and pointed them at us. A colleague who had just arrived in East Timor asked me what we do in a situation like this. I didn't know.

'What can we fucking do? Nothing,' I answered.

The soldiers left and the family kept the body. They told us about more killings. Down the street, the UN representatives were checking if the rooms they had booked for the election monitors had fans, and they were enjoying lunch. It was none of their business—they were there to organise an election.

IN MANATUTO, a young man at the church wanted to show us the remains of the militia's victims. We drove out of town to a deserted beach and he ran to the spot. A pile of rocks on a rock-strewn beach, two chewed-off white bones protruding from either end; hands and feet. He apologised, realising now that dogs had chewed off the remains, it wasn't much of a photo.

VIQUEQUE WAS the same. We drove all day to get there and got stuck in the landslide that had isolated the town for months. The driver said we could get through, and we ploughed straight into the mud until the car sank up to its axles.

About 100 East Timorese helped us manhandle the car out of the mud and across the landslide.

We arrived and the police held us up with questions, registration and warnings. The local priest I saw in November wasn't there. He had left the day before after Kopassus troops shot three people in broad daylight outside his church. Another five people had been killed in the same way during the previous two weeks, and in early May, the local CNRT chairman was executed by Kopassus in the main street. Many people had fled, about 1,400.

We drove to Uatolari and the people told us two students had been killed in the previous week, and again many people had fled.

No-one had written in the visitors' book in Viqueque

since I'd been there in October the previous year. The land-slide had cut the town off for most of the rainy season. In the meantime, the local military had not been very success-ful recruiting militia and openly resorted to killing people themselves.

They formed a group called 'Team 59/75 Junior', a refer-ence to an armed rebellion in the area in 1959 against the Portuguese. Most of the members were serving in the military and didn't even bother to change out of their uniforms when they were 'working'.

Viqueque is a remote place, and they didn't worry about pretence. The market had been burned down and there was nothing in the town except armed men, road blocks and blackened power poles angled crazily along the main street, wires still hanging off them. It looked like there had been an earthquake. But the military had burned the market down because the town had been an enclave of pro-inde-pendence activists; that was what they told us when we asked them. In fact, the market was burnt down because they were punishing the people—showing them who had control before the UN's arrival. That was supposed to be the following day.

━┝━◆┝━0━◆┝━┥

THE NEXT day, I saw a man I recognised from the free-speech dialogue days in Lacluta. He pulled me aside and told me three men were killed by Kopassus in the main street of Lacluta two days before.

'They tied their hands behind their backs and beat them with rifle butts until they dropped, and then the officer shot them all in the head—right there,' he said, pointing to a building further along the street.

There were soldiers milling about and at a meeting in a

building on the main street they were telling the people to support autonomy. Lacluta was only a small village of about 300 people. Since that killing, 54 young people had fled to the mountains.

'If you don't go to the campaign, you get locked up,' said the man, before loudly giving me directions back to Viqueque as a soldier walked along the street towards us.

As we watched photographer Dean Sewell trying to eat what looked like ox stomach-lining and intestines for lunch back at the only restaurant still standing in Viqueque, a man approached. Without even sitting down, and looking nervously out the window as he spoke, he said in English, 'Here it is very bad at the moment, they are killing anyone who does not support the Indonesians and the military, and I think it will get worse as the time for voting gets closer.'

He said the military was telling the people they would attack the UN, and they were saying the delayed arrival was because the UN was scared.

The fragmented details of events we were getting were just the latest in months of similar violence.

><+>+<>+<+><

DRIVING BACK to Dili, about 200 people were blocking the road in the village of Vermasse with 44-gallon drums. They surrounded our car, thinking we had come to help, and were jumping up and down screaming, '*Viva Xanana! Viva Timor Leste!*', and waving machetes and spears.

The night before, a military truck from nearby Baucau had stopped, and soldiers had leapt out and chased two youths into the bushes; they'd shot one dead and injured the other, then took the body and the wounded boy to Baucau. The people were expecting the military to come back, and they were determined to defend themselves.

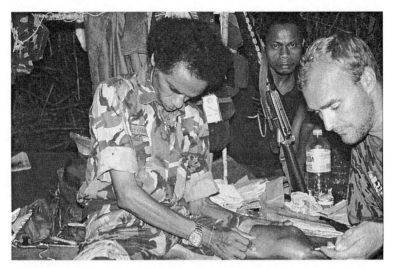

British doctor Chris Duke treats 22-year guerilla-war veteran David Alex, the Falintil commander, in his secret camp near Baucau in January 1997. Alex disappeared in 1998 after being captured by the Indonesians. (John Martinkus)

Following the fall of Suharto in May, East Timorese demonstrated openly for independence in Dili in June 1998. For the first time since 1975 the demoralised Indonesian military did not respond to such displays with violence. (Ross Bird)

Indonesian Brimob police withdraw from the Alas region on 27 November 1998, following the first waves of militia terror. 'The Indonesians have made no provision to control the rifles they have handed out. There is no order, no control, no law here,' said one resident. (John Martinkus)

At a Mahidi militia rally on 23 February 1999 in Cassa, militia leader Vasco (bearded, centre) and Indonesian Marine Sertu Kifahzin cheer the pro-Indonesian leaders. The 4,000-strong crowd were transported to the site by the Indonesian military. (John Martinkus)

28 May 1999: The body of 25-year-old Julio Caetano Ximines is carried into his house the day after Indonesian troops opened fire on a religious procession near Baucau. Julio was shot in the head and two other youths were seriously wounded. His mother (left) had refused to hand over the body to soldiers from the unit who had shot him. The UN was due to arrive in Baucau the following day. (Dean Sewell)

Aitarak militia fire on pro-independence supporters in Becora, Dili on 26 August, the last day of campaigning in Dili. Five people had been shot dead and a number wounded including a Reuters photographer who was shot in the leg. Pro-independence supporters and foreign journalists were targeted by militia and rounded up by police. (Jason South)

A man weeps moments after his village of Memo, near Maliana, was destroyed by militia on 27 August 1999, the last day of the official campaign period. At least three villagers armed with spears and knives were killed trying to fight off the militia. Injured villager Amaral Lopes said, 'This is not campaigning. This is slaughter.' (John Martinkus)

East Timorese being marched through Dili by Indonesian military on 6 September 1999. 'They are going around and shooting and burning down houses. It is the military, the Indonesian military that is doing this,' said one East Timorese UN staffer. Around 250,000 East Timorese were either forced to leave or fled for their lives. (Steve Tickner)

By 7 September 1999, more than 2,000 East Timorese were sheltering in the UN compound. Militia thwarted attempts to secure supplies from the UN warehouse, and water and power were cut. UN staff and leadership agonised over whether to abandon the refugees or try to stay. (H. T. Lee)

10 September 1999: The majority of the UN staff evacuate in Indonesian military vehicles, along with local staff and their dependents. The refugees in the compound and all but 12 of the staff (who stayed until the peace-keepers arrived six days later) were successfully evacuated on 14 September. (H. T. Lee)

Australian soldiers disarm and arrest Aitarak militia in sweep operations in downtown Dili on 21 September 1999, the day after the first of the INTERFET international peacekeeping force arrived. (David Dare Parker)

Local witnesses say retreating militia were responsible for throwing this unidentified man (photographed on 6 October 1999) to his death from a cliff outside Ainaro after hacking him with machetes. The corpse is just one of hundreds discovered after the peacekeepers' arrival. (Max Stahl)

East Timorese view the remains of ten people incinerated in the back of a truck by retreating militia or Indonesian military at Tacitolu, outside Dili, on the road to the West Timor border on 26 September 1999. (David Dare Parker)

Indonesian troops leave East Timor via the INTERFET-guarded docks in Dili in October 1999, 24 years after the invasion of East Timor. The last Indonesian troops left on 31 October. (David Dare Parker)

Thousands of East Timorese welcome home their resistance hero Xanana Gusmão on 22 October 1999 after his seven years in prison in Jakarta. 'There is much to do to recover, to save our homeland, to save ourselves,' he told the crowd. 'All of us must try to let go of the bad things they have done to us. Tomorrow is ours.' (Andrew Meares)

They showed us the blood on the ground and the spent shell casings, and gave us the names of the victims; they even named one of the soldiers responsible for the shootings, and gave us his unit number. The Indonesian police refused to come out of their post, and the East Timorese people were shouting and screaming, working themselves up for a confrontation with the returning military. We left them as it got dark; they were waiting out on that road, burning tyres, piling up rocks and rolling the 44-gallon drums into a road block. It was only a matter of time before a military truck came back.

IT WAS at about this time that Quintão came to see me with a story from the town of Laleia, east of Dili. The local head of the SGI, an Indonesian officer, had called a meeting of all the young men in the town. At the meeting, he had demanded all the youths join the local militia. One of the youths, Frederico Xavier, stood up and said, 'We agree to join, but we don't want to make war like the militia in Liquiça.' The officer had lost his temper and pulled out his pistol and put it to the young man's head.

'You think we are afraid of the UN?' he ranted, before telling all present he would personally kill anyone he saw approaching the UN when they arrived. Quintão was about to be employed by the UN, and in the end they sent him to that area.

The head of the UN mission, Ian Martin, had finally arrived in Dili, and there was a flag-raising ceremony to mark the opening of the UN compound in an old teachers' college. Thousands of East Timorese crowded around the entrance. The crowd was excited and students banged on the doors of the governor's car as he arrived. Other pro-autonomy representatives got the same treatment.

David Ximenes stood on top of a car and tried to calm the crowd. The blue UN flag was raised and the crowd went wild and started shouting a version of the East Timorese national anthem, '*O Ramelau*'. The noise was deafening and people were pushing against the police, who were holding them back. Ian Martin was yelling through a megaphone: 'I am grateful to you for your welcome, but I want to ask you now to disperse from our compound . . . If you respect the UN, please disperse quietly . . .' But you could barely hear him. The Timorese were so buoyed by the opening, they just keep singing and shouting, '*Viva Xanana! Viva* UNAMET*! Viva Timor Leste!*'

It was finally happening, the UN were there. They were going to get rid of the Indonesians.

▷┼◆▷─O─◁◆┼◁

JOAQUIM AT Yayasan Hak told me their only human rights worker in Suai was arrested at the beginning of April after he had reported 200 people killed in the area. No-one had been down there since, and I used the imminent arrival of the UN in the town as an excuse to go there.

The road was free of traffic and road blocks as we left East Timor and followed the border south. We weren't stopped coming back over the border, but there was a whole series of checkpoints to the west of Suai between the border and the town which were manned by men with automatic weapons and who wore no discernible uniform, just bits and pieces of military cast-offs.

Father Hilario was glad to see us, and our arrival sent him racing around looking for bits of paper on which he had written down lists of those killed in the last three months since a journalist had been there. The refugees in the church had left. Hilario said that in March the militia had been constantly threatening to attack and had stabbed some people on the road outside the church, so he had instructed them to leave. Hilario and Father Francisco started to go through the lists of details; they spoke in a hurried way, as if they would never get a chance to finish.

Francisco produced three hand-drawn maps. 'This is where they have dumped the bodies,' he said, and showed me the spot. There was a lake between the main road and a small village called Salele, about 18 kilometres west of Suai, almost at the border. Francisco and Hilario both insisted that 400 to 500 bodies had been dumped there in the previous three months, since the Lak Saur militia had taken control of the area at the end of February.

It was a huge figure, but they insisted it was correct. They had information from the militia themselves who had taken part in the operation and then confessed to the priests, hoping for some kind of redemption. The people were brought from Dili, Bobonaro and nearby Betun, and some from the mountains. They were killed and dumped in the lake, which the two priests said was full of crocodiles. It had been going on for months. They also had two other maps on which graves were marked behind the military head-quarters in Zumalai and in an area of pine forest near the town of Mape, to the east. They said at least 40 people from Bobonaro were buried in those graves.

Hilario painstakingly went through the other details, naming the leaders of the Lak Saur group who were mostly from towns just over the border in West Timor. He stopped at one name: Alippio Mau. 'He raped a girl, Azelia, last week in Mela on 31 May. He held a gun to her head—write it down, it is important,' he told me. We went on writing down details of attacks that had taken place since February. There were two groups responsible: Lak Saur for attacking villages and Suai from the west, and Cançio's Mahidi, doing the same from the east. The information filled the pages of my notebook—dates, names of victims, names of those responsible. 14 March, Oebaba village, Luis Dos Santos and Fatima Da Silva, killed, their six-year-old daughter raped then killed, Lak Saur responsible. 27 May, Duarte Belo, Vicente Soares, Caetano Gusmão, beaten to death and killed with machetes in Suai, Mahidi responsible. João Ximenes and Bernadino Simao, university students, bodies dumped beside the river Lo'omia, north of Zumalai, 11 April.

We went on writing it all down with a frantic urgency. It wasn't that safe for anybody in Suai to be out after dark, and it was getting late in the day, so we didn't have much time. Lak Saur had been coming into town recently and torching houses at night.

Father Hilario laughed at the suggestion that the militia could have been acting independently of the authorities. 'They give them guns, money, transport,' he said. 'The reality is, they are behind the plan—the whole thing is a plan. Down here, they have a name for it—*Operasi Sisair*—it means 'clean sweep'.

'They say after the election they will kill us. I hope the United Nations arrive quickly—this is all still going on now.'

One of the photographers asked if there were any dead or wounded people to photograph. Hilario and Francisco discussed it and then told one of the young workers at the church to take us to see another churchworker, Venanzio Amaral.

His face was a mess—puffed up and swollen, with the deep purple rings under the eyes you get from a broken nose. He couldn't walk, but when we entered the small house, he made the effort to stand, and you could see tears of pain forming in his almost closed-over eyes.

He had been attacked the day before in the market by five militia; they beat him with iron bars until he was unconscious, because they knew he worked at the church. He had broken ribs and arms, but there was no hospital in Suai. It was closed by the Indonesians, who ordered the doctors to go to West Timor. One East Timorese doctor remained and had done what he could. We took photos and his family thanked us, then we went back to the *losmen*, via the market where youths wearing black Lak Saur T-shirts and carrying machetes eyed off our vehicle.

The next day we drove east to Zumalai and stopped outside the building shown on Father Francisco's map. There were militia wearing black Mahidi T-shirts standing around. I tried talking to them, but they wouldn't say anything. Then Vasco, the tall bearded Timorese who had shouted at me at the rally in Cassa, stormed over. The others moved away and he glared at me. I told him I was going to see Cançio and he pointed at the road. We were being thrown out of town.

Vasco was in charge of Zumalai, and if the story of the bodies buried behind the military headquarters was correct, then he was responsible. He looked damned sure he wasn't going to let anybody wander around. Ironically, he later unsuccessfully tried to save Father Hilario from being killed by the militia in September after the ballot. But for that act, the militia turned on him and killed him as well.

<hr />

DRIVING INTO Cassa was like stepping back into a medieval kingdom. Cançio's Mahidi militia, dressed in black or khaki T-shirts, manned small bamboo shacks that lined the road and became more numerous the closer you got to town. The men stood at full attention as we drove past, and some saluted the vehicle with military precision. We were going to see the leader, and were treated with respect. We drove straight across the football field and could see activity on the balcony of Cançio's house. We joked that they were probably putting their guns away.

Cançio and Nemezio were there, and welcomed us enthusiastically. They had both just returned from the meeting of all the pro-integration leaders in Bali and were eager to talk. Cançio told me that of all the militia groups, General Adam Damiri had told him Mahidi was the best, the most disciplined. I egged him on. What about the Besih Merah Putih (who were responsible for the 6 April Liquiça church massacre)? Cançio rolled his eyes as if to say: 'What a mess.' And I nodded in agreement.

'Many people want to join us now because autonomy is the best way,' said Cançio. He was even speaking certain phrases in English; it was as if they had been given media training in Bali, and now was his first chance to put it into practice. He was acting like we were old friends.

'I tell my people that their strength is in their heads and not their hearts,' he said, clutching his biceps at the word strength, putting his hands on his head, then crossing them on his chest at the word hearts. He finally ended with his hands resting on his thighs. He repeated this strange little sequence several times. I asked him more about Bali.

'Well they, the central government, make an evaluation on the groups based on their ability to ensure peace and provide security, and we were the best. You see, we are not like the Besih Merah Putih. We stop arresting, killing; we stop torturing. I made a promise to stop kidnapping people, to stop torturing.

'We have guns, not to kill people, but to defend ourselves. We have to show the people we are as strong as Falintil.'

He started talking about restraint and compromise. I

asked him about the students his men had killed in Zumalai.

'They had five guns, it was a conflict,' he said. 'Mahidi has stopped activities in Zumalai, we must forget the past to create peace.'

We continued talking round in circles and I could see the others were getting restless; there was nothing for them to photograph. As we were leaving, Cançio said: 'We are the kings here, me and my brother, we are blue-blooded here in Ainaro. We have to look after our own, and if the UN make trouble, we will have to respond.' He said it matter-of-factly.

Cançio, his brother and the men hanging around were all dressed in military-style clothes. I noticed that even Cançio's Ericsson mobile phone on the table, useless out here in Cassa, had a camouflage faceplate.

The men saluted us as we left, and raised the flimsy bamboo road blocks they had placed at the other end of town.

>-+◆>─0─◆+─<

EARLY THE next morning, we finally made it to the closed town of Hatolia. The operation that had concentrated on the town had ended, and most of the people had moved on, further into the hills. The 5,000 refugees didn't feel safe there and it wasn't hard to see why. A young guy wanted a lift to back to Sare, where he had come from. We agreed and stopped outside his house so he could grab some things. Within minutes, two soldiers on a motorbike came flying down the hill and tried to grab the kid as he ran towards our car. He disappeared and the soldiers, after searching the house, turned on us and demanded to know what we were doing there. They were young and aggressive and escorted us to the police station.

An hour later we got out of there and headed north. The road got progressively worse and we were driving across shallow rivers.

We passed Sare, where the refugees had come from—forced out by the operation that caused them to move south. The state of the road worsened until it wasn't what you'd call a road anymore, and we were driving through a wide riverbed. We picked up a track leading to the river bank on the other side. It led to a village, smashed and deserted. There was a school with torn school books all over the floor; there were yellowing public health posters on the walls of what must have been the clinic. All around were empty, smashed houses.

It was Lissa Dila, cleared out by the Besih Merah Putih months ago—not a thing had been touched since. As the others took photos, a woman came out of a burnt building carrying some corrugated iron. She was very old and covered in soot. Our driver tried speaking Tetum, but she didn't even speak that—which probably meant she'd never left the hills around that village, where a different dialect was spoken.

She stood in front of us crying, the only inhabitant left there. She had been too old to move on and not important enough to kill.

There were destroyed, abandoned houses all the way back to the highway. When we emerged onto the main road, startled militia waved us down. They were positioned at the turn-off to stop people going to the destroyed area, but we had come around behind them. We were the first foreigners to see the total destruction they were capable of, and we told the driver to just get us out of there.

⊱─◆─◆─◆─⊰

ON 10 June, Ian Martin made a visit by helicopter to the two regions of East Timor worst affected by the militia violence—Maliana and Suai. I got a seat in that helicopter.

In Maliana, we waited outside the meeting between Martin, the local military commander, Siagian, and the *Bupati*, Guilherme Dos Santos. We could hear raised voices speaking Indonesian. It was the *Bupati*; he was an emotional man. I'd seen him speak at militia rallies in Balibo and Atabae, where he had talked about the perils of independence and pledged his allegiance to Indonesia.

Peter Bartu, who was to become the UN political officer for Maliana, later told me that the *Bupati* had been screaming, 'You do not run Bobonaro, this is my province! You are my guests and you will do as I tell you!' at Ian Martin.

After the meeting, Martin told us that he'd had 'a very good discussion with the *Bupati* and the chief of police'. 'We talked about the pro-independence leaders that are in the police station, and about how they can go back to their homes with a guarantee of security.'

The local CNRT office had recently been attacked and the leaders were in police custody, where most of them would stay until after the ballot. They were then killed— still in protective custody.

Ian Martin had continued: 'Some of the worst reports of military and militia violence have come from here in the Bobonaro regency. We have received assurances that this will cease in the campaign period.'

The UN was due to open its Maliana office the following week.

><+>-0-<+><

THERE WAS no-one except military and police to greet the helicopter when it landed in Suai. While Ian Martin met with the Suai *Bupati*, Herman Sedyono, the police commander, Lieutenant Colonel Gatot, and Lieutenant-Colonel Mas Agus Achmad—all later accused of crimes against the people of Suai—I ran down to the church. Father Hilario was not there, but Father Francisco immediately took me around the back to show me a wounded man, Carlos Munis, who had just walked to Suai from Beco, about 20 kilometres away. He had been shot on 31 May but it had taken him several days of walking only at night to get to the church because he was weak from loss of blood.

Father Francisco told me the Lak Saur had told everybody in Suai that if a demonstration had been staged during the UN visit, they would be killed once the UN left. They were also telling the people that if the autonomy vote didn't win, they would all be killed. For good measure, they burnt down three houses the night before we visited.

After the meeting, Ian Martin said the military and police had told him there were no recent or current security problems in Suai, but he added, 'Of course, we have quite specific information regarding the operations of militia and we have certainly made clear once again that it is only the police that are in charge of security and not militia or whatever they are called.'

The military and police did acknowledge that there had been a problem in January (6,000 frightened refugees in the church) and that a 'self-defence group' (the militia) did exist in the area, but they assured Ian Martin its activities were being monitored and it would not prevent the UN opening their office in the next week to 10 days.

I was starting to get it. The UN weren't going to confront any of the security problems of the East Timorese; they were just going to make sure the ballot took place.

CHAPTER EIGHT

29 June 1999
Maliana, East Timor

MALIANA WAS ALWAYS going to be a problem for the UN, and within three days of its office being opened, it was attacked. The attitude of the local authorities under *Bupati* Guilherme Dos Santos was belligerent and obstructive. The position of the region of Bobonaro, at the northern end of the border with West Timor and straddling the major road connecting East and West Timor, made it a strategically crucial area. The Indonesian authorities, fronted by long-term supporters such as former pro-Indonesian commander João Tavares, had made it a very strong militia area, and killings of known pro-independence supporters in nearby Cailaco had been widespread during April.

The region of Bobonaro had always been included in a possible 'breakaway' part of East Timor that the pro-Indonesian leaders had been threatening to create if they were forced to accept an independent East Timor following the ballot.

ABOUT 200 militia had gathered on the football field across the road from the UN's fortress-like office in Maliana on Tuesday 29 June. At 10 am they charged the building and pelted it with rocks, smashing windows and the front office.

About 50 East Timorese and UN staff hid in the compound. The five unarmed UN civilian police were powerless to do anything other than run out and assist the wounded Timorese at the front of the compound, and drag them back behind the heavy steel doors—severely dented by the large rocks being hurled against them.

An Australian UN police officer leapt over the back wall and ran to get help from the Indonesian police. He demanded they act to stop the attack, which ended when 20 armed Indonesian police were eventually deployed.

It was over in less than 20 minutes, but the abruptness and ferocity of the attack rattled the UN officials. Three staff, including a South African electoral official, were evacuated back to Dili that day by helicopter.

⊷⊶●⊷⊶

BACK IN Dili, I heard about the incident from a colleague in Jakarta. Later that day, the UN confirmed an attack had taken place, but the details they gave were very vague. At the Dili heliport, the South African woman looked shaken. She just stood, clutching a plastic bag full of clothing and a sleeping bag, waiting, unsure of what to do next.

No car had been sent for her, so we offered to give her a lift back to the Dili UN compound. She limped to the car—a rock had hit her leg. The Sri Lankan electoral official who was with her explained what had happened in the brief attack, but refused to allow us to quote her because UN personnel were under strict instructions not to talk to the press.

From then on, relations between the UN and the press were supposed to be a lot more formal and structured, as the UN tended to downplay the threats against its mission. Everything had to be first cleared through their spokesman or the public information office, and we were told that we weren't to revisit original sources after speaking with authorised spokesmen.

Later that night, Ian Martin made a statement in which he said he'd expressed his concern about the attack to the head of the Indonesian police task force who was supposed to be responsible for the mission's security. 'The large size of the rocks thrown indicate [the attack] was not spontaneous,' he said.

In Maliana the next morning, I saw what he'd meant. A large rock had been thrown into the front office so hard it had lodged in the opposite wall. Peter Bartu, now the senior district UN political officer for Maliana, continued working at his desk and pointed proudly to the rock. He told us the UN would not be evacuating—just moving out some nonessential staff in the short-term, leaving five people on the ground.

When I told Bartu that his own translators, students from Maliana, had just told me they'd recognised some local Indonesian soldiers in the crowd who attacked the office the day before, he simply replied: 'Well, that's it, isn't it? First they destroy the office, then they scare the local staff, and pretty soon you can't do your job.'

Outside, two UN helicopters buzzed over the town in what they told us was a 'scheduled road survey'. It looked to me, however, to be an obvious show of strength. There wasn't much else the UN could do.

Across the road, militia still milled about on the football field. One junior leader, Paulo Fereira, proclaimed he'd led the attack because he wanted the UN to leave. Indonesian police had been conspicuously stationed outside the UN compound. Pro-independence supporters had stayed inside the police station—they had been outside the UN compound at the time of the militia attack to report the burning down of their own houses by the militia the night before.

THE UN had already moved the vote back from 8 August to the weekend of the 21st because of security concerns and obstruction from the local authorities, and it looked as though it might have been necessary to reschedule again.

The following day in Viqueque, 15 armed militia entered the UN workers' residence and threatened them with weapons. Seven staff were relocated to Dili. Comments like 'Well, there goes another mission,' were starting to be heard around the UN compound in Dili.

The most serious attack happened in Liquiça on Sunday, 4 July at 4.30 pm. A humanitarian-relief convoy—the first to deliver food and medicine to the displaced people in and around Sare, behind the destroyed and deserted villages of Guico and Lissa Dila—was returning to Dili via Liquiça. As it stopped in the town centre, the militia attacked. They ran alongside the convoy screaming, banging on vehicles and smashing windows. They shot one man, a driver from Yayasan Hak, wounding him seriously.

Some of the members of the convoy fled to the police station and military barracks, others to the UN office in town. Several East Timorese members of the convoy were beaten. An American NGO worker, Max White, told how he had watched a militia man beat a New Zealand UN military liaison officer in an attempt to get at an East Timorese man who was sheltering behind him. The tall

New Zealander had refused to move and just stood there, taking the beating, not allowed to respond.

An attempt to evacuate the UN staff from Liquiça by helicopter was thwarted when stones were thrown at it as it tried to land at both of the only two possible sites. Two Australian police officers later confirmed to me that they'd been shot at by militia as they sped down to Liquiça in response to the attack. By the end of the evening that day, all 50 UN staff, including local employees, had been relocated back to Dili. Seventy-two of the convoy members had been escorted back safely, but six remained unaccounted for at the time. All but one of those missing turned up the next day, having made their own way back to Dili.

The next day was all statements, press conferences and responses to the latest violence. And it looked like the incident was going to stall the whole voting process, or at least hold up voter registration, which was due to begin the following week.

Indonesian police chief Colonel Timbul Silaen claimed members of the convoy had been armed. Remembering what had happened to the investigation convoy on the way to Alas the previous November, where the same excuse had been used for a similar attack, I half expected the colonel to say there were Falintil guerrillas in the convoy. But he didn't—that was left to Major-General Zecky Anwar, a former high-ranking Indonesian military intelligence official acting as a military liaison officer to the UN mission later in the day.

A clumsy attempt to plant a homemade pistol in the car of Dan Murphy, the outspoken American doctor who had been with the convoy, had taken place. The idea that Dan would be carrying a homemade weapon to attack militia was ridiculous, and it never went any further—except as a bad joke.

Ian Martin made some strong statements about the incident, and, in Australia, New York and Jakarta, the Indonesian government was urged to put an end to the violence. But Martin would still not come out and say what we all knew to be true, and was supported by a mountain of evidence—that the Indonesian military was well and truly behind the actions of the militia.

What he did say was, 'There is certainly a pattern of incidents and threats to UN personnel, as well as to their activities in different places, and that's a major concern for us . . . and I am not in a position to say whether it's a concerted strategy and who is concerting it, but it is certainly happening in a number of places.' He would not draw a link—of command or financial backing—between the militia and the Indonesian military. They still wanted to keep the bargaining leeway. It was inconceivable that the UN didn't know who was attacking them, and why, and with whose direct support.

Over the next week, more assurances did come from the Indonesian government that the attacks would cease and that voter registration could go ahead as planned. They even agreed to send an extra 1,300 Indonesian police to East Timor to provide further security for the ballot.

One night out at Pedro's place in Becora, I was talking to one of his relatives from Aileu about the situation and whether the ballot could go ahead. He claimed the militia were planning to repeat the recent wave of attacks on the UN in Aileu. I told him that unless something actually happened or he had some kind of evidence, I couldn't report anything. So he promptly went out to his car and came back with a pile of papers, one of them a faxed order signed by Suprapto Tarman, the *Bupati* of Aileu—former Kopassus officer from Java. It read: 'If there is any UNAMET conducting their work without reporting to the police or the

military and, after 6 pm, they are to be searched, if possible
beaten up, stoned and their cars destroyed.' Then, for the
benefit of the militia: 'The Indonesian military is always
behind you and want to live or die to protect integration.'

The order was dated 3 July, the day before the attack on
the convoy in Liquiça. It was quite possible that this order
to attack the UN had been rescinded since the Liquiça
incident, because of the international pressure on
Indonesia, but the document clearly showed a planned
harassment campaign had been initiated and coordinated at
one level by the local Indonesian civil administration.

Pedro's relative produced another piece of paper. It was
an order form for 100 automatic rifles from an Indonesian
military base in Java, Kodam III Siliwangi in Bandung. At
the bottom of the order, the *Bupati* had authorised
payment of 530 million rupiah for the purchase and
delivery of the weapons. It was dated 15 May and I was told
the weapons had been delivered and were now in the hands
of the AHI militia in Aileu.

The next day, Sebastião translated the documents
properly for me and I showed them to the CNRT and to
Joaquim at Yayasan Hak. They all agreed that the documents were genuine so I wrote a story that caused quite a
stir because of the direct links it showed between the civil
administration and the attacks on the UN.

That night, a colleague called to tell me that the UN was
going to deny the authenticity of the document at the next
morning's briefing.

Competition in Dili between journalists had become
intense. As more arrived to cover the voting process,
alliances were formed and broken as information was shared
or withheld according to professional and personal rivalries.
Mine had become a front-page story and everybody wanted
a piece of it. I sensed that Wimhurst, with the UN having

seemingly stopped the attacks through diplomatic pressure, and certain journalists, whose editors by now would have seen the story on the wire and demanded a match, all had their reasons for calling the document fake and burying the story. Which is exactly what happened at the following morning's briefing. Wimhurst stated emphatically that the document was fake.

ON 15 July, a day before registration for the ballot was due to begin, I went to Maliana, knowing the *Bupati* there had made many threats to boycott the process. The CNRT leaders were still in the police station, where some of them had been since the militia had begun killing people in April.

'Three months and three days I have been here because of the militia,' Manuel Magalhaes told me in the police headquarters. 'They destroyed my house, and the military and the militia, they have told me they will kill me if I leave here.' The three leaders, who were the original CNRT coordinators for Maliana, had been there that long. Manuel said he felt quite safe in the police headquarters—it was a large area with the main building in the centre and barracks off to the side in front of the garage area. Along one side of the car park, there was a row of three rooms where the CNRT people were staying, along with the young people who fled the militia attack on the UN compound. There were about 30 of them in there.

Manuel seemed to have faith in the Indonesian police and their sincerity in providing security for the ballot. He was visited regularly by UNAMET staff and seemed to be in good condition. But he was eventually killed after managing to escape the massacre in that same police compound that happened on the night of 8 September, following the announcement of the ballot result and the UN evacuation from the town. Manuel was among 12 people who got away from the police station as militia worked their way through the refugees who had sought shelter there while the town was destroyed around them. The militia, wearing balaclavas and working with swords and machetes identified and killed those involved with CNRT. Forty-seven were killed according to witnesses interviewed by Australian journalist Jill Jolliffe, one of the first to reach the town after the massacre.

The same witnesses described how the killing was done by militia, with police and Indonesian military standing behind them with guns. Police commander, Major Budi Susilo, ordered all those in the compound to watch the killing in silence and then supervised the loading of the bodies onto trucks.

The 12 who got away fled to a nearby lagoon but were found by the Indonesian military the following morning after a shepherd alerted them to the presence of the men. They were all killed and their bodies thrown in the sea at nearby Batugade.

But that was more than two months into the future when Major Budi greeted us in Maliana, where we'd gone to report the start of registration. He was glad to see us and went through the security preparations he'd made for the first day of registration.

'We are ready to protect the process,' he said. 'We have 300 men in the region of Bobonaro and we will have men at 20 of the registration centres.'

He seemed young, smart and efficient, and told us that the hotel we were staying at was a good choice. There were UNAMET people there and he had men deployed to protect the place all night.

He was right about the hotel. The local UNAMET workers dubbed it 'The Sheraton'; it had a wide balcony with excellent views across the mostly flat town which was overlooked by a massive peaked mountain on the other side. Maliana was a prosperous place, with rice paddies and farmland that stretched back west along a fertile floodplain to the Malibaca River which, further along, formed the border with West Timor. At one point, the border is only about five kilometres from Maliana, and West Timor can be seen across the river from the village of Memo.

The local priest in Maliana, Father Tavares, identified that area to the west of the town as a major transit point for Indonesian troops into East Timor. He told me that as many as 600 Indonesian troops had passed through the area at night during the past week.

'Their presence here is to frighten the people,' he said. 'In Cailaco they have road blocks today. From Maliana to the border there is no security. There is no way the CNRT can campaign here.'

He went on to tell me about the killings in Cailaco, which had been going on for months. Another 12 people had been killed recently. The priest said the Cailaco killings were mainly carried out by East Timorese who worked with SGI and the local military.

One man, João Koli, who had killed at least two people in Cailaco in April, had been bragging that the Indonesian military had instructed him to kill UNAMET staff. The priest was worried because he thought this man was quite capable of doing it; he'd killed two men—Armando Belaco and Antonio Basilio—in Cailaco in April, apparently of his own volition and without instruction from the Indonesian military, because he'd thought they were Falintil. Armando's daughter had witnessed it and recounted the details . . . she said it had been like watching a buffalo being butchered.

>-+◦+-<

EARLY NEXT morning, the registration centres opened and we went to Bobonaro, a crumbling old Portuguese hill town in the mountains south of Maliana. The people seemed subdued but determined to go through with the process, despite a visit two days earlier from pro-Indonesian leaders, including *Bupati* Guilherme, who told them they had to vote autonomy.

The Austrian UN civilian police officer, eyeing off a group of youths in a truck who'd been yelling at people waiting to register, said, 'If we come under serious intimidation problems, we will pull out.' It was obviously bothering him that he could only make sporadic contact with Maliana on his two-way radio.

In Maliana, the intimidation seemed to have confined itself to a 40-minute tai chi session by the local Indonesian military on the oval outside the UN compound, and we continued on to Balibo.

A rally had been planned there for the following day, 17 July, to commemorate Suharto signing the bill to integrate East Timor into Indonesia in 1976. Guilherme Dos Santos was there making preparations, along with members of João Tavares's family.

Guilherme took time out to tell us how the requirements for the UN registration were flawed and that the people didn't have the two pieces of documentation required. Next came a rhetorical question: 'If all of the people protest this, and don't take part in the ballot, what about the UN position then?'

Warming to his theme, Guilherme said that even he, the *Bupati*, had only one piece of identification—his Indonesian one!

'I promise I will kill any member of UNAMET, especially the Australians,' he continued, becoming quite animated. 'If UNAMET is not neutral, I will kill them.' He was leaning forward, jabbing his finger at us.

I had heard him and I understood, but I wanted Jiji, who was translating for me, to check what he'd said and make him repeat it.

'Write it down,' said Guilherme, forcefully tapping my notebook, 'I promise! I will kill them.'

⊳─◆─○─◆─◁

BACK IN the car, driving to Dili, Jiji was laughing. 'He really shouldn't have said that—you're going to report it aren't you,' he said.

'Of course, he told me to,' I said, laughing as well, and told him to drive faster so I could make an early Friday deadline for the Australian papers.

If anything, Jiji was pro-autonomy. His brother, Mario Viera, was a representative of the FPDK in Dili, and sometimes filled in for Basilio as a spokesman. Jiji had driven us down there for money and occasionally helped us with translating. At the time I didn't believe him when he told me he was not interested in politics and didn't trust him. Later I found out he was actually pro-independence but hiding it to gather information in his work with the FPDK. To take one of the openly pro-independence students to Mailiana at that time would have been asking for trouble— they would have been threatened or beaten, or worse.

If the meeting with the *Bupati* had been a set-up, then somebody in the FPDK wanted to discourage and weaken the *Bupati* by having him give me stupid answers that would put him on the wrong side of the real authority in Bobonaro, the military.

⊳─◆─○─◆─◁

BACK IN Dili, I sent off the story detailing the *Bupati*'s death threats and within the hour a representative from the newly established Australian Consulate was around at the hotel asking me whether Guilherme was serious. I told him what had happened and repeated the conversation; there was no secret about it, the story had already been published.

'Right, let's see what we can do about this,' he said as he left.

The next day I missed my ride to Balibo for the rally. By the time I arranged another lift and got there, the rally was almost over.

It was the usual kind of militia rally: red and white Indonesian flags everywhere, a stage, local dignitaries lined up on chairs at the front. But this time, the VIPs were joined by three UNAMET military liaison officers, from Australia, England and Sri Lanka.

The speeches had finished and there was a crowd of journalists around *Bupati* Guilherme, all asking about the death threats and his threats to boycott the ballot. He denied ever threatening anyone, and when David O'Shea from SBS pointed at me and repeated what I'd quoted him as saying—that Australians would be killed if they were not neutral—the *Bupati* flew into a rage of furious denial.

Guilherme came towards me through the crowd saying he was going to throw me out because I hadn't told the truth. Obviously he'd been told by someone higher up the chain of command that he couldn't go around making those kinds of threats any more.

Everybody went to the Portuguese fort at the top of the hill to have their lunch. A heavy-metal band made up of militia from the Lak Saur group in Suai played down on the oval. They looked the part in their wide-brimmed hats, long hair and fringed suede jackets, and the music reflected the mood of the crowd.

At the fort, João Tavares said that this wouldn't be the last party he'd attend to celebrate East Timor's integration with Indonesia. 'We have won. We have been Indonesian together with 200 million Indonesians. This year's celebration will not be the last,' he said.

▷─◁▶─○─◀─▷

SEBASTIÃO CAME up to me where I stood with other journalists milling around outside after the Monday morning briefing at the UN compound in Dili, as we normally did when nothing particularly interesting had been announced. He had been doing some work translating documents for the UN public information office, and he looked angry and agitated. He motioned me over to one side, away from everybody else.

'If they didn't fuckin' believe the last one, let's see them deny this,' he said, handing me some folded sheets of paper.

The week before, he had helped me go through the other document—the incriminating fax from the *Bupati* of Aileu had been excited to think we'd finally established some undeniable links between the Indonesian government and the attacks on the UN. And when it had been denied by the UN as a fake document, Sebastião blamed the UN for duplicity and, being Timorese, was furious with the games that were going on. They were costing people's lives—those of his countrymen.

No sooner had he handed me the papers, when a public information officer, followed by Geoff Thompson from the ABC, walked over to see what was going on. Sebastião went back into the office and I walked off with Geoff—after what had happened last time, I thought I might as well let Geoff in on it.

As we translated the document in the restaurant at the Resende, by now joined by several other journalists, we realised the bombshell that we had in our possession: it was a blueprint for the Indonesian evacuation of East Timor.

Dated 3 July and signed by H.R. Ganardi—who turned out to be the special assistant to the Indonesian government's coordinating minister of internal political affairs, Feisal Tanjung—it was entitled 'General Assessment If Option One Fails'. It listed the reasons why the result of the ballot would be for independence, and what the Indonesian response would have to be.

'Our former optimism has turned to doubt,' the report said. 'It would not be wrong to predict the worst-case scenario, that special autonomy will be rejected.'

But the real impact of the document was in the measures it recommended as a result of this assessment: 'An immediate plan to be made to evacuate all Indonesian public servants and migrants to the neighbouring province of Nusa Tenggara Timur [East Nusa Tenggara, West Timor] before the announcement of the ballot result; the various elements of the TNI to be put on alert and prepared for action near the evacuation areas; Nusa Tenggara Timur to be made ready to receive huge numbers of refugees; the planning and securing of evacuation routes and the destruction of facilities and other vital objects as the Indonesians pull out.'

It was the last recommendation that was the most chilling. 'Facilities and other vital objects,' what did that mean? There weren't that many facilities and 'vital objects' in East Timor—barely passable roads, a very bad telephone system that was almost nonexistent outside of Dili, a power supply that was unreliable and still not available in many parts of the country.

At the same time as planning a withdrawal from East Timor, the document recommended that full support of the pro-integration forces had to continue. 'The government's commitment must be confirmed through empowering the pro-integration forces,' it said, adding that those elements placed great hope in an injection of strength from the Indonesian government to conduct an 'Operation of Sympathy'.

Well, that part was already happening, and it was obvious even in Dili in July that the militia were better funded, armed and organised than ever before. The crunch was how these 'elements' would respond to the evacuation of their prime backers and the destruction of their infrastructure. And what exactly was the concrete outcome of an 'Operation of Sympathy'?

After we all ran with the story, with many reassurances to editors, the document was declared a fake by the Indonesian government. The UN said it was 'analysing the contents of the document—but was not questioning its authenticity' and the Australian government also said it was checking the authenticity of the source.

Soon after the ballot and the subsequent turmoil in East Timor, the author, Ganardi, would admit that he had written the document, but at the time he denied it.

In Timor we had previously no real idea of the scale of the preparations and plans the Indonesian authorities were putting in place to deal with a pro-independence referendum outcome. The document hinted at them, the signs were all around us, and soon the predictions of chaos would be coming from both sides.

＊＊＊

TRAVELLING DOWN to Suai was becoming more difficult. Leaving East Timor involved thorough border checks at Batugade in the north, and when you re-entered the territory on the southern border, there was a police post, an immigration post and an army-militia post. At all three, your papers would be checked and, in some cases, people would not be allowed to re-enter East Timor for visa discrepancies.

But the posts weren't really to check on incoming travellers, they were to prevent people getting out. The people in Suai were literally backed up into the south-west corner of the country. The strength of the Mahidi group in Ainaro, Cassa and Zumalai meant the road to Dili, and even the road over the hills to Bobonaro and Maliana, was blocked. To the west of Suai, Lak Saur and the military blocked the way to the border.

When the UN arrived in Suai, about 700 people immediately went back to the church. Over the next two weeks they were joined by 800 others, some who came in on UN-organised convoys to escape the violence in the villages.

The situation at the church grounds and in the half-built cathedral was now a permanent institutionalised version of what had been happening in January. 'Every night they want to attack here,' Father Hilario told me. 'We have no guns here. We see them outside in the street. Last night at about 8 o'clock two kijangs [pick-up trucks] full of weapons and men, and some on motorcycles, were outside shouting that they would kill us. If the UN were not here, they would have done it already.'

This was normal now, and there was none of the panic that had caused the woman to smother her child accidentally, back when it had all begun. Now the people just milled around and sat in what were now more or less permanent tents and shelters. In the cathedral steeple above the town, people had cleared out the loose bricks and made themselves their own family areas. Some had radios or guitars and one man had arranged a kind of an office with a typewriter and a desk made from a board and some bricks.

Hilario told me how they were still trying to contact people who were hiding from the militia violence in the forest, to tell them to come to the church grounds, where he believed they would be safe until the ballot. He already knew what the local military had planned for those in the church, no matter what the result was because inside his house there was a man who had just deserted from the local military.

Anito Cardoso, the deserter, still looked like a military man even though he was dressed in civilian clothes and slightly unshaven; he still had the small, neat moustache and the stiff back of a soldier.

Anito had been an East Timorese member of the local Indonesian military command, Kodim 1635. He joined in 1989 and his loyalty was never questioned—you could see he was still proud of that as he spoke. But now he was hiding in Hilario's house after being imprisoned for 42 nights and escaping as his guards slept—he'd heard they were planning to kill him.

He had been arrested after his house in the nearby village of Tilomar had been burnt down by militia in April. His brother-in-law had gone to the mountains to join Falintil, and Anito had been accused of supplying them with weapons. He continued to deny that he was guilty of that even as he told us the military's plans in the area.

His commander, Lieutenant-Colonel Achmad Mas Agus, told the men every day to prepare for the aftermath of the ballot. When autonomy wins, he said, the army 'will kill all those who support independence and stay in the church.'

Anito also informed us of how the leaders of Mahidi and Lak Saur met every evening at 9 pm with the commander, and how all the militia leaders and the troops were told that Suai and Maliana would become bases for the fight for integration after the ballot.

They were also told to move their families across the border, so that they could return to fight for autonomy. Anito said the Indonesian commanders told them about the troops waiting in West Timor and on the two nearby islands of Flores and Alor, ready to come in and join their fight. They had spoken about 12 warships near the island laying mines. They were told not to worry—the airforce was moving planes including fighter jets, into Kupang, and the military no longer wore uniforms, but were infiltrating East Timor in large numbers.

Anito was most affected by the way Timorese soldiers in the military were continuously threatened by their superiors and told that if they did not support autonomy, they would be killed.

In their nightly meetings with the commander, Anito revealed, the militia were told to wait and to be prepared to carry out operations after the ballot.

'Every day they speak about this,' he said. 'The *Dandim* [commander] tells us every day, everybody—soldiers, servants and their whole families—must vote for autonomy. If you don't vote for autonomy, they will throw you out of the military and kill you.'

Anito was now in a very bad position and had no alternative but to hide in the church until such time as he could slip away. The road blocks on either side of town were manned by his former comrades who now had orders to kill him on sight. His revelation that the military commander gave direct orders to the militia leaders on a daily basis was nothing new. But the fact that the soldiers themselves were being told to move out their families and to be prepared to kill all independence supporters after the ballot clarified what was referred to in the Ganardi document as an 'Operation of Sympathy' on the part of the military. In blunt terms, this meant widespread killing organised by the military, no matter what the result.

THE NEXT day, journalist Ian Timberlake and I went to see Lieutenant-Colonel Achmad Mas Agus, who was extremely accommodating. We asked our questions and got the response that it had been 'peaceful here in Covalima, the only problem has been the people who were upset with UNAMET for taking down the Indonesian flag and replacing it with the blue UN flag at the registration posts.'

'It is terrible they should have another flag pole,' he said. 'The people here think it offends the Indonesian dignity.'

There was, he said, absolutely no relationship between the military and the militia, and the weapons the militia carried were from the Portuguese time. When we pointed out that they were M-16s, he said, 'No, I don't know about that,' and smiled.

Ian asked him why his men in the street were still armed, as there had been an agreement announced by the UN that all Indonesian troops would refrain from intimidation by not brandishing weapons outside of their barracks. Clearly, the agreement was meaningless; I remembered leaving the briefing during which it was announced, and Ian pointing out a soldier in the street who was armed and saying, 'That's a violation.' He was going to count every violation he saw, and for a while he did.

Now Ian wouldn't let this point go with Achmad Mas Agus. He was pedantic enough to be the only journalist still keeping figures on the violations to this latest agreement. Mas Agus replied, 'That is because there are many crocodiles in Suai—we have to defend ourselves from the crocodiles.'

Then, as we were leaving, he said, 'Crocodiles can be men as well, can't they?' Yes, Colonel, they can be, I thought as I shook his hand when we left.

><+>-0-<+-<

WE DROVE through to Zumalai on the long, flat road through the fields. It was a relief not to be lurching from side to side on mountain roads. At one point on the side of the road, there was a small, skinny Javanese man wearing the pointed bamboo hat of a peasant. On a pole across his shoulder he carried a wide selection of brand new shirts, each in its individual plastic wrapper. It couldn't be—they couldn't still be doing the same thing. Not now in 1999. An old story went that Yunus Yosfiah—then a special forces captain, but more recently the Information Minister for the Habibie government—had hiked around East Timor prior to the Indonesian invasion in 1975, collecting military intelligence on Fretilin positions. He had disguised himself as a poor, humble Javanese shirt hawker. Surely they wouldn't be needing that kind of information now. But there was that man, down near Zumalai, plodding along with the shirts over his shoulder. Impossible? Maybe. Slightly surreal. Definitely.

><><><><

CANÇIO CARVALHO wasn't in Cassa when we arrived, but his brother Nemezio was more than happy to tell us why Cassa was the only place where registration for the ballot was going along very slowly. The UN registration post had been closed for the first two days of registration, and when it opened was surrounded by militia. His complaints were the same as those being voiced in Maliana—about the necessity of having two pieces of identification. He was threatening to boycott the registration and the ballot.

Nemezio lived in terror of Falintil coming down and killing him, or at least that was what he wanted us to believe. He was sitting in his living room listening to the incredible static on a two-way radio which a voice would occasionally interrupt.

'That's them, that's Falintil,' he would say, listening to the noise intently. He reminded me of a paranoid drug dealer with a police scanner.

There had been an incident on the first day of registration that had kept the registration offices in Cassa closed. Some of the Mahidi men had gone to a small village near Zumalai and surrounded a house, intending to capture the occupant. But the villagers had fought back and apparently killed one of the militia with a well-aimed rock to the head. Nemezio had called it a Falintil atrocity, and said that if he didn't order a response to the killing, his men would take things into their own hands.

He kept talking about how he would be forced to use his weapons; about how he would have to call out his 7,000 militia and be forced to initiate an attack and boycott the ballot.

'Then, if we don't follow the popular consultation, we won't receive the result and we are back to our basic position of integration with Indonesia,' he said. The possibility of that happening in that part of the country was real. If there was anywhere the militia could do that, it would be down in the south-west. The sheer number of militia at posts along the roads and milling about in Cassa and Zumalai would be enough to stop people voting.

Two days before, the chief of the UN civilian police contingent, Australian Commissioner Alan Mills, had made a special trip to Cassa to get things moving along and lean on the two brothers. After an hour and a half of civil discussions with Nemezio and the local military and Indonesian police commanders, Cançio had joined them and flown into a rage, physically launching himself at Commissioner Mills—a large and solid man with the typical physique of a middle-aged policeman. The two had to be separated by the Indonesian liaison officer present,

Colonel Plastica. Later, one of the party told me that Cançio appeared to be either drugged or in such a state of irrational fury, he was literally frothing at the mouth.

Back in Dili, Mills told me that, 'it's hard to know exactly where the truth lies in that area'. They had simply told the brothers to use their influence to allow the registration to proceed, he said.

The story of that incident made me feel particularly disinclined to be anywhere near Cassa or Cançio when the ballot result became known. If he'd behaved like that towards Commissioner Mills in the presence of high-ranking Indonesian military, I could imagine what he'd do to a stray journalist. Cançio's reputation for savagery would only be enhanced by what happened later in Cassa and the surrounding villages.

SAM, THE local photographer who worked for Associated Press, came and got me from the Tourismo—he said there'd been a killing by Falintil and the Indonesian police wanted to show us the body. The police were waiting outside and drove us out of town towards Liquiça to a small village called Ulmera about 10 kilometres away. There, laid out in a small hut, was a horribly hacked corpse surrounded by terrified relatives and militia in civilian clothes. The police told us the victim was João Nunes, a 25-year-old unemployed man who had been stabbed 22 times.

The family looked with fear at the Indonesian men in civilian clothes who carried small submachine guns and pistols, and the Indonesian television cameras recorded the sombre scene in the grass-roofed hut. João's blood was still sticky on the table, and the flies buzzed in the hot and stuffy low-roofed room.

I was told a story by Major Joko Irianto of the Indonesian police about a wedding party that was attacked by Falintil—20 of them with 30 guns—in the mountains behind the town. According to him, they had been looking for someone else and had found and killed João. As a result of the young man's death, there would have to be an operation to find those responsible, he said.

It was all wrong. There was no wailing and the people who lived in the hut stood nervously at the back of the room as the camera crew and I were shown the body. The mysterious armed men who purported to be mourners displayed not an ounce of grief. They had just stood around with blank faces, wearing sunglasses.

Outside were some of the East Timorese members of Besih Merah Putih. Shabbily dressed, wearing red and white headbands and holding spears and machetes, they were the ones who you would normally have seen manning the road blocks and posts along the road west from Dili through Liquiça.

The police major shepherded me past the mourners and walked me back to the car. It was obvious to me what was going on and who was in control; the armed Indonesians had treated the militia as though they weren't there—they were running that particular show.

Later, a UN civilian police officer in Liquiça confirmed what I already knew: João was not a Falintil victim, he was just another young man who had refused to join the militia.

The next day Sebastião told me he had seen me on the local television news looking over the latest supposed Falintil victim. They had filmed me and run it on the nightly news to lend credibility to the story.

THE ROLE of the UN civilian police was supposed to have been to advise the Indonesian police on security and to carry out investigations alongside their Indonesian counterparts. The UN police were hamstrung by the fact that they were unarmed, which meant they had to rely on the Indonesians for security. If a planned investigation involved someone connected to the militia, the UN civilian police were usually given the run around.

Two Australian police asked me whether I could think of a really strong case to present to the Indonesian police as a test to see if the Indonesians could be brought to prosecute militia-related violence. I told them about the students from the polytechnic whose bodies were supposed to be buried out the back of the house of Mateus Carvalho, the militia leader in Hera, and we organised to interview the same staff member who'd recently come to me to confirm the story.

As he ran through it with them, and one of the Australian police tried to employ standard murder-investigation procedures, the witness became increasingly intimidated. He knew the UN police worked with the Indonesian police, of whom he was understandably frightened, and so the story he told the Australian police officer was different to the one he'd told me. We slogged on through a few meetings where the same thing happened, and it became obvious the case wasn't going anywhere.

Without an absolutely watertight case, the Australians couldn't force the Indonesians into an investigation, and when everybody was so terrified of the authorities the difficulty of convincing a witness willing to testify without really having the means to protect them later was too great. In this case, the main source of information regarding the murders was a serving militia member, and we couldn't talk to him directly.

Another difficulty was that the UN police had no way of knowing where information they handed over to the Indonesians was going. It was highly likely that if the intention to base a case against Mateus Carvalho was revealed, the bodies would simply be moved from behind his house. Hera was by then a major encampment for the new police being sent in to boost the Indonesian effort to provide security for the ballot, and the place was full of Indonesian police as well as militia, and there was an Indonesian military base there, too. There was no way anything could be done in the area without their knowledge or permission.

IT WAS after a morning meeting with the police and the witness that we heard shooting in the market. Ian Timberlake and I went up there. As we approached on our motor scooter, militia and Indonesians wearing plain clothes and carrying weapons charged at us and forced us to turn and flee. We headed around the corner and it was just as it had been. It was just like back in May. Shooting, confusion, and all of a sudden the market was full of Indonesians in plain clothes waving guns, yelling at militia and forcing people away.

That afternoon, two East Timorese were wounded with machetes and one Indonesian from Lombok was stabbed in the chest.

Militia were suddenly running about, kicking and stoning UN vehicles that happened to be going past the busy intersection. 'Fuck you UNAMET!' they shouted as they beat on the cars. Jose Belo was there in the market by chance, and saw how quickly the situation was turned into a show of anti-UN violence by just a handful of militia in the crowd.

After about 30 minutes, the Indonesian police came out from their headquarters, not more than 50 metres away, to 'restore order'.

In the hospital, the uncle of the stabbed man from Lombok told us his nephew was not part of the militia, he was just unemployed. In the Motael clinic, the two East Timorese men who'd been attacked by the militia told us they had no idea why it had happened. The police told us it had been a dispute between the pro- and anti-independence groups, and that they had arrested five men who they thought were the pro-independence people who had started the trouble. Later, Eurico Guterres claimed one of his militia had been killed (even though the guy from Lombok wasn't dead at the time) and demanded revenge on the pro-independence people who, he said, had started the problem.

It was like a game and everybody had their own version of events according to their allegiances. Even the police had their own agenda, and weren't sharing that with their UN counterparts. That day, 26 July, a further 899 police arrived in Dili to provide security, and another 400 followed the next day.

I was in Becora when the bulk of those police moved from the port out to their temporary camp in Hera. Truck after truck loaded with the brown-uniformed and heavily armed police passed through the suburb. People ran from the main road. Mothers grabbed children and hurriedly closed doors and windows. Men got off the roadside where they normally spent most of the day.

'It is like another invasion, all over again,' said a Timorese youth who was standing next to me as the column of trucks went by. The Timorese made no distinction between the police and the army.

ON 30 July, Alexander Downer made the first-ever visit of an Australian foreign minister to East Timor. The Australian press contingent was invited along to the opening of the Australian Consulate. It was the first time a consulate from Australia had existed in East Timor since 1971, and it was a chance for the journalists in Dili to sound out the attitude of the Australian government at a time when things were showing all the signs of lurching towards an inevitable violent conclusion.

As soon as Alexander Downer had said it, most of us realised it was just a simple mistake: 'The cantonment idea is a very constructive idea. It is going to be very hard to achieve what is sometimes called disarmament in a short time period. I think the cantonment of Falintil and the militia groups is a positive step whatever happens in the ballot.'

What he was talking about was the cantonment plan between Falintil and the UN. Falintil had agreed to concentrate their guerrilla forces in four camps throughout East Timor if, in return, they would not be forced to hand over their weapons. They also agreed to voluntarily restrain themselves from carrying out violent actions. But what Alexander Downer got wrong was the idea that there was a concrete plan for the militia to do the same. The fluid urban-based militia organisations were not really conducive to being corralled in a camp, and there was no real commitment on the part of the Indonesian police or military to do so either. And why should there be? They hadn't finished their job yet.

Downer did use the opportunity, however, to remind the Indonesian government of the enormous damage that would be done to the country's reputation if the ballot was not conducted in a peaceful way. But his evasive comments regarding what would happen after the ballot suggested that the Australian government's position was vague and noncommittal. 'Assuming that it [the ballot] is a success, phase two will be a very dangerous period. The Indonesians will still be responsible. What we are looking at is maybe an increase in the UNAMET civpol [civilian police] presence,' which wasn't very comforting coming from the Foreign Minister and showed the reactive nature of Australian policy towards the whole process in East Timor.

Later that night, all Australians in Dili were invited to a function at the Hotel Resende. There was free Australian wine and beer, and Downer gave a speech thanking all the Australians for their work in the difficult and dangerous conditions of East Timor. He also said he was confident that in the coming months we would all acquit ourselves well because Australians were 'a tough people'. After the speech I felt rather morose, thinking that if that was the best spin he could manage to put on things, it must have been worse than we realised.

━━◦━━

EDUARDO FINALLY showed up at the Tourismo to take me to the main cantonment camp up in the hills behind Manatuto a few days later. It was getting dark as we finally reached a point where the car couldn't go any further. We were in a river valley that suddenly got narrower and water filled its base. On either side the hills had closed in, and the wide, flat rock floor of the riverbed that had once been an excellent road had become too rocky for us to continue.

Over 100 people stood around in the darkness unload-ing a truck and dividing up the supplies into portions that could be carried by each person. Eduardo, who was in charge, was trying to figure out a way to attach a brand new wide-screen colour television to a long bamboo pole so it could be carried up the river without getting wet. No-one had thought to bring a rope, so some of the young men began twisting together reeds to make some cord.

Eduardo had come a long way in the Falintil organisation since I'd met him in Kupang in mid-1997, when he'd given me the details of the capture of David Alex. After that he'd returned to Dili and narrowly missed arrest, and had been forced to flee to the forest and live with Falintil. There he'd become a trusted member of the Falintil inner circle of commander Taur Matan Ruak, who had taken over as field commander of Falintil after the accidental death of Konis Santana in late 1997. With Falintil secure in their cantonment in a place called Waimori, in the hills south of Manatuto, east of Dili, they were making themselves comfortable at their first permanent camp that wouldn't be under threat of attack due to the cantonment agreement. That was why Eduardo had been sent to Dili to get the television and, of course, a satellite dish.

Even though they had an agreement with the UN saying they wouldn't be attacked by the Indonesians, Falintil hadn't let their guard down. The Waimori camp was a natural fortress. The only way to approach it from the north was to walk up the river valley.

As the young men with us cursed each other and splashed around in the river trying to keep the television and dismantled satellite dish dry, young Falintil recruits stationed high above on the cliffs overlooking the valley called down for us to identify ourselves. Eduardo cleared things with them, and we continued to splash our way noisily up the river. Soon, a column of about 40 civilians passed us going the other way and quietly exchanged greetings. Further along we stopped with another group who were huddled around a fire on the sandy beach on the riverside.

East Timorese are susceptible to cold, especially those

who live in hot and humid Dili. Most of the people with us were from the city, and everybody was wet and cold, and didn't want to move from the fire. So Eduardo had to sharply remind a few people who was in charge, and to get them moving. It was his responsibility to get the equipment to the camp. As we continued along the river, we passed more groups of armed Falintil soldiers who whispered challenges as we approached.

It was about 2 am when we finally crossed back over the river, which had by then widened out again, and in the darkness we could make out a whole series of bamboo and straw huts built right down to the water's edge. There were over 100 huts and men, many with long, wild hair and wearing bits and pieces of Indonesian camouflage uniforms, stared out at us. There were guns and equipment lying around everywhere, and a small fire burned, hidden behind a wall of green leaves. We sat down and had some coffee, and some huts were cleared out for us to sleep in.

In the morning we realised we were in just one small corner of the camp. It was divided up into roughly three areas. Falur's fighters from region three were down by the river where we had slept the night. Those from region two, normally stationed further east behind Baucau, were over on the other side of what was a football field and parade ground, next to which was the small compound of the commander, Taur Matan Ruak, and his guard.

It was a village constructed entirely from bamboo, straw and rough wooden shelters. Huts were built in rows and sections were divided by the organisational breakdown of Falintil. Units were kept together and family members were able to visit their relatives for the first time. There were about 500 guerrillas and about 300 families and refugees living where just over a month before there had been a flat piece of land on a bend in the river.

Taur Matan Ruak, Falintil's commander in East Timor, walked up from an early morning wash in the river. He casually introduced himself in English as he wiped water from his face. We would have time to talk later, he said, but first he had to get ready for the morning parade. He was shorter than I'd imagined and had shaved off his beard; he didn't look anywhere near as fierce as he did in the posed photos I'd seen of him holding his gun. He'd been fighting since 1975 when he was 19 years old.

The whole marching band of the Indonesian Territorial Battalion 744 had defected to Falintil and the mostly older men had brought their instruments, mainly drums and bugles, with them. They set up and played a martial marching song to which around 200 Falintil soldiers—many wearing the new insignia designating which region they belonged to, and with the blue, white and green of the Falintil flag sewn onto the shoulder of their Indonesian uniforms—marched around the parade ground.

These were guerrilla fighters, and their marching left a little to be desired, but they were intensely proud and it was a serious ceremony. I recognised some of the younger ones from 1997 when I had been in David Alex's camp and, to be honest, I was surprised to see them still alive. There had been a lot of deaths reported among that group immediately after Alex's capture in 1997, and I had never been sure who had died.

The parade came to a halt in front of the flagpole and they presented arms and then saluted as the Falintil flag was raised. Taur Matan Ruak returned the salute. He was standing outside his hut, which was in a roughly fenced-off area behind the flagpole. Two guards with machine guns stood at the entrance and I noticed another heavier machine gun set up and manned in a hut out the back, covering the building from behind.

The hut had wooden walls and no windows. Its roof was made of sheets of orange plastic covered over with branches, which allowed some light through to the inside. Satellite phones, two laptop computers and a stereo sat on the large bamboo 'conference' table, with benches around three sides, inside.

There at the main cantonment camp, things were secure and the guerrillas could afford to relax a little. But, Ruak told me, the situation in the two camps in the west was not nearly so comfortable. Despite the cantonment agreement, they were still facing attacks from Indonesian military and elements of the police. Three days before, TNI, Polri and Besih Merah Putih had attacked the village of Boarema in the west near Hatolia and captured two villagers who worked with Falintil, as well as shooting another two. The Falintil fighters escaped, but only just.

There had been other problems in that same area throughout July, which was one of the reasons they had to establish two cantonment camps. There were too many people seeking refuge with Falintil in that area, and the two locations, one near Bobonaro and the other near Ermera, were separated by the strong militia area near Maliana and Atabae. It was a strange strategy to concentrate all their forces in four places and then tell the Indonesian authorities and the UN exactly where they were. But it also made sense—Falintil wanted the ballot to take place peacefully, and they wanted to deny the militia and the Indonesian authorities the opportunity to use their existence as a pretence for operations or to blame them for violence they themselves had carried out.

'Our position here is a self-defence position—if they attack, we will respond. It's their decision, we will not run away from a fight,' Ruak said.

When they moved to the Waimori camp at the start of

July, they had dealt with the local military post by surrounding it and telling the 14 Indonesian soldiers inside that if they left their post armed or did anything against the local population, they would be surrounded and disarmed. When we'd arrived, the Indonesian troops had just stood there, demoralised and outnumbered, with their hands on their hips, and watched us.

The huge supply operation involved in feeding everyone at the camp meant there was a continuous stream of vehicles travelling along what used to be a back road to a dead end at the river. A few days later, I saw the Indonesian soldiers standing in front of their post, watching as East Timorese struggled with a broken-down earthmover they had brought in to extend the road right to the camp.

THE REGISTRATION period for the ballot was almost over. Around 430,000 East Timorese had already registered—almost 90% of the eligible voting population—and Ruak didn't seem to think he really needed to bother risking a confrontation by registering his few hundred men. Most of the refugees in the camp—mainly students who had fled the violence in the towns—had already walked the five hours to the village of Liaruca, where I had seen them come out of the hills in a long line a few days before. That was high in the central mountains, and the scene had a spectacularly epic nature about it—the ragged line of long-haired students and a few Falintil fighters with guns, all wearing a weird collection of clothes against the cold mountain air, suddenly started streaming out of the mountains to register at a remote post. Agus, an Indonesian journalist who was later murdered by militia, was with the students filming them. He had been up with Falintil for two weeks where rice, a few vegetables and occasionally some buffalo meat were the staples. He was desperate for something processed to eat. I gave him some cheese and biscuits, which he immediately devoured.

There was an air of victory in the camp in Waimori, and Taur Matan Ruak had no doubt that independence would be the result of the ballot. He stressed that they, Falintil, didn't need to do any campaigning in the official campaigning period that was about to begin.

'Violence will happen after the consultation period [but] the responsibility must be in the hands of the United Nations. If we act, it will be called civil war,' he said.

For the first time ever, many of the people in the camp were able to see friends, family or comrades in a situation of relative peace and security. Two young women told me how they'd started working for Falintil when they were very young, in the early 1980s. They had come from Laga in the east.

One of them told this story: 'We used to take them corn and old clothes in the mountains. During that time, everybody who worked with Falintil got captured. Fourteen of my family were captured by the Indonesians, so they sent us two girls to make contact with Eli. We found him but we didn't tell the Indonesians, and they took some of the older women away and tortured them. It was very bad in '84—those who had family in the jungle had to be killed, and we had to move to Dili. Eli stayed in the forest.'

She was talking about Eli Foho Rai Boot, one of the region's three commanders who was sitting with us. It was the first time she had seen him since then, and he was beaming. He was one of the original East Timorese who had served in the Portuguese army before 1975 and had formed the core of Falintil's fighters. He had been in the forest ever since then.

Later in the day, Eduardo finished putting up the satellite dish and the colour television. They set it up under a canopy, with bench seats made of tree branches that got progressively higher towards the back, so you were balancing with your feet off the ground but you could see over the heads of those in front. It was the second dish and television that had been brought to the camp. The first one was so popular, they had to get another one. Most of the people there had been living in the mountains for years, some since 1975, and when they turned on the television in the afternoon, we sat there with them in the forest and watched CNN. The cantonment in Waimori had felt like the most secure place in East Timor.

⊷⊶⊷○⊷⊶⊷

THE OFFICIAL campaign period for the ballot started on 14 August. The parties signed an agreement beforehand with clauses such as 'participants should not shoot, stab, beat or otherwise intimidate those involved in the campaign process'. This, of course, had no effect on what was happening in reality.

As the campaign started with a noisy pro-autonomy rally in a dusty field near the airport in Dili on 14 August, 12 students set out to begin the low-key doorknocking campaign that CNRT had recommended for Liquiça, 30 kilometres west of Dili. They got as far as the village of Ulmera. Indonesian police, the safeguards of the ballot process as agreed by Portugal, Indonesia and the United Nations in the 5 May agreement, stopped the car, destroyed it, and beat five of the students with iron bars and gun butts at the scene and then again later at the Liquiça police station. The five were released to be briefly hospitalised in Dili, but nobody ever found out what had happened to the others.

The following day was CNRT's turn to campaign in Dili, and about 3,000 people turned up to the opening of a new CNRT office on the foreshore in Dili. Manuel Carrascalão returned from self-imposed exile and addressed the crowd, and a message was read from Xanana Gusmão to the cheers of those gathered there.

Later that night, Jose Belo called me from his house in Becora. There was shooting going on all around the area, he said. It was soldiers from Battalion 745 keeping people awake, expressing their displeasure at the start of the pro-independence campaign.

Tuesday 17 August was supposed to be a day free of campaigning. There was supposed to be a ceremony outside the governor's office on the foreshore to commemorate Indonesia's independence, but residents of the Bidau and Audian areas, and those near Dili's two main hotels, were woken by sustained bursts of automatic weaponfire at around 5 am.

The ceremony at the governor's office to honour Indonesia's independence went ahead with a full military parade of over 1,000 soldiers and a flag-raising ceremony. Representatives from the UN, including Ian Martin and the Australian consul, James Batley, as well as all the high-ranking Indonesians, attended the ceremony, which included the reading of Indonesia's declaration of independence and the singing of the national anthem. Afterwards, East Timor's Indonesian-appointed governor, Abilio Soares, was emotional and crying when he addressed reporters.

'Don't you doubt it, this it not the last [such ceremony]—this will be forever. We will continue in the Indonesian context forever,' he said before moving back into the governor's office building.

The head of the Indonesian task force for security for the

UN ballot, Agus Tarmidzi, was more circumspect when asked if he thought this would be the last such ceremony held in Dili. '*Inshallah*,' was all he said—'God willing.'

But across the road, militia from the Aitarak group were stopping cars and harassing people. They soon formed a convoy and headed off in the direction of the CNRT office in Audian, where pro-independence leader David Ximenes appealed for calm from the hundreds of supporters who had lined the street and the office's two-level balconies as trucks, cars and motorcycles with red and white Indonesian flags waving passed in a noisy convoy. They moved past three times shouting pro-Indonesian slogans to provoke the people gathered around the CNRT office.

Standing on the first-floor balcony, David Ximenes shouted to the crowd to disperse to avoid a confrontation.

'We are not provoking the situation, they are,' he said. 'Look, they shot at us here this morning,' he went on, pointing to a bullet hole in the window behind him.

It went on all morning. The pro-autonomy people rode past on motorcycles and in trucks, occasionally brandishing a weapon, and yelling at the CNRT supporters near the office. Three Australian civilian police stood around outside; the Indonesian police they had called for assistance two hours earlier hadn't arrived. A small boy went to raise a CNRT flag as the trucks and motorcycles went past again, but someone in the crowd pulled it out of his hands. They didn't want to provoke the militia.

It went on all week. The next day, the militia from Halilintar and Dadurus Merah Putih attacked and ransacked the local office of the University of East Timor's Students Solidarity Council in Maliana. They then moved on to where the students were staying and wounded two with machetes. The students were in Maliana to carry out the low-key pro-independence campaign that was planned to avoid confrontation with militia by only sending teams of students back to the areas they fled from earlier in the year to simply conduct voter education sessions.

One session in the nearby town of Ritabo ended with one student being stabbed and the house they were using burnt down. The militia in Maliana started openly parading on the main street with automatic weapons as Ian Martin visited the town.

The violence continued. In Suai, militia attacks forced more people to flee to the church. There were already 2,370 sheltering there as the first attempt to campaign for independence brought on a stone-throwing attack by militia against those at the church. A UN vehicle was smashed when the driver tried to intervene. The next day in Manatuto, 10 militia and a Kopassus officer attacked and shot to pieces the local CNRT office.

In Dili, Eurico Guterres carried out another disarmament ceremony as the attacks continued, handing in 10 modern weapons and over 200 homemade pipe guns and spears. He vowed the weapons would not be seen on the streets again.

Two days later, two US senators and a congressman came for a lightning visit. After all the moderate statements made by the UN and the Australians, it was good to hear someone propose an obvious solution to a rapidly deteriorating situation. Canadian reporter Ian Timberlake and myself were the only ones who bothered to go out to the airport when the Americans arrived and left. They had flown in and travelled down to Suai and Maliana. In Suai, the refugees in the church were without water because the *Bupati* had used his influence to turn off the supply, so the senators demanded to see him and ordered him to turn the water on again.

After seeing the situation down there, Senator Tom Harkin simply said, 'I just know they need some forces down there with blue helmets that are armed, because this situation could get out of hand. As the UN told me, there could be a bloodbath down there before, during and after the ballot.'

At last someone had seen what was obvious and had said it. But it was too late, even though the Americans had said outright that it certainly looked like the militia and the military were closely associated, and that they would be recommending peacekeepers as the only solution.

Ian Martin told us that, 'it's certainly true that a level playing field in terms of campaigning has not been established, in the sense that the CNRT are in many areas not able to campaign openly or even move from door to door. So that is a matter of concern.' But Martin also told us not to forget how the East Timorese had dealt with the difficult conditions served up to them in the registration period, and how they would probably face the continued intimidation with the same determination.

The violence continued to get worse. I managed to get hold of a car with *Guardian* correspondent John Aglionby and we headed out of town westwards to Maliana late in the day. The road was busy with overloaded trucks leaving East Timor, and we saw one go off the side of the road and topple over the embankment as we passed it.

In Balibo, new checkpoints complete with guardhouses had been put up hastily in the middle of the town. They were manned by what looked like TNI troops but who wore pro-autonomy vests over their uniforms. But they still carried M-16s.

It was dark when we got to Maliana and the town appeared empty. People had been crossing the border to Atambua since the violence of the previous week. Rumours of an imminent attack on the 100 or so UN workers based in the town were circulating, and there had been a lot of shooting at night near their residences. The UN staff believed the weapons cache of João Tavares was about to be distributed to the local militia, and on 23 August when Major-General Zecky Anwar—widely believed to be a high-level organiser of the militia—visited, he was greeted by local militia leader Antonio Meta, who was carrying an M-16.

There were reports of deaths in nearby Batugade and Memo, and it was known that militia in Lahomea had killed a man under the orders of Lieutenants Sutrisno and Yusuf. TNI soldiers had been heard discussing their intention to kill UN staff and had threatened them. At meetings in the square in Balibo, militia had been chanting, 'We want war'. Indonesian soldiers were sending their families across the border to Atambua.

Only one man remained in the Maliana CNRT office. The others had left after one day of attempted campaigning, deciding it was too dangerous.

'We are looking to God for an end to the intimidation,' said Jose Andrade, who had remained there because his legs had been injured in an earlier attack. The militia had tried to break in the night before to get him, but they couldn't get through the barricaded door. He was killed later.

At the Maliana military headquarters, Captain Rosidin told us that the people leaving town were just migrants, and that the militia members out the front had just come around to play billiards and eat noodles.

The local priest predicted 27 August as the day they would attack the pro-independence supporters and the UN; the UN representatives said they were expecting trouble on the 27th; all the students who were still in the town said they had an evacuation plan for the 27th. The local military said nothing would happen on the 27th.

THE NEXT day, 25 August, people were hurriedly packing possessions and boarding vehicles to get out of Maliana. The militia announced they were going to seal off Maliana like they had when they'd attacked on the 18th. Ian had been there then, and had told me about the road blocks on the way back to Dili where he heard militia, armed with automatic weapons, discussing whether to kill him or not.

About an hour and a half away by road, the 187 Falintil fighters in the cantonment said they wouldn't respond, no matter what happened in Maliana. They couldn't, as they were under orders from Xanana. They knew exactly what was going on in Maliana—37 militia had already fled to their camp, two of them having admitted to being forced to kill people by the military; one of them killed his schoolteacher.

'They don't want to go back to Maliana, they will be killed—we let them stay here,' said the commander.

We crossed the border to Atambua. The road was still busy although it was late at night and it was very hard to find a hotel room there. The town was full; there were soldiers everywhere.

The next day in Suai, 55 people set out from the church to campaign for independence, insisting they had the right to do so, and saying they would exercise it and return to the church, where more than 2,000 people were sheltering.

In the church, they talked about the Indonesian warship they'd seen off the south coast, and the low-flying fighter jets that buzzed the church two days previously. They'd thought they were going to start bombing. The militia had been drilling with weapons near the church, and talked endlessly about the civil war that would begin after the ballot. They even called across the wall to the church compound, saying they would kill the people inside.

WE STOPPED in Cassa to see Canção Carvalho one more time before the ballot.

'If Falintil does not come forward to accept autonomy,' he said, 'we will go back to our baseline, which is integration, and the 5 May agreement may as well be ripped up, because there will be a bigger war than ever before.

'What can the UN do? Bomb us here in Cassa? They would bomb both sides.'

It was getting late and we had to leave. Canção admired our battered four-wheel drive and told us to drive fast. The militia man at the post saluted and didn't bother to hide his gun.

As we climbed the steep hills leading back up to Ainaro, I realised we had no brakes. I stopped the car in Ainaro and discovered the brake line was hanging off—disconnected.

▻◅▸◦◂◅

IT WAS almost midnight when we got back, and we stopped for a beer at the Hotel Dili. It was booked out with journalists, in town for the ballot. Gino Favarro had constructed plywood cubicles in the old dining hall and was renting them out as rooms. But the place was deserted when we arrived.

'Where is everybody?' we asked Gino.

'We got attacked by militia—most of them have gone to the Mahkota.'

I didn't believe he was serious at first. But Dili had seen the worst day of violence since April. The militia had run riot on the last day of campaigning in the capital. Five people had been shot dead and a number wounded, including a Reuters photographer who was shot in the leg. The violence had gone on all afternoon, and pro-independence supporters and foreign journalists had been pursued by militia and rounded up by police. Everybody seemed shaken.

EARLY NEXT morning, John Aglionby and I headed to Maliana for the last day of campaigning. All the way we passed trucks full of militia with red and white flags and headbands, spears and homemade guns. They waved their weapons at us as we passed. At Batugade, more trucks were parked by the road after coming from the direction of West Timor. We calculated we must have seen at least 3,000 of them by the time we got to Balibo.

At the football field in Maliana across the road from the UN compound there were rows of buses and trucks, all covered in red and white flags. On the ground were pro-autonomy hats, pro-autonomy T-shirts and, ominously, pro-autonomy matches. Young men on motorcycles raced up and down the wide main street. On the podium, *Bupati* Guilherme Dos Santos was speaking to the enthusiastic crowd of more than 4,000 people.

A British UN military liaison officer told us the village of Memo about three kilometres away was about to be attacked. We took the back route and found ourselves in the small village on a hill. The people were out on the streets watching. Everybody was looking in the one direction, towards the sound of massed motorcycles.

The people of Memo were ready for the attack. Armed with rocks, spears, machetes and swords, they rang warning bells as the 60 militia on motorcycles approached.

'We are all waiting and ready for them—we've been told they are coming here to attack us. We will not let them destroy our homes,' said Anacleto Lopes, holding a sword and a rock as he watched the motorcycles approach.

Women and children ran away. As the first motorcycles went through, the men of the village ran forward with weapons and positioned themselves to retaliate. Then five minibuses full of pro-Indonesian supporters stopped and as they all got out, the village men ran up and started smashing their vehicles. As the pro-Indonesian supporters retreated, more than 40 automatic weapon shots were fired at the villagers, still venting their anger on the vehicles. They smashed everything they could on them and tipped over two of the minibuses.

Women and children emerged from the houses gathering stones; men ran screaming orders to each other, and the makeshift alarms of metal pipes which hung on trees were rung as the whole village prepared to fight back.

Men came running out holding clubs with nails driven through them, spears, machetes and knives. One stocky man ran past us with a shovel.

We jumped back into the car and sped into Maliana, arriving just as the rally was being told of the outrage of their people being attacked. Some young militia among the crowd raced to their vehicles and headed out to the west of the town in a long convoy to extract revenge on the village of Memo.

Out in the bare, dried-out rice paddies, a column of several hundred scared and angry militia, armed with homemade pistols and knives, walked towards the pillars of black smoke that marked Memo.

It was like a column moving up to a medieval battle, with the swords, the spears, and rough wooden clubs they were carrying, and the noise of screaming that rose from the village as the line of nearly a thousand young men got out of their vehicles and walked towards the fighting.

We went as far as we could towards the fighting but an angry militia with a pistol started yelling at us. Then an

Indonesian on a motorcycle, obviously military, waved us back angrily.

The town of Maliana was now deserted as we drove back through to get to the other side of the village. I stopped to shout through a report at the telephone exchange and we headed back out through to the side of Memo held by the pro-independence people who lived there.

The pro-independence villagers had just beaten back the militia, and we walked down the hill past the still burning trucks and houses. The owners wept by the wreckage or yelled at us that the militia and the Indonesian police were to blame.

A group of East Timorese women tried to support another who had collapsed screaming in grief outside her burning house, where the thickly congealed blood of her dead husband glistened. His body was still inside but no-one would go inside the now fiercely burning building to pull him out.

As relatives tried to salvage what they could from the burning house, they explained to me how Paulino Lopes had been hacked to death by a group of pro-Indonesian militia as he ran into his house away from the approaching mob. His neighbour, Bernadino Lolitu, had met a similar fate; although the Indonesian police later claimed he had survived the multiple machete wounds to his chest inflicted by the militia.

All around, houses burned as their owners emerged from hiding with their eyes streaming from the thick smoke and grief. They stood around in shock; some waved swords and shouted angrily.

A group of friends were trying to help a man who had collapsed from grief. A woman told me how the militia had held a knife to her throat and asked for her money, then burned down her house; the militia had just left suddenly and the house was still burning behind her. There were thick blood trails leading from the road into the bush, and spent shell casings on the ground everywhere.

Amaral Lopes, a middle-aged man who had just lost his house and whose family were among the 50 or so villagers who were still missing an hour after the attack, looked around at the village and said, 'This is not campaigning, this is slaughter.'

The locals were saying the Indonesian police had been firing up the hill at them to cover the retreat of the militia, and they didn't know how many other people had been hit.

One villager, Caetano Guterres, told me later how Raoul Dos Santos, his neighbour, had been shot dead by an Indonesian police bullet as the police attempted to storm the upper part of the village.

'It's clear the police were working with the militia,' he said. 'They were shooting at us and walking in front of the militia as they came up the hill.'

Further down in the village, some Indonesian police drove up and—almost for our benefit, it seemed—told us they were conducting an investigation into the fighting between the two sides.

Back in Maliana, the local police commander, Major Budi Susilo, told us his men hadn't fired any shots—they had orders not to. He said he didn't know how many people had been killed or injured. It wasn't their policy to deploy people to small villages, according to him, and the whole thing was just an emotional outpouring in reaction to the campaign.

We went to tell the UNAMET people what we had seen, and they told us it was the village of the *Bupati* Guilherme that had been attacked. It was the only area that hadn't obeyed his order to attend the rally, so it had been targeted.

Shortly after we left the UN house it was surrounded

by militia, who fired automatic weapons all around it throughout the night.

In Balibo, the road block was in place, but they waved us through. At the crossroads, militia were standing in a line testing homemade weapons. The flash from the crude gunpowder charge in what were basically muskets was blinding, and I thought they were shooting at the car.

There was another road block by the police post in Batugade, blocking the way to Dili. When we pulled up, the police ran out and told us to come inside. They said the militia at the road block had been involved in the attack on Memo that day, and they knew we'd been there. They wanted to kill us and to burn our car. Apparently the militia had lost some people too.

We had no choice but to accept the protection of the Indonesian police, who earlier in the day we had seen shooting at civilians to cover the actions of the militia. We sat in the tiny police post all night as the drunken militia cried out obscenities against Australia and death threats against ourselves.

John tried to explain to the police he was English not Australian, while outside bottles were smashed and drunken militia screamed, 'We fucking kill you Australia.' But nobody was listening to him and the militia eventually left in the direction of West Timor in the early hours of the morning. We drove as fast as we could on the empty road back to Dili at 4 am.

The campaign was officially finished. The ballot was two days away.

CHAPTER NINE

30 August 1999
Maliana, East Timor

WE STARTED OUT for Maliana at about 3 am on 30 August to get there in time for the start of voting at 6 am. It was pitch black as we headed out of Dili, but there were already militia at the road block outside of town. They did nothing to stop our three-car convoy—I was travelling with the Australian parliamentary delegation that was in Timor to observe the ballot process. The office in Sydney and my AAP colleague in Dili, Karen Polglaze, had not liked the idea of me going down to Maliana again after I'd gone missing overnight when I'd been reporting the attack in Memo. But I was given the go-ahead after the delegation decided to spend polling day there. Laurie Brereton, the Federal Opposition spokesman for Foreign Affairs, had been pressuring the Australian government to send peacekeeping troops to East Timor and, as Maliana had been the most volatile and hostile part of the country, he decided that was where he had to be for the big day.

To be honest, I expected to see a repeat of the violence of the 27th and was sure the militia wouldn't allow the voting to proceed. At best, I thought there would be militia intimidation at the polling booths, and at worst, all-out attacks on those waiting to vote. But the scene was very different when we arrived just before the main polling station opened.

All the way down to Maliana, along the winding coast road that clings to the cliffs high above the sea heading west towards the border, we had seen people walking in the pre-dawn light. Thousands of villagers were walking to the polling stations, so that they'd be there, ready to vote, when they opened. There was fear in this action—the fear that something would happen before they got a chance to vote. But also the desire to get it over with as soon as possible, and then head straight back to the supposed safety of the villages, where they had no real protection—other than the opportunity to run to the forest if the militia or the military came through.

I was told later that some people from the more remote places walked all night to get to the polling stations as they opened, and the scene that greeted us in Maliana was that of over 3,000 people waiting patiently to vote, already forming queues at 6 am.

The *Bupati*, Guilherme Dos Santos, was the first to cast his vote, of course, followed by militia leader Antonio Meta, then a few other militia leaders. After that, things began progressing normally, and the large sporting hall across the road from the UN compound filled rapidly with people; they pushed through the doors in a crowded but orderly queue.

A UN military liaison officer told me how, after we'd left three days earlier, the militia had surrounded the UN house and fired shots into the air all night. They had been so close, he told us, he saw the muzzle flashes just over the fence. That had been happening all around town ever since, at places where the nearly 100 UN staff in Maliana were staying. But the night before the ballot, it had been quiet and no trouble had been reported anywhere in the area. When he had gone down to the polling station at 4.45 am on the 30th, he'd found several hundred people already waiting in the darkness to cast their vote. More than 2,000 people had fled Maliana because of the violence during the previous week, but the liaison officer believed they were all back to cast their vote and then depart again, before any trouble started.

In the hills above Maliana it was the same. Hundreds of voters came down from the villages and spent the night at the small church that served as a polling centre in the tiny village of Odomau Atas. Jean Feiselmoser, the American UN worker at the post, was overwhelmed.

'Because of all the threats, because of all the shooting and the violence here in Maliana, because it has not been a quiet, peaceful place, we just didn't know what was going to happen here today,' she said.

She didn't even know whether her local staff were going to turn up. But they did. And the scene at the picturesque hilltop church was orderly and calm as the villagers, many of whom had family in the local Falintil cantonment, sat on the ground in lines waiting to vote.

The parliamentary delegation was all smiles and dished out encouraging comments, saying the day was 'an over-whelming demonstration of the East Timorese people's will to express their wishes in the vote that has so long been denied', and other such positive sentiments.

They were right, it was a moving scene. Even in Memo, where I'd seen such chaos only three days earlier, the people were queued up at the schoolhouse. They looked a little tense, but they still seemed to be voting without fear of reprisal and appeared unaffected by the recent terror.

In Balibo things were a little different, but the people still queued. Militia milled around in the main square at the house of a local leader. They were lined up not to vote, but to get paid. The young men were too intent on getting their 150,000 rupiah (Aus$30) to pay much attention to me as I watched them get their names ticked off the list by the local militia leader. As soon as the man paying them saw me, he quickly hid the pile of money underneath some papers and shooed everybody out of the room.

At the polling post, there was some pushing and yelling going on, and some militia were videotaping the crowd. Earlier, the militia had been checking people's documents and telling them they couldn't vote, but that had stopped when the UN intervened. Nobody was really sure of what the UN could or couldn't do, so the militia just sort of hung around looking nasty.

Laurie Brereton wanted to make a speech outside the house where the five journalists were killed in 1975. There had been some confusion over which house it was, and I inadvertently directed him to the wrong house—where he started talking into my taperecorder, as there was no-one else present.

'Particularly on this day,' he said, 'some Australians should come here and think about those who died.'

The security officer from the consul had caught up with us.

'It was through the denial of the circumstances surrounding the deaths of the journalists . . .'

But we were both watching a group of militias walking menacingly up the street towards us.

'Peacekeepers, they should be considering it now . . .'

The security officer interrupted Brereton. 'Look, that's enough sir—we have to move,' and the rest of the planned statement was quickly forgotten as we walked hurriedly away from the house and the approaching militia.

The Zimbabwean UN civilian police officer outside the Balibo polling station looked despairingly at the unruly and noisy crowd, some of them calling others militia and being taunted by them.

'Even if they are here, we cannot recognise the militia. There is not much I can do, except keep the crowd moving,' he said.

But, generally, things went well all over East Timor on ballot day. As we sped back to Dili through Maubara and Liquiça, the streets were deserted. Even the polling centres seemed almost empty by early afternoon, as the majority of people had voted in the morning. Everybody was waiting.

The day was so peaceful that, back in Dili, the major story of the day had been the detention and expulsion of the Australian *Sixty Minutes* television crew, and that was what all the journalists talked about that night.

The next day, journalists, UN staff and observers were all beginning to think that the whole nightmare scenario of the militia rhetoric might be just that—a lot of empty threats. People were speculating whether it was in the interests of the pro-autonomy groups to maintain peace, since they might still get a share of power if the ballot was close; or whether the military was responding to the international pressure, that kind of thing. But that talk was mainly confined to the garden at the Tourismo.

Outside, the militia were already roaming around the foreshore and were armed with spears and machetes. I asked them what they were doing and they said they were trying to blockade East Timor.

'We have been told to stop the people leaving by boat,'

said one of the militia who were standing with knives on the beach. It seemed ridiculous. There were only three of them, and it looked like the largest thing they could have stopped was a canoe.

Other militia threw rocks at the now smashed and deserted CNRT office on the foreshore. The only effect that had was that a few of the journalists who were staying at the Hotel Dili, virtually next door, moved into the already overcrowded Mahkota.

One street away at the Aitarak's headquarters at the Hotel Tropical, the more senior inner circle of militia were gathering. They were generally physically bigger than the rank and file, and rode flash motorcycles and wore military-style clothing. They didn't carry machetes or spears, or wear the scrappy red and white headbands associated with the poorer members who had obviously been press-ganged into what they were doing. These guys were aggressive and assertive, and were ordering people onto trucks. The procession of motorcycles and trucks soon moved out with a lot of noise and smoke and revving of engines. The convoy wound slowly through the centre of Dili to the military hospital in Lahane.

Militia outside the hospital stood around waiting for their leaders. They were there to pick up the body of one of their own, who had apparently been killed by pro-independence supporters at the barricades in Becora that had appeared again on the day before the ballot.

They were talking to each other about how the 'communists' had sliced up one of their leaders. The body had apparently been found that morning in the river in Becora.

I rode back to Dili with the militia in a convoy. They all gathered in the back hall of the Hotel Tropical. The body, covered in mud and flies, was on a piece of plastic at the front of the crowd. Journalists were ushered into the room and pushed to the front, where militia jostled each other for a glimpse of the body.

It was a place we'd never been welcome in before. Students had told me about being brought to this room to be tortured and beaten. The militia crowding all around us were angry and I noticed a few were armed. I could see the bulges under their shirts, and one guy loitered at the back with a shotgun.

This time, the body really was one of theirs—that of Placido Ximenes. He had been killed by pro-independence people at Becora. They ordered us out of there.

Outside in the street, I stood next to a car parked in front of the headquarters. The window was down and inside there were three men. On the seat between them was a box, and one of the men was taking pistols out of it and handing them to the other two. He was loading and reloading the pistols, then clicking out the bullet clips, showing the others how to do it. They shouted at me when they saw I was watching.

At the airport that afternoon, Eurico Guterres walked in with about 10 militia and stopped two East Timorese and one ethnic Chinese family from boarding the only commercial flight to leave from Dili that day.

Most of the UN officials, diplomats and journalists, eager to leave now the polling was over, stood by, oblivious to the militia and what they were doing. But one Australian UN volunteer who was leaving on the flight tried to intervene.

'I had someone bleed to death in my arms last week,' he told a journalist. 'I know what these people are leaving for. I can't believe these people are not being allowed to leave.'

Outside, more militias waved away East Timorese trying to enter the terminal. 'We are here to control the people because we don't want the CNRT to get to Jakarta,' said one militia. Meanwhile, the Indonesian police did nothing to stop the militia—they said they'd asked them to stop, but had been ignored.

Militia then blocked the street behind the Tourismo with barbed-wire barricades and, armed with handguns, some stood guard. The street, Jalan Antonio De Carvalho, runs behind the residence of Bishop Carlos Belo; the Tourismo is at one end and a military barracks and the governor's office at the other. Nobody made any attempt to remove the barricades.

In Gleno, the militia was already acting. They'd shot at the helicopter that had come to pick up the ballot boxes, burnt down 10 houses, and killed one local man who had been working for the UN. The Indonesian police did nothing to stop the militia. A 17-vehicle UN convoy eventually evacuated the 150 foreign and local staff.

That night, journalists and some UN staff had a party on the roof of the Mahkota. As TV reporters ran through their stand-ups that were beamed live around the world through the four satellite up-links on the roof, we sat around and got drunk. They were all reporting the 'tense but calm' or the 'remarkably peaceful' atmosphere surrounding the historic ballot. At that time, most of the 165 registered foreign journalists in Dili were still there, along with more than 80 Indonesians. There were almost 100 media staff, photographers, technicians and unregistered journalists in town as well. The date set for the ballot and the violence in the campaign period had led to a huge influx of reporters in the last week before the vote, and the demand and price of everything—from rooms to cars to translators—had trebled. Big news agencies like Reuters and Associated Press rented houses and had their own two-way radios to get over the communication difficulties, as the regular phone system crashed due to the demand.

There were also 400 volunteer UN electoral monitors

who had assisted with the polling, and many were still wandering around, as well as the 280 electoral observers brought in by IFET and independent observer teams from organisations such as the Carter Centre. Add to this the UN civilian police contingent, the UN staff and other interested parties such as church groups and diplomats, and the total number of foreigners in East Timor immediately after the ballot was well over 2,000.

It was a big party and it went on until late. There were a lot of people, the music was loud, and everybody was winding down from a busy and intense period. Also, because there hadn't been the expected serious outbreak of chaos, people were ready for a big night; they had all been stressed for weeks. But even as I was riding my bike back through the deserted streets in the early hours of the morning, I noticed the militia were still blocking the road.

THE NEXT day, I spent hours out at the police headquarters. The Indonesians had arrested some Australians, accusing them of being provocateurs. They had been in Zumalai on ballot day with what the Indonesians were calling 'pro-independence literature'; it was actually just voter education material from the UN. It was Dr Andrew McNaughtan and two other people I knew from Darwin, Jude Conway and Sally Anne Watson. I laughed for a moment thinking how the Indonesians had, in a way, got the right people if they were after activists, although their reasons for the arrests were spurious. (They eventually had a harrowing trip back to Dili, and told me about the road blocks between the border and Dili, and how militia and the military had stopped all vehicles.)

THE ROAD east from Dili was also effectively blocked. In the late afternoon, I went up to Becora with Karen Polglaze. We drove up to the highest ridge, where you can look back at Dili on one side and down to Hera on the other. At the top of the ridge there was a crowd of men. They had spears, knives and swords. They said they were pro-independence and they were guarding the ridge against the militia from Hera—Mateus Carvalho's men had been out shooting earlier in the day. We left them there on the ridge waiting to be attacked. From the top of the hill you could see the road to Baucau; there was no traffic coming from the east, and fires were burning in Hera.

The three Australians, still in custody at that point, were among the safest people in Dili that afternoon. A running battle was taking place outside the UNAMET compound. Militia with guns and machetes advanced up the street towards the UN compound. Pro-independence East Timorese ran forward with rocks. The militia advanced and then pulled back, then came forward again. By this time, there were more than 100 journalists in the crowd outside the compound, and more kept arriving as things became more chaotic.

As the militia advanced, they caught one man and knocked him to the ground. What happened next was sickening; it was caught on film by APTN cameraman Daniel Furnard. A group of three militia killed the man with repeated full-arm swings with machetes. One would walk away, and then come back and casually hack another time into the lifeless body. It is horrible, gripping footage of a brutal murder, carried out in a casual manner.

The chaos near the compound continued and BBC journalist Jonathan Head was caught on film by CNN being attacked by militia, who broke his arm. Three East Timorese were killed in the violence. Almost all the journalists in town were there by then, and fled *en masse* into the compound along with about 300 Timorese. The Indonesian police eventually arrived and began to escort the journalists in the compound back to their hotels on their trucks, with an armed escort.

I had missed all of this—I'd been stuck out in the police compound and they wouldn't allow us to leave. When I eventually got away, I went to the Mahkota with Geoff Spencer from AP to look at the footage. There were people and equipment spilling into the corridors all over the building—it was like a madhouse as everybody was trying to file stories about the violence. All through the corridors and in every room, everybody seemed to be watching that same horrible footage of the man being hacked by the militia.

If the Indonesians had wanted to cause panic among the journalists so that they'd leave, they couldn't have produced a more effective tool than that piece of footage. It was replayed over and over again. It had happened so recently and so close to where everybody was, and the footage was so graphic, that the effect, planned or not, could be seen all over the faces of the people at the hotel.

It was a relief to get out of the building, away from it.

James, one of the volunteer UN observers, burst into my room at the Tourismo early on 2 September. He had just tried to get out of Dili on a public bus to Kupang. First, the militia had come to the bus terminal and checked everybody's ID. Then, just outside of Dili, they were all checked again, and everybody had to get off the bus.

James had spent a lot of time in East Timor and spoke Indonesian and Tetum. At each road block he told the militia he had nothing to do with the UN, he was just a student trying to get back to Kupang. It had worked until he got to the third road block outside of Dili. There the

Besih Merah Putih ordered him off the bus and one of them had hit him in the neck. An Indonesian man came out of a hut wearing full military uniform but with no identification marks. He pulled out his pistol and put it to James's head, saying that he knew James was with the UN and would kill him. James talked his way out of it, all the time his UN observer ID hidden in the document folder the officer was now looking through. The officer took 200,000 rupiah from James and sent him back to Dili. He hadn't been able to get more than 20 kilometres out of town.

It sounded like what Andrew and the others had told me about the road blocks. Kopassus in uniforms with no identification markings had taken over the road going west. The endless stories we'd heard about the infiltration of plainclothes Kopassus across the border now made sense. They were being deployed to seal off Dili.

I had barely started typing up James's story when he burst back in again, this time with two photographers. They were all out of breath, panting.

'Militia downstairs. Five with guns. They just ran in and started yelling,' said James, in a panic.

We stayed quiet, listening to the shouting and doors slamming—they were downstairs moving about. Thinking they might come in at any time, I called the office in Sydney and sent a report to the copytaker.

After we'd heard a car screech out of the driveway, we went downstairs. The hotel staff looked shaken, and were just starting to stick their heads around from the back of the kitchen or up from behind the reception desk. Sharon Scharfe, a Canadian UN observer, had been alone in the dining room when the militia came in. They yelled at her and kicked her. The staff said they were looking for a journalist with a red hat. Finding no-one but Sharon, they'd left.

That morning, I'd been up early to take my bike around the corner to put air in a tyre. The mechanic, who I knew because I was always having problems with my scooter, told me not to go out that day. He was Sulawesi, and the militia had told him they were going to kill journalists that day. *Wartawan mati hari ini*—Kill Journalists day. I repeated the phrase to some people over breakfast, and it caught on.

At the Mahkota, the BBC had announced plans to charter a plane for the following day to get its people and equipment out. There were spare seats, and about 70 foreign journalists signed on to leave. Most of the Indonesian journalists also left Dili on 2 September, taking advantage of the Indonesian military-supplied C-130 transport plane they were offering for free.

Plans to withdraw the UN volunteers and the IFET election observers were also stepped up, with 340 of the UN volunteers to be moved out by Friday 3 September. The result of the ballot was going to be announced on Saturday 4 September, two days earlier than scheduled, because of the threat of violence, and the majority of the observers were to be gone by then.

I went around to Yayasan Hak. Miraculously, they were still working. Joaquim was putting together a report on violence in Oecusse which had apparently begun the night before the ballot. According to the report, around 50 people had already been killed there. They had only just received information about houses being burned down and CNRT members being attacked before the ballot. He was still trying to finish the report, but he kept getting interrupted by phone calls and questions. Everybody in the office was moving at a feverish pace. Packing things, typing, running from room to room. I was trying to grab the Oecusse report details before he had even printed it out, while Joaquim was telling me about the latest rumour they'd heard about the return to Dili of the notorious ex-Falintil commander Lafaek—with a supply of 800 weapons for distribution to the militia. He also told me about four people killed in Hera at Mateus Carvalho's road block and about a further 22 people who'd been kidnapped and detained at the same place. The office was surrounded by militia—and it would be attacked that night while some of them, including Joaquim, were still hiding upstairs where they had been working.

The IFET office was full of people organising to leave or coming in from the regions. The observers from Manatuto had just returned after the local UNAMET military liaison officer said he'd had information that 1,000 weapons were about to be distributed and they should leave. The *Bupati* and the police chief would guarantee no-one's safety. The UN followed them out a few days later.

All over Dili that day, the only people outdoors were militia, or those who were leaving. They left for the west in vehicles piled high with belongings. The suburb of Becora was almost totally deserted. The militia had moved into the area and the people no longer stood on the street to fight them; they either left for the mountains behind Dili or stayed in their homes. We could no longer go west or east without getting hauled out of our vehicles. The road south, which only really headed inland, took you down to the militia areas on the south coast. Other than that, there was only the sea or the air, and people everywhere were thinking of ways to get out.

Every day, the stories and reports from other parts of the country were getting worse and on the Friday, as we waited in Dili for the ballot result to be announced, convoys of mud-streaked UN vehicles with smashed windows started coming into town from the west.

The Maliana convoy drove straight through town to the

UNAMET headquarters. The 40 international staff and 14 locals looked severely shaken. The town had been destroyed around them beginning on Thursday evening. Militia rampaged through the town and spent the night firing their weapons wildly at random. Two UN drivers were killed by militia, and the remaining local staff had gone to the police headquarters for protection.

'Today there was chaos in Maliana. The whole town was thoroughly destroyed. Hundreds of houses have been destroyed,' said one of the UN staff before he was bundled off for debriefing.

I asked one of the local staff who came in with the convoy what had happened, and he told me that it wasn't only militia involved—they had actually seen the Indonesian military taking part in the destruction.

'Nobody will welcome the result in Maliana. The dogs have control of the city,' he said angrily. Maliana had been his hometown.

UN spokesman David Wimhurst was in shock as he told us that Maliana was burning and that the militia had engaged in an all-night rampage of destruction. Next came Same. The convoy came in full of IFET observers who described driving through the burning village of Holo Rua as they had left Same. UN police had told them at least 15 people had been killed. Militia and military were on the streets.

Another team of observers was attacked coming back through Becora as they returned from the east. Militia put a gun to the head of an observer and smashed another in the head.

In the IFET office, everything was chaos. Observers came in from all over East Timor and the capital, too frightened to stay in their homes. Four IFET personnel were listed as missing as they tried to cross from Maliana to West

Timor. They turned up later, but at the time all we knew in Dili was they had called from Maliana in the early afternoon saying the town was being destroyed.

'The town is ablaze. I am just about to go on the convoy,' was the last message Australian Mark Green had got through to the office.

I saw Pedro sitting in the IFET office. He didn't know what to do. There were militia in Becora and he didn't feel he could safely go home. His wife and youngest son were supposed to have come and met him, but they hadn't turned up. Pedro asked me to go to Becora and tell the people staying at his house to get out of there. He knew his place was targeted and he was worried about the Australian UN observers who, as far as he knew, were still out there.

There was a group of people in the street near a police post further up from Pedro's place when we got out there. We could see a white person waving to us from inside a house, and then being forced back inside. Militia started walking towards us from the police station as another carload of journalists approached. There was a shouted exchange when the militia ordered us to leave just as the other group was piling out of their car. The militia ran forward and kicked the journalists a few times. Everybody ran for their cars and left, and the street was empty except for the militia and the police. The houses seemed deserted.

Back at Pedro's house, the three Australians who had been working as observers and one East Timorese woman from Darwin were still there. There was nothing between the militia on the road and Pedro's house and it seemed a very vulnerable place to be at the time. When they decided to leave I went out to get the car but all I could see was the blue four-wheel drive retreating back to town and the militia approaching from the other direction. I screamed down the mobile to Karen Polglaze back at the hotel to have the car sent back—Becora was the last place on earth I wanted to be stuck that afternoon. Eventually the driver came back. Everybody was starting to panic.

LIQUIÇA WAS overrun by militia on the Thursday. The UN pulled out late on the Friday after houses were burned and one American civilian police officer, Earl Candler, was shot by Indonesian police as they drove out of town. That led to an evacuation, and UN helicopters came under fire as they tried to land.

The press hadn't been told about that until later, after the announcement of the ballot result. Although the situation in the regions was disintegrating rapidly and almost every one of the eight UN offices was surrounded and shot at by militia that night, we didn't hear about most of it until later. The UN was making every effort to keep the people who had been evacuated from the regional offices away from the press until after the result was announced.

As 70 members of the foreign press decided not to wait for the announcement and left on the BBC-chartered flight, Wimhurst appealed to the other foreign reporters to stay.

'This is the wrong time to be leaving, that is all I can say,' he said. 'Your presence throughout the process has been absolutely crucial,' he continued, but added that no-one—particularly not UNAMET—would be able to guarantee anyone's safety in the territory.

At the Resende, a Korean photographer and his Indonesian assistant asked me how far it was to Maliana.

'In normal times,' I told them, 'about three hours. But I don't think it's a good idea—you know, road blocks.'

They looked at each other and said, 'We will go now,' and

paid their bill and left. I saw one of them about a week later. He was staring vacantly and was brought into the UN compound by the Indonesian police. He didn't say anything for a few hours, and then when he finally answered my questions about what happened, all he could say was: 'I have never so nearly died so many times than the last few days.'

That afternoon in Dili, people started buying what little was left in the shops. I stood in one supermarket watching Indonesian military in plain clothes buying boxes of noodles and bottled water. They were moving quickly, running in and out to the car. Outside, a huge black plume of smoke was coming from a burning house near the cemetery, but nobody looked up—they were too intent on buying whatever remained in the shop.

Foreigners, too, were running into the shops buying whatever they could—water, cigarettes, tinned food . . . whatever they had. Suddenly, everybody was driving fast, talking quickly, arguing.

I went looking for petrol and at the only stall open lines of people were filling their tanks and plastic drink bottles with petrol. Everywhere, people had heard that the result would be announced the following morning, and they argued with each other in queues waiting for food, petrol, water . . . everything.

The East Timorese on the street had tight facial expressions as they waited, eager to get off the streets before dark, but knowing they still had one last chance to get something—anything—to eat or take with them. Militia carrying weapons went past on motorcycles. Real guns now, not the homemade muskets they used to parade with.

At the Tourismo, journalists were walking in with cases of beer, and boxes of water and food, preparing for a long stay. The Australian ambassador to Jakarta, John McCarthy, convened a security meeting in Fairfax correspondent

Lindsay Murdoch's room. He advised us against leaving. He told us that the Australian government would be in charge of an evacuation if it took place, and that they did not think the security situation warranted one. He did recommend we take up a collection to pay the Indonesian police stationed outside the hotel—just to pay for their food and drinks, to ensure they remained neutral.

Outside, Margarita Tracannelli, an Australian who worked with CNRT, and Helio Tavares, an East Timorese who had been living in Australia, were trying to give a message from CNRT to the journalists: 'A major assault on Dili is planned for tomorrow to be carried out by Kopassus and Intel. They will try to kill those high profile leaders of the resistance movement,' said Helio.

'We have people in the Indonesian armed forces, and the intelligence they are giving us says that is what is going to happen as the vote is announced.'

'We are telling our people to get out to the mountains where Falintil has some chance to protect them.'

Dili's population was already responding. People were making their way through the suburbs and up into the hills behind Dili, on foot and in the darkness.

'The main concern of CNRT is to warn the people,' Helio added.

Some correspondents were already responding to the situation by helping those Timorese they knew. I knocked on one door and found Antero and João from the Students Council sitting in a friend's room. They were laughing and kidding at being overly dramatic, hiding behind the door whenever someone came in. But it was serious—they couldn't go back to the office, the militia had already been there that day.

⊢⊷⊶⊙⊷⊶⊣

IN THE last four days since the ballot, our world had shrunk unimaginably. Travel outside Dili was out of the question. Everything west seemed to be collapsing. Maliana, Gleno and Liquiça were all in control of the militia and the only other armed troops out there were Indonesian. Even certain parts of Dili, such as Becora and Taibesse—where there were military bases—were out of bounds. Journalists seemed to be running around Dili in ever-decreasing circles trying to get information. From UNAMET, CNRT, IFET, Yayasan Hak; all the offices that were now in a state of disarray with people camped on floors, phones ringing, convoys coming in with bad news from all over East Timor, people packing, yelling, pushing, telling each other to get out of the way. Questions were answered tersely by officials: 'It is difficult, we don't have any information. The truth is the security situation is changing, there is panic. We can't confirm anything at present.'

Shops were closed, banks were closed, people talked only of leaving and the ways out. And all the time, there were more militia on the streets, wandering around or roaring past on motorcycles. Those foreigners staying in houses dared not to return to them, and people spent the night in the major hotels on the floor of other people's rooms.

IN THE morning, I had a flat tyre on my scooter again. I drove it slowly to the only place that was still open to fix it, on the road to the airport. Already, the place was full. Militia in their black T-shirts and red and white headbands were revving up their bikes; tuning them, making last-minute adjustments, filling up with fuel and oil. They eyed me off as I filled the tyre with air. I knew that within hours they would probably be attacking the UN, or the people in Dili, or us. There was a moment when one looked as though he was going to come over, and his friends were watching, as if expecting him to take the lead and attack me. Then the guy turned back to his motorbike and the moment had passed, and the mechanic hurriedly told me to leave, waving aside the money. It was all about to begin, but not *quite* yet.

THERE WOULD have been more than 200 journalists in the ballroom at the Mahkota. UN staff, observers—foreign and Indonesian—diplomats and a number of East Timorese made up the rest of the crowd. Banks of television cameras and lights and photographers crowded the front of the room. Ian Martin took his place at the table and quickly began to read the announcement.

'The Secretary-General is currently making the following statement to the Security Council on the result of the vote in East Timor,' he said, and then, after praising the courage and determination of the East Timorese people who had participated in the ballot under difficult circumstances, he read the result: 94,388 in favour and 344,580 against the proposed special autonomy. The people of East Timor have thus rejected the proposed special autonomy and expressed their wish to be in the process of transition towards independence.'

Martin went on to tell the crowd that 'the coming days will require patience and calm from the people of East Timor' to prepare for a period of peace and prosperity. He called on the government of Indonesia to ensure a successful culmination towards the process by carrying out its responsibility to maintain law and order in the territory, and then promised the East Timorese that the United Nations would not fail them in 'guiding East Timor in its transition to independence'.

That was it, the East Timorese had voted 78 per cent in favour of independence. We had all expected an independence win, and there it was. Indonesian television cameras were pointed directly at the crowd of journalists who were standing and watching the announcement. Everyone was at pains to register no emotion at the announcement, although many of us, especially those of us who had been in East Timor for a long time and seen the consequences of Indonesian rule, had hoped for this outcome. Everywhere, people had blank expressions of impartiality—looking at the floor, at their notebooks, but not at each other. The East Timorese who were present mostly worked for the UN and did the same. There was no outpouring of emotion, just a businesslike efficiency as everybody remained in place until Martin had finished his address.

Karen Polglaze was there filing for AAP, and suddenly I had nothing to do. Outside, people were milling around. Those reporters who had to file were on their phones, and the few Timorese there didn't seem comfortable about showing their joy at the announcement with so many Indonesian officials and police present. Across the road at the harbour, people were already queuing to board Indonesian ships that had arrived to take people to Kupang.

I got a ride down to Bishop Belo's house. In the garden there were already about 1,000 people taking shelter behind the wire fence. A young girl came over to talk to us by the fence. 'The Bishop doesn't want us to show how happy we are because of our safety, but I am so happy, but we cannot go anywhere, we cannot show our happiness too much,' she said, and then moved quickly away.

Behind her I could see the Bishop waving at some other people to move away from the fence. He didn't want any problems and refused to speak to us.

We went across town to the house of Leandro Isaac in

Lahane on the southern side of town at the base of the hills to where people were fleeing. The streets were deserted; there was only the occasional fast-moving vehicle. There was nobody on foot. Leandro's door was open and I walked in to be greeted by his wife, in tears. She hugged me and told me he was out the back of the house, all the while telling me she was so happy with the result. But she whispered it, as though afraid to say out loud that the independence vote had won.

João Alves and Leandro Isaac were loading their car, preparing to leave. Leandro was going to the Mahkota to make one last comment to the journalists. Alves was hurrying us along. They knew that at any moment the backlash would begin—and as the two public CNRT leaders in Dili, they were prime targets for the militia.

'East Timor is already a winner,' said Leandro grandly, barely able to contain himself. 'They have decided for themselves. Today is the end. Today the East Timorese people stand equal with the other countries of the world.'

Alves was hurrying Leandro along and turned to me. 'What are you doing, anyway? We are going to the mountains, and we are advising all our people to go to Dare,' he said.

I hadn't even thought about leaving. I asked him how he felt about the result.

'Of course, it is a victory for us,' he said, still loading the car, 'but we have to get through the day alive.'

We followed Leandro back to the Mahkota. Something strange was happening there, and the police were urging people to stay indoors. Barricades were being put up near the port and now the TNI as well as the police were around. I left on my motor scooter with English journalist Joanna Jolly and headed to the Resende, as usual, for something to eat. But as I sat down to eat at the table by the window, I could see the militia, now armed, moving up and down the street outside. The waiter asked us nervously what was happening. We told him: independence 78 per cent. He crossed himself, brought our food, and told us to eat quickly.

There was no-one else in the dining room. All life in Dili seemed to have stopped. The reception area was empty, as was the street outside except for the occasional militia member on a motorbike. It was the same waiter I had talked to months earlier when the militia first made the death threats against Australians. He had laughed then, but now he said we had to go and we had to be careful.

Outside, there were two people waiting with bags. One was the waiter from the Hotel Dili, who was from Kupang and worked for Gino Favarro. Gino had just left, boarding one of the Indonesian boats in the harbour bound for Kupang. Gino was married to the niece of Yunus Yosfiah, the Information Minister. He had told me that he would know when to go—when he got the word from Yunus, he would pull the plug and be out of there. The hotel wasn't worth his life, he had said. Now he had gone and the West Timorese waiter had no idea what to do.

Similarly, the sole Australian tourist who had been staying at the Hotel Dili had no real idea of what was going on. He had told me he had come to Dili for the diving. I told him to leave at the first opportunity.

Joanna and I rode extremely fast back to the Tourismo. Now I was scared. The militia were gathering in the street outside their headquarters and they were wandering all through the now deserted Hotel Dili. It was too nerve-racking on the bike; I kept feeling like a bullet was about to hit us at any moment. The militia were just watching us go past, and I started going way too fast out of fear that they would just start shooting.

Karen was back at the hotel and we took the car to the airport. All along the road to Comoro, which was also the main road west out of East Timor, people were packing vehicles, queuing for fuel and driving west. Occasional shots sounded out but nobody even looked up from what they were doing. It was not their problem anymore, they just had to get out.

At the airport, Indonesian military personnel were loading a C-130 Hercules. The families of soldiers, laden with possessions, were being walked up the ramp. I stood there watching with Helio, who was also flying out; there was still one regular commercial flight to Bali, and he was on it. So too, it turned out, was Eurico Guterres—he sauntered into the waiting lounge and we journalists crowded around. He ended up conducting interviews using the previous CNRT spokesman, Helio, as a translator. He said he was just going to Bali and would be back the following day. We joked that he was just going to personally get his orders for the destruction of Dili from his commander, General Adam Damiri (whom he had once told me was the only authority he recognised). Eurico heard us and glared.

⊶—◦—⊷

WHILE WE were out at the airport, a drama was unfolding at the Mahkota where the majority of the journalists were staying. The police and Indonesian military had effectively sealed off the building. No-one was able to leave and if you went in there it was very difficult to convince the police to let you out. The police and military suddenly became very uncommunicative to those inside, insisting they couldn't leave. As the journalists waited inside, wondering what was going on outside to cause this, two militia walked through the police lines and one took a shot at the foyer with a homemade weapon. The other walked up to the building and smashed one of the glass doors with a machete. Inside, camera crews caught everything from the foyer. Photographers on the roof took shots of the military leading away the militia, gently holding them by the arm.

When we tried to drop a journalist off near the barricades, she was kicked by the military until she got back into the car and we went around to the other side. The streets around the Mahkota were the only ones in the whole town sealed by the military, and the operation seemed to be working. The Indonesians wanted the journalists to leave. They had sealed off the hotel and organised the militia attack, then they turned off the water supply to the hotel later that day. Inside, the people felt very vulnerable. One of the militia who had come to the front of the hotel had clearly had a grenade in his hand, and the police and military had done nothing to disarm anyone until after they had done their acts of violence in front of the cameras. Most major news organisations made the decision to charter aircraft and leave the following day.

Things were still relatively normal at the Tourismo. Food was still being served, the bar was open and the phone lines and water continued to work. People were busy filing stories and working. Afterwards we sat in the garden and drank beer. The main topic of conversation for most people was whether to stay or leave. Agence France Presse and CNN had both chartered planes for the following day, and there were plenty of seats. There was also a commercial flight to Bali.

The conversations went around in circles. 'Look, we can't call anyone here, we can't move around, we really could be covering this better in Bali.' 'Besides, look, I really think it is over. I mean, the announcement has been made, hasn't it?' And on they went, everybody coming up with a variety of reasons to leave, but at the end of it, what happened later that night negated any reason other than self-preservation.

At around 9 pm the shooting started. First it was far off, out across the canal in the area towards the beach. We climbed on the roof and listened and watched as a few houses went up in flames. They seemed to be using incendiary bombs or grenades. There was a big boom, then another building would go up in flames. At first, because it felt far away and gunfire wasn't uncommon at night in Dili, people weren't too concerned. Then it began to get louder and closer, and people went inside.

It was intermittent, and would sometimes stop for 30 minutes or so. The police, to whom we had all contributed a nominal sum to ensure our security, remained out the front of the hotel.

But then, after midnight, the level of gunfire rose again. This time it seemed to be coming from right behind the hotel. We could hear trucks moving and shouting and all the time an infernal racket that sounded like a fully-fledged gun battle taking place in the back streets behind the hotel.

The glow from fires closer to the hotel could now be seen and I tried to keep reminding myself and others that it was only a psychological game by the militia and TNI to make us leave. There was no gun battle—everybody out there was on the same side: militia, TNI, Kopassus, police. Falintil were in their cantonments far from Dili. There was no fighting, no civil war. We had been reporting one-sided intimidation and violence for months. It was no different now. It was all bullshit just to make us leave.

Then the police around the hotel started firing. Against who—the night sky?—I didn't know, but it was an incredible noise, frightening and close and loud. Was the firing being directed at us? But nothing was breaking, no windows smashed, nothing—not one bullet hit the hotel.

Around 3 am the firing rose to an incredible crescendo then, abruptly, stopped altogether.

—————•—————

IN THE morning, almost everybody was leaving. Those who had been undecided had had their minds made up by their employers or the previous night's shooting. A lot of people wanted to stay, but were being ordered to leave because the flights on Sunday were the last charter flights out, and no company wanted to be responsible for leaving their employees without a means of escape.

I spent a lot of the morning trying to catch up on my neglected expense account, which seemed absurd, but necessary—I had to claim money from Karen, who was leaving. I had no cash left and now there were no banks. I had a problem. I'd been doing work for Associated Press and they were leaving as well. All of a sudden I had loads of food, booze, a satellite phone and a luxurious suite at the Tourismo with two working phone lines, but I wasn't going to be able to enjoy it.

People waited nervously out the front of the hotel for the police trucks to take them to the airport. The shooting had also taken place around the Mahkota, and it was virtually emptying that morning as well. Everybody was leaving and many were leaving behind local people they had worked with for some time. There was a tremendous amount of guilt among those going, and people were being exceedingly generous to the East Timorese who had no charter planes coming to take them away. On several occasions, money was given to me by departing journalists to pass on to mutual East Timorese friends. Some people were in tears as they climbed onto the trucks. Everybody believed they'd never again see the East Timorese who remained.

As the trucks were going out to the airport, I got a terrifying phone call, but I didn't know who it was from. It was a female voice in English screaming, with gunfire in the background.

'This is not a fuckin', joke! Get the fuck out of there while you can! There are militia everywhere and they are fucking serious!' was what she shouted, and then she hung up or the signal dropped out. I never found out who made that call.

▸┼◂▸─◦─◂▸┼◂

THE PREVIOUS night's shooting had spooked everyone. We had no way of knowing if that sustained ferocious gunfire had actually been directed at people. I fully expected to see bodies piled up on the streets in the morning, the noise had been so intense.

When I woke, I had heard a different sound. Hundreds of voices—children crying, and women, and men. The sort of low chatter of hundreds of people gathered together.

At the end of the landing outside my room, the low wall overlooked the ICRC headquarters. In the garden there were hundreds of people asleep and lying around or sitting, talking, walking around, cooking food—they were refugees who had come in during the night as the militia and the military roamed through the nearby neighbourhoods shooting and setting fire to homes. The neighbouring compound was Bishop Belo's residence, and there, too, the gardens had filled with people, about 3,000 of them. Collectively, there were about 5,000 people sheltered in the two compounds next to the hotel, and in the morning, when the shooting had stopped, I found that reassuring. More kept arriving all day.

Agence France Presse stringer, Ian Timberlake, was

always taking notes. It used to bother me that I was missing something. He would be writing and, well, he was my competition. What was I missing out on? That morning, as he waited outside the Mahkota to catch a truck to the airport, he watched three militia on a motorcycle—two with guns—ride through the police lines to the front of the hotel. He wrote in his notebook: 'These people are truly evil and there has been a sick feeling in my stomach thinking about all the people probably killed last night.' Not long after, he said, he crossed out 'truly evil' in case they checked his notebook before he got to the airport.

><+•>-0-<+·<

THOSE OF us us who remained met in the same ballroom of the Mahkota that had been used to announce the result of the ballot just over 24 hours before. The window to the street was cracked; it had a big bullet hole through it from the militia shooting incident. Empty drink bottles and water containers were scattered on the floor and the press releases announcing the ballot result were scattered every- where. Militia wandered in and out of the foyer next door, and nobody knew whether the police would attempt to control them or not. Heather Paterson, who had the onerous position of media safety officer in East Timor for the International Federation of Journalists, set about writing lists of all those who remained. There were about 27 of us who would not be evacuating that day, and it was decided we would stay at the Tourismo. Most of us were staying there anyway, and the Mahkota looked downright dangerous, with hostile militia on the street. In the foyer on the way out, I ran into Ian Martin. He was hurrying out the door carrying his computer and a small bag.

'I can assure you I am not leaving,' he said. 'I am just

grabbing some essentials to take to the compound.' He could assure me, that was laughable. After listening to him in press conferences for months, and his endless references to the 'assurances' he had received from the highest levels that the Indonesian government was serious about its security commitments, he was assuring us that he wasn't leaving. I really never expected to see him again after that.

'Fuck, have they all gone?' asked Wimhurst when I told him who had evacuated. He was shaking his head. He couldn't believe that all the major news services had left. No-one had told him. There were only three of us there as Wimhurst ran through the updated situation report on the state of the mission.

'At 9.15 am yesterday, the result was announced throughout East Timor,' he began, and then ran through the state of the regional offices.

'At 10.15, our office in Same was co-located with the police and the army after it was surrounded by militia. The Indonesian military escorted our staff to the landing zone and at midday, 22 international staff and 22 local staff were choppered out. In Ainaro, 13 international staff and 15 local staff were evacuated to Dili. Five homes were reported destroyed and two people confirmed killed. The town is now under the control of the militia.

'Aileu 4.15 pm, 22 international staff evacuated, two local staff, they drove themselves. Liquiça, 4.05 pm yesterday, 16 international staff were in the police compound and there was an attack on the compound by militia walking through police lines. One police officer, American Earl Candler, was shot trying to drive to Dili.

'At 5.00 pm the Indonesian police offered a chopper. We declined. At 5.05 we flew the injured man to Dili and at 5.35 we flew 15 international staff to Dili, coming under fire from the ground.'

He continued and gave us the details for Ermera, which was evacuated two days before the announcement, and Oecusse, which was also evacuated before the announcement. The other regional offices of Manatuto, Baucau, Suai, Viqueque and Lospalos were reported to be calm, but shots had been fired at the UN residence in Baucau. The night before, the Portuguese delegation in Dili had been attacked at their house in the suburb of Audian. The militia, accompanied by the military, had been reportedly attacking Becora. And this morning there were reports of police ordering East Timorese to board trucks for Atambua in West Timor.

'All UNAMET staff in Dili are now located at the HQ,' he concluded. There were about 400 left at that stage, after another 50 had left that day.

We asked if it was true that American civilian police officer Earl Candler had been shot by Indonesian police.

'It is fairly widely accepted that it was Indonesian military or Brimob that carried out the shooting. There were more than 20 rounds in the vehicle,' he said.

The Indonesian police assigned to protect the UN were now shooting at them.

Outside in the compound, East Timorese staff who had ventured outside that morning reported that the people were terrified by what was happening.

'They are going around and shooting and burning down houses. It is the military, the Indonesian military, that is doing this, and ordering people to leave for the docks and for West Timor,' said one exasperated East Timorese UN staffer.

'My whole family is leaving on one of these boats. They told me that after the shooting at their houses, the soldiers told them to pack and wait for a truck, and then they came back and shot again because they were too slow,' he said.

'District by district, this is why there is so much shooting.'

Military trucks and militia on motorbikes sped through the empty streets. Here and there, small groups of people could be seen walking to the dock area, carrying bags.

It was a serious breakdown of security. The UN had basically been run out of half the country, police were shooting at them, and most of Dili was a no-go area. We went back to the Tourismo.

I got a call from Tim Johnston, the Reuters correspondent. The company had ordered him to leave. He was at the airport waiting to evacuate. 'Do you want a car?' he was yelling. It was a bad line. 'Of course, but please don't tell me it's behind the Mahkota,' I replied. 'Okay, you know where it is—in the carpark behind the Mahkota. I'll send the keys to you,' he said and hung up.

The Mahkota was crawling with militia. They were looting all the abandoned possessions now that the UN and the journalists had gone.

A nun brought back the keys from the airport for me. Having a car would be invaluable. All the drivers had left with their vehicles, and anything on the streets was rapidly disappearing as militia and people who looked decidedly like Indonesian military had begun breaking into parked cars and stealing them. An Irishman called Sean was the only one prepared to walk down to the Mahkota and get the car with me. We walked about 50 metres down the road and watched the militia further down the street.

'No I don't think this is a good idea,' he said. I agreed and we ran back to the hotel. We convinced someone to give us a lift down there and they dropped us by the car, a big four-wheel drive. As I fumbled with the keys, some militia and soldiers started running towards us. We opened the doors, jumped in and started it. The loudest stereo I had heard in a long time burst into life; it was playing

Queen, 'I want to ride my bicycle'. We drove off at top speed, as the soldiers were now shouting for us to stop. We had gone around the corner before I could get myself together enough to turn off the stereo.

Later in the day, the fact that we had the car safely inside the gates of the Tourismo made me decide to stay there. But the Australian ambassador and the military attaché arrived at the hotel with an Indonesian police truck to take us to the UN compound. It was about 5.30 pm and they told us that if we stayed we would have to take our chances of going through another night of gunfire and possibly an attack. I changed my mind at the last minute, and decided not to go with them. I felt that the Australians were only doing the Indonesians' work for them—clearing us out of the way to the compound where we would probably never be able to leave. There were plenty of others who felt the same way, and we decided to see if we could stay another night in the hotel. Throughout that day, those of us who remained were told over and over to go to the airport by whatever authority we happened to run into. The Indonesian military and police actually picked up some of the journalists wandering around and took them to the airport. Other journalists who had no intention of leaving, found themselves at the airport unable to get back to town, and forced to board the charter flights.

Most of the staff at the hotel had left by then, and the owner, Alex, was permanently engaged in discussions with the police. More money was handed over and we began lending our mobile phones to the police guards to make calls to their family in Jakarta or Surabaya, or wherever else in Indonesia they were from.

James Dunn, the former Australian consul to East Timor in Portuguese times, was one of those who stayed at the hotel. He spent a lot of his time talking to the Indonesian police, reasoning that if they were familiar with us they might be more inclined to protect us later. James also told us of a similar time he had spent there at the Tourismo during the UDT, Fretilin coup in August 1975—and that even then, and in the December invasion by the Indonesians the same year, the hotel and the adjoining compounds had been spared. I immediately told that to the office in Sydney to reassure them, but it backfired badly on me later.

Not long after the journalists who left the Tourismo arrived in the UN compound on the Sunday afternoon, they were witnesses to horrible scenes. Adjoining the UN compound was a school that had large grounds and was used mainly as a carpark by the UN. Now that school was full of people seeking protection from another night of militia violence. Shooting began on the far side of the school, carried out by militia or military. The people panicked, thinking they were about to be massacred, and began charging the razor wire-topped wall of the compound. Children were hurt as their parents passed them over the razor wire, people were badly cut as they jumped over themselves, and there was a lot of blood. The shooting and the panic continued for almost an hour and the psychological effect of people throwing children over razor wire to make sure they were in the safety of the UN compound was not lost on the UN staff inside.

At the Tourismo, things were relatively quiet. We could hear the shooting across town and see fires burning out towards Becora, but for a while at least it seemed we would not see a repeat of the night before. Most of those who were there gathered together in one room. There was not a lot anybody could do. To go outside was to invite trouble, as the shooting continued; sometimes close by, other times barely audible. But it was always there, constantly and all night.

At about 2 am, the shooting became sustained and closer, like the night before. I went outside and the police were nowhere to be seen. I could hear the whoosh and subsequent explosion of grenade launchers destroying buildings and the ever-present rattle of automatic weapons. Weeks later, when I finally got to go and have a look at the beach area, I realised that the militia had walked along and blown up all of the old Portuguese-era concrete beach shelters with grenade launchers. Some of the shelters were big, tacky concrete clams, and they had been flattened.

The shooting came very close and I ran, bent double, along the landing. I could see figures at the back of the hotel and the flashes of their weapons. Nobody else was around. They were either asleep, or lying terrified in their rooms. Jacinto, a student I had known since the student 'dialogues' in 1998, had turned up at the hotel that afternoon. He hadn't known what to do after the previous night's shooting, and had come to see if we could get him out. He was in my room. He thought we should take the car and go to the UN compound.

I called the compound and managed to speak to Wimhurst.

'Stay where you are,' he said. 'We are in the same situation. There is shooting all around our compound—about 500 to 1,000 shots in the last two hours. They are shooting tracer rounds into the hills behind, we believe from a heavy machine gun. It would not be safe to approach. We don't have any people outside at all. Wait until morning.'

I called the Australian Consulate. They were in the same position, surrounded by gunfire and had no-one outside. An Australian doctor, Kevin Baker, and his wife, Liz, were out at the Don Bosco centre in Comoro. They had hundreds of refugees with them, sheltering from the militia and military who were driving through the streets.

Shooting had begun and they were burning houses.

'We are getting the same treatment,' said Kevin. 'We are just going to wait until morning and sit tight.'

There was nowhere in Dili that was quiet, or free from the shooting. All the foreigners remaining were in one of four places, surrounded and terrorised. The East Timorese were being told to be ready to leave for Kupang in the morning. Military trucks with loudspeakers were being driven up and down the main roads and, interspersed with shooting and grenade blasts, East Timorese were being told to leave for West Timor in the morning, or they would be killed.

At 4 am the phone in my room rang. It was the Australian Consulate. They told me to advise everyone to be ready for evacuation.

CHAPTER TEN

6 September 1999
Dili, East Timor

THE ROYAL AUSTRALIAN Air force was flying in Hercules C-130 transport aircraft from Darwin to carry out the evacuation. They would start arriving at about 10 am and would have the capacity to take out up to 350 people throughout the day. Foreign nationals only. The Indonesian military had said that they would ensure the road to the airport was secure for those taking part in the evacuation.

We arrived at the airport with no problems. It was around 9 am but there were already over 100 people waiting—people who had previously vowed to stay were leaving. For most of the observers, NGOs and UN staff, there was no point in trying to stay. The people they were there to help were now being forced out of the country or fleeing to the mountains. But some of us felt we had to stay. We had to see what would happen after everybody left. In my mind, there was no question—we had to stay, there was no-one else left.

On the way out to the airport, we had seen the Indonesian military trucks full of civilians heading towards the port. In one side street I saw a family being ordered onto a truck at gunpoint. The road to the west was full of overloaded vehicles heading out of town. It looked as though they were depopulating the whole city.

>-+-<>-O-<<-+-<

MEREDYTH TAMSYN, one of the UN observers who had returned and spent the night at Pedro's house in Becora, talked of the military shooting in the neighbourhood: 'All night they came back, Indonesian soldiers driving up and down the street—shooting, firing rocket-propelled grenades, bazookas.' The soldiers were talking through a loudspeaker, telling those people still in their homes to evacuate. 'They were shooting mostly in the air, but they shot our dogs in the front yard,' she said.

UNAMET staff began to arrive to be evacuated. They were down to 200 staff and civilian police staying in the compound. The previous night, around 40 people had injured themselves coming across the razor wire, and there were now more than 1,000 refugees in the compound.

The remaining UN staff joined the main evacuation that day. Some expressed dismay and anger. 'They've got a refugee crisis in the compound and they won't even let us stay to help with it,' said one Australian heading for the aircraft. The last of the IFET observers were leaving as well.

TNI troops arrived and stationed themselves across from the terminal in the carpark. We were told we'd have to go soon if we wanted to leave, and an Australian official suggested that if we weren't going to join the evacuation, our presence wasn't welcome at the airport. They didn't want any problems with the TNI.

I walked out to the car with the others who were going back to town. We had managed to pick up another journalist—Robert Carroll, an English correspondent for a Macau newspaper—who'd just flown in on what had to have been the last commercial flight into Dili via Suai. It was an insane time to have arrived—just as everybody else was fleeing and the city was about to be destroyed. He asked if I knew of anywhere he could stay, and he went back into Dili with us.

Because so many journalists had left, those of us remaining were picking up everyone else's work. Anybody working for radio was filing stories constantly.

Driving back into a town that had been overrun by militia and the military, and which was rapidly being depopulated, made for good radio—the journalists in the car with me were talking furiously into their mobile phones as we drove back. I noticed a motorcycle with two militia next to our car, just behind the driver's door. The guy on the back was carrying what looked like a large shotgun. When I realised it was a grenade launcher, I slammed on the brakes just in time to see the guy fire; the grenade flew in front of our car, and the others didn't even notice, they just kept talking into their phones.

We went to the Motael clinic to see if we could get any figures on the casualties from the previous night. The place was all locked up and I had to bang on the door before a Timorese nurse came and told me that the doctors were across the street.

The doctor who came to the door demanded to know who I was before he opened it. And I could understand why. It was a bad area, and as we drove in I'd seen militia with guns wandering around in side streets, going in and out of houses.

When the doctor opened the door, I was immediately

taken aback—he was standing there with nothing but a pair of leopard-skin print underpants on. Another doctor came to the door—also wearing only underpants. The day was getting worse.

Despite their apparel, I asked them what had been happening, and they described what kind of wounds they'd been treating.

'We had 10 gunshot wounds yesterday, some to the head,' one of them told me. 'These people are not aiming to scare, but kill.'

'We had three brought in yesterday already dead from bullets,' the other said.

One man had been brought in late the night before with seven machete wounds to his chest and head. He had later died, they said.

The clinic had also been surrounded and shot at by the military the night before. The soldiers had tried to force their way in, but the nurses barricaded the doors with furniture. No patients had arrived since then.

The two doctors were volunteers from *Medicins Du Monde* (Doctors of the World), and they were the only surgical team left in Dili. They had been waiting for their replacements to arrive, but probably weren't going to stay much longer after I told them about the evacuation.

Aside from the Indonesian military hospital, which had probably been evacuated by then, there would be nowhere else in Dili where a gunshot or stab wound could be treated.

Outside the clinic I saw Father Barretto—the head of Caritas—standing, stunned, in the middle of the road. I knew him well, but he just looked at me as though I was from another planet.

'I thought all the foreigners were gone today,' he said. And, before I could say anything, 'We are waiting for the worst. No-one can stop the Indonesian military. No-one is powerful enough. There is no help from outside. Nothing will stop this.'

He walked away, back into the clinic, as more gunshots echoed in the nearby streets.

><+>-0-<+><

THERE WERE now 15 journalists at the Tourismo, and we gathered in the AP room. I'd never seen some of them before. I didn't know what they'd been doing, or where they had been. Some of them had just arrived. Among them was Max Stahl, who had filmed the Dili massacre in 1991. He appeared suddenly and began filming, quite at ease in the extremely dangerous conditions.

We had a quick meeting of sorts, and exchanged what we had been able to find out that morning. I sat down to write a piece and people were running in and out of the room. All of a sudden, there was a tremendous amount of shooting directly outside in the street. It went on and on, and we could hear people shouting orders, trucks rumbling by and screams, but mostly just gunfire blasting away very close by. It sounded like magazine after magazine was being emptied into the air.

Jacinto ran doubled-over across the room to the window. We were all sitting on the floor by then, and he beckoned me. Hesitantly, we looked outside. In the street, almost directly in front of us, a TNI sergeant was holding an M-16 in one hand and firing single shots into the air. At the same time he was screaming at militia and other TNI troops to move forward, pointing down the road past the Tourismo to the ICRC compound and the house of Bishop Belo. There were soldiers, police, trucks and militia all over the street. Everybody seemed to be firing into the air or towards the ICRC compound.

Max and Carmela Baranowska ran into the room and told us that the ICRC compound next door was being attacked. They ran out to do more filming.

I knew from the others that the two compounds were crowded with people after the previous night of shooting. The number seeking shelter there had risen to 5,000 in Belo's compound and 2,000 in the ICRC. So, over 7,000 people had been surrounded and were, at that moment, being attacked. I crawled under the desk to call the AAP office in Sydney.

When I got through, they put me on hold. I asked for a copytaker, but instead I got the two news chiefs and a company lawyer. I was on a conference call. Before I could go ahead, they just wanted to make one thing perfectly clear, they said. Because of my status as a stringer, as opposed to a full-time employee of the company, they just wanted me to know that I had absolutely no responsibility to the company and they had no responsibility for my well-being. Did I understand that correctly? Yes. Of course.

I asked them if I could send a story.

'Now just hang on, we just want to make sure you understand our position,' they said.

'Yes, I know, I know,' I told them. I said it loudly because of the amount of gunfire in the background.

'What's that noise?'

'Well, they're attacking the ICRC compound next door, and I believe they're also attacking the house of Bishop Belo,' I said.

The night before, I'd told the same editor that there was no problem—if something happened at the hotel, I would just jump the wall to the ICRC. Unfortunately, I now had to report that the ICRC compound was being attacked and the people were being driven at gunpoint along the beach.

They recommended strongly that I evacuate.

At that particular moment, evacuation wasn't exactly an option, so we all hid in the toilet. The gunfire got louder and louder, and it really did seem that the militia, soldiers or police were standing on the path in front of the hotel, firing as closely as possible to the building without hitting it.

There were 13 of us in the toilet, and it was extremely stuffy.

The firing outside eventually stopped, but it still went on further down the street and we could hear shouts and footsteps along the first-floor landing outside the room we were in. Doors were being slammed and we could hear them getting closer.

We all looked at each other, each person wondering what the soldiers or police or militia—whoever was going through the place—would do when they found us in the toilet.

It was the police who opened the door and told us to come out. We had to leave immediately, the militia were attacking, they said.

'Quickly, don't worry about your things,' they said.

The door to the next room, which had belonged to Kyodo, the Japanese news agency, before they left, was open. I walked in and picked up one of the cases of beer stacked near the door and gave it to the police officer. We suddenly had 40 minutes to pack and to leave; the militia attack had just been delayed.

That was barely enough time for most of us, since some people had to do radio crosses and others had to send stories. I called Wimhurst to see if we could still go to the compound. He said no problems, as long as we brought our own food, water and whatever else we needed—the compound was already running out of supplies.

I got to work with Sean, and we packed as much as we

could get into the car. We were able to gather up a lot of things that were left by everybody else who had had to leave in a hurry. The Kyodo room was like a supermarket. We knew that we wouldn't be coming back—and that the place would be looted.

I tried to kick down a door to get a friend's computer for her, but an Indonesian police officer cocked his weapon and barked at me not to damage the property. That, under the circumstances, seemed a bit absurd.

The Australian ambassador arrived with the defence attaché. They had been driving to the Tourismo because they'd heard it was under attack. But they were unceremoniously shot at as they approached the area, and had to return with an escort.

Half of the people in our group at the hotel had decided to evacuate, and the rest of us wanted to go to the compound. We formed a convoy and headed off slowly. The road was still crowded with people; they had been forcibly marched out of Bishop Belo's house or the ICRC compound. Belo's house was burning, and we could see thousands of people streaming back along the foreshore, heading for the port. Behind them walked soldiers with their weapons raised.

The convoy turned right along the beach to avoid the crowds and we drove back through the suburbs behind the hotel. Buildings were burning. We passed military trucks, with people packed into the back, heading for the harbour, and a column of people, mostly women and children, being walked through the centre of town by the green-uniformed military.

There was no way the Indonesians could claim they were not forcibly evacuating the population. The photographer next to me was busy taking pictures that would be front-page images all week in the Australian press—uniformed

Indonesian soldiers marching crying women and children out of Dili.

The Indonesians would later claim that the soldiers were protecting the civilians from the rampaging militia. But the militia on the street seemed to have a uniform remarkably similar to the TNI, perhaps with the addition of a black militia T-shirt or maybe a red and white bandana. They were just soldiers, TNI in militia dress depopulating Dili.

▷┤◁▷─○─◁▷┤◁

THERE WERE barbed-wire road blocks at least 200 metres from the UN compound. The convoy was stopped and we had to get clearance to enter. Shooting continued in the suburbs all around us, and another column of women and children were marched past, these people being allowed to enter the compound.

The compound itself was backed up against the hills that surround the capital. It was a former teachers' college and the buildings formed a circle around a central open area. Along one side was the school from which the refugees who had thrown themselves over the wire the night before were fleeing. The school grounds was a big wide open area filled with UN vehicles.

There were Indonesian police guards outside the school and further along the street there was a road block manned by more police. Beyond that we could see military trucks and soldiers or militia walking about with guns. There was still a lot of gunfire all around, and the sound became a continuous background noise—sometimes close, from the guards themselves, or further away, from the soldiers or militia beyond the road blocks. The continuous, irrational gunfire that reached periods of intensity then fell away was designed to panic those in the compound—and it worked.

The people who had moved to the compound in previous days came out to greet us. They—colleagues and friends, Timorese and foreigners—were relieved to see us and wanted to talk about what we had seen that day. Nobody had been out into the city, except those who had left to join the evacuation.

When we arrived, there were about 1,500 people in the compound, along with about 200 UN staff. People were everywhere, sitting in small groups on the ground or under the verandas of the buildings. In the main auditorium, where the UN used to hold meetings and press conferences, families were asleep on the floor or just sitting and listening to the gunfire. Outside the public information office where we used to attend daily briefings, journalists had set up their computers and were working. UN civilian police, evacuated into the compound from Maliana, Suai and Ermera, had strung up hammocks or sat on the ground. Inside the office was chaos; phones rang and were left unanswered by the UN staff, who were still working, competing for desk space with the 30 or so journalists still there. There were computers, cameras and sound gear everywhere—thousands of dollars worth of equipment lying around under desks on the floor; there was nowhere to put anything. Any available space was immediately taken by someone and used as a work space. Tins of food and empty drink bottles littered the floor, and everybody just got on with his or her work and ignored the confusion. And all the while there was the constant and infernal racket of gunfire in the background.

Wimhurst ran up to meet me as we unloaded the car. I thought he was glad to see me, but he just desperately wanted a cigarette. I gave him the pack. He looked like he needed it; he was unshaven and his clothes were dirty.

Everybody looked worn and worse for wear. Most of the

UN staff had been called into the compound on Saturday after the announcement, and had been there ever since. Many had been living in houses around Dili—houses that were now being destroyed. They had been marked with paint to identify them as targets for the militia. The UN personnel still in the compound had little more than the clothes they were wearing when they came in.

But personal appearance was the least of their worries. Wimhurst asked me what the conditions were like on the way to the airport, and I told him about the chaos—about the forced depopulation of Dili that was going on. He was leaving on the last evacuation flight that day, and was about to head off to the airport. He insisted he was not evacuating, just 'redeploying within the mission area'.

'So you're flying to Darwin?' I asked.

'Yes, I am redeploying within the mission area. Darwin is considered part of the operational area,' he replied haughtily.

I laughed. It seemed he was being a little pedantic by not saying he was evacuating, but it wasn't the time to be talking about it in the schoolyard, with large numbers of bullets being fired into the air nearby.

All of the regional UN offices had been closed, except for the one in Baucau that had been surrounded and shot at and was in the process of being evacuated. The foreigners in Dili who had been located by the Indonesian police were now either at the airport being evacuated or at the UN compound. The Australian consular staff were the exceptions, still in their fortress-like building, but there were only a few of them left—the Australian ambassador, John McCarthy, was joining the last flight of the day.

THERE WERE many familiar faces among the Timorese in the UN compound. Sebastião was there, and Antero from the Students Council, and Jose Belo had turned up. They had all come to the compound as a last resort—they knew, being East Timorese who had worked with journalists and UN staff, that they would be killed by the militia if they were caught on the street. Antero, who led the student demonstrations for months in 1998, had effectively been in hiding since April '99, but had returned to East Timor for the ballot, despite being one of the most easily identifiable student leaders. The hatred of the militia for the students was almost beyond politics. The militia, recruited from the lowest economic groups, despised the students for their ability and their potential.

The UN employed many of the brightest students simply because they spoke English and, in some cases, were computer literate. The fact that many of those students held strong pro-independence views and had previously been involved in the pro-independence rallies and demonstrations in Dili was always pointed to by militia and Indonesian leaders as evidence of the bias of the UN. But the fact was, the students were the only ones qualified to take the jobs on offer.

Three local staff had already been killed by the militia in Maliana and Gleno, and there had been no indication that any mercy would be extended to those sheltering in the UN compound. They sat around nervously debating the situation and tried to decide whether to take the chance of leaving the compound after dark and fleeing into the hills behind it. But the hills were being raked with gunfire by the police and troops surrounding the compound.

Ian Martin called a press conference to try and explain the UN position. It was after dark and continuous automatic gunfire continued around the compound. As we waited on the first-floor landing outside his office, fires burning across the city could be seen and tracer rounds flew across the compound in the dark, aimed at the hill behind—the only way out.

The almost 30 journalists present were in no mood to go easy on Martin. Most of us had been rounded up that day and had seen exactly what was happening outside, and we were horrified by the destruction and the obvious involvement of all branches of the Indonesian military. The UN position had always given the Indonesian government the benefit of the doubt when apportioning blame for the violence. Always, Ian Martin had spoken of the assurances he had received from the Indonesian government and how he was satisfied with the process. The violence was never directly blamed on the Indonesian military or government.

But Martin must have realised his previous diplomatic treatment of the situation would not work any more, and he looked nervous as he stood in front of us and asked if we would respect his right to go off the record on certain questions. Of course we agreed—and the questions started; more like angry statements of disbelief and outrage than direct questions.

Lindsay Murdoch's question trailed off into, 'It's an absolute disgrace what is happening out there. It has got to be one of the greatest crimes of the century . . .'

Ian Martin looked taken aback, but managed to say with a weak smile, 'I agree with the premise that the situation is absolutely appalling . . .' and went on to say that pressure was being put on the Indonesian military to get the situation under control 'at the highest levels'.

Somebody else countered, 'What makes you think putting pressure on the military which is actively engaged in this violence will make any difference at all? What makes you think that pressure will do anything?'

This was the first point at which Martin wanted to go off the record.

'One of the pictures put to us is that there is a major problem in the TNI regarding East Timorese in the TNI, and what has been happening is related to that,' he said.

I couldn't believe it. There were no East Timorese in the Indonesian military with a rank higher than major. Even in the two units that contained most of the East Timorese soldiers, 744 and 745, the East Timorese were still in the minority and the highest rank of most of these troops was sergeant. Martin was reverting to a tired version of the 'rogue elements' theory that only certain units and officers were involved in the violence and they were operating outside of the Indonesian military command structure. It was absolute rubbish, but it was the line the UN—or Martin—had decided to take.

Three weeks earlier, at a closed 'off the record' briefing for the print journalists in Dili, Ian Martin had elaborated on the view that it was only certain entrenched officers and units who were involved in the violence, and who actively supported the militia. At the time, I suggested the extensive movements of Indonesian troops and the activity of the air force and navy in West Timor as evidence that they were going to carry out a large coordinated operation and evacuation not unlike that predicted in the Ganardi document back in July. There was no way such a large operation could have taken place without the authority of the highest level of the Indonesian military. Martin had brushed aside my comment at that time, but now extended the same scenario to explain away the violence happening outside.

'One of the things we are looking at,' he said, 'is to bring more troops into East Timor to block the troops on the ground—I think three battalions have been brought in. What can best be hoped is those troops have not been involved with what has happened here in the last three months, and that they may be more loyal to Jakarta policy.'

He was telling us that the only hope at that stage was to bring in more of the troops we had just watched destroy the capital and forcibly evacuate the residents—the people who had stood around shooting into the air outside our compound to terrorise us into leaving. It was insane. Even as he spoke we could hear automatic weapons in the background, and he was telling us more Indonesian troops were the answer.

'What do you expect of these new troops and how do you think they can get the other troops in line?' asked veteran freelancer Tom Fawthrop, his voice quivering with suppressed anger. 'Do you expect them to shoot their own soldiers?'

An exasperated Martin replied, 'I'm simply saying the only areas I can see any real possibility is if Jakarta might be able to get the situation under control. If that is their genuine intention.'

It was a slim hope, and when we asked if there was any way the UN mission could be saved from total disgrace because they'd been forced to abandon the East Timorese to their fate, Martin simply replied, 'I don't know. I don't know.'

Finally, somebody asked what we were all thinking: 'Do you feel the position is safe staying here?'

To which Martin replied with a weak chuckle, 'Do you?'

The joke fell flat and everybody waited for him to give his real answer.

'I think we are reasonably safe, because we do have quite strong protection out there from people I believe have been genuinely ordered to maintain protection of this compound by those who understand the consequences if it were attacked. But I can't give you an assurance that that will hold,' he said.

Richard Lloyd Parry of the *Independent*, angered by Martin's glib responses, asked, 'So, if people were to start coming over the walls and firing automatic weapons at people, what would happen?'

'I think that is obvious,' said Martin, lost for words. He simply meant that if people jumped over the wall and started firing automatic weapons at us, then people would be firing automatic weapons at us. 'I can only make judgments hour by hour,' he continued. 'I think you understand the dilemma we are in and to press me hard on that is, if you understand it, not very helpful, because on the one hand—if you understand how important it is to the people in East Timor and to the East Timorese in this compound that the international personnel of the United Nations remain—and yet you understand there is a high level of risk with that, then you know that is a pretty heavy burden to carry.'

Martin was trying desperately to tell us to back off from making him state the obvious. It had become clear that he, and the United Nations in New York, hadn't quite made up their minds yet whether or not to abandon the 1,500 East Timorese in the compound.

After Martin's shambling response, Di Martin from the ABC asked, 'What do you say to those downstairs who say if the UN evacuates they will be slaughtered?'

To which he replied, 'What can I say, except the UN is very committed to staying? We do not wish to evacuate.'

▷─┤◆├─◇─┤◆├─◁

OUTSIDE, THE Indonesian police 'protecting' the compound were still firing their weapons into the air. Fires continued to be lit all over the city. The UN had no answers. The situation was as it appeared on the surface. They were being harassed and bullied by an Indonesian military that was determined to destroy the city and the rest of the country, and to do it away from the prying eyes of the international community and the media. The UN was powerless to do anything to change that, and nowhere was that powerlessness more apparent than amid the scared and angry East Timorese trapped in the compound with the equally scared UN staff.

Ian Martin had admitted at the press conference that they had had no contingency plans for the Dili headquarters to be turned into a makeshift refugee camp—a fact which was becoming increasingly apparent as drinking water and food supplies dwindled. The whole compound was crammed with East Timorese with nowhere to sleep or sit other than on the ground between the UN offices and the vehicles that filled the centre of the complex.

THE SHOOTING outside the compound reached new levels of intensity the following day. The Australian government continued the evacuation with a flight in the afternoon. After the depressing press conference that revealed the tenuous nature of the UN presence and another night of continuous gunfire, another group of journalists decided to leave. It was true that we were now basically trapped in the compound with hundreds of East Timorese who believed they were going to die if the UN pulled out.

Ian Martin called a meeting of all the local staff that morning to assure them they would not be abandoned, but the tension on their faces as they left the meeting showed that he had also told them events may have become out of his control.

I WALKED out into the schoolyard through the metal gate in the wall that was being watched by a Dutch civilian police officer. He was the last line of protection against what was going on outside—and he was unarmed.

The shooting had been going on all day and most of the refugees in the school had stayed inside the buildings. Indonesian police armed with automatic weapons wandered between the buildings and stood at a road block at the entrance. Beyond that was another road block on the street, manned by soldiers and police, and beyond that buildings were burning and you could make out Indonesian military trucks and soldiers moving around on the street. The police officer at the gate told me I couldn't go any further. He pointed his finger at his head and twirled it around. 'Are you crazy yet?' He was grinning as he asked.

Back in the compound everybody was working at a furious pace, whether writing or doing constant phone interviews. The phones were still ringing in the public information office. People would walk in, pick up the nearest receiver and do an impromptu interview. Some journalists were doing back-to-back interviews, and people were calling, asking if anyone wanted to do something for such-and-such network or radio station.

The racket outside continued and seemed to get louder every time the UN wanted to send a convoy out to the airport. The cars sent out to try and get food and water from the UN warehouse were forced back by a ferocious level of gunfire that drowned out conversation. As they drove back into the compound, the UN staff in the convoy were wearing flak jackets and looked shaken.

People began taking shelter behind buildings and running doubled-over through the open part of the compound near the main gate. The sound of the shooting had changed. The shots seemed to be entering at a lower trajectory and a few of the cars in the centre of the compound had been hit by bullet ricochets.

'This is classic psych war stuff,' said an English military officer, one of the unarmed military liaison contingent. We all knew that, but it didn't make it any less unnerving.

Individuals responded in different ways. Some became loudly defiant, like Tom Fawthrop, who I saw standing out in the open amid the racket bellowing into his mobile phone above the noise of the gunfire: 'As long as the blue [UN] flag is flying, I shall remain.'

Some others just stopped working and decided to leave on the next flight, while others slipped away to decide if they could stand it for another day. Everybody was tense and most of us were short-tempered. Some of the journalists argued with the UN officials, blaming them for the predicament. And all the time, the gunfire continued.

East Timorese came into the compound from outside and updated us on what was happening. One man told me he saw the suburbs of Audian and Santa Cruz being burnt down house by house, and the people were being driven to the dock area. He had been forced by the military to go along. 'There were thousands of people at the dock and more arriving in columns on foot with Indonesian military forcing them at gunpoint and firing above their heads,' he said.

The people were being told they were being taken across the border to Kupang and Atapupu, and others were being told the ships in the harbour were going as far afield as Irian Jaya, Ambon and Surabaya. Trucks crammed with East Timorese and armed military were still leaving the town for the west, he said.

Aida Ramos Horta Asis, the sister of Nobel Peace prize-winner José Ramos Horta, also came in that morning.

Typical of the kind of person being targeted by the militia and the military, she had left her house with her five children before the announcement of the ballot result and gone to the house of another family.

'We are surrounded by soldiers,' she said. 'If we tell them who we are they will shoot us.'

She told us how a soldier called Thomas from the Indonesian navy had broken their door down and asked them why they supported independence when Indonesia had done so much for them. He also told them that after the 13th, East Timor would be razed to the ground. 'It will be turned into a level plain,' he had said before he threw her out of her house and started smashing everything up.

The soldier also demanded to know where her husband was. She said she didn't know, which was true—he had gone before the announcement, telling her not to wait for him, but to save the children.

The soldier had also told her not to go to the UNAMET compound.

'Tonight, we are going to bomb UNAMET,' he had said.

The last note I have of that interview is the final statement she made: 'UNAMET should look after us because we are still alive. Don't let us die.'

Sebastião, who had been translating Aida's interview for us, started sobbing bitterly and said he had to go and check on his family. Their house was in Taibesse, behind Santa Cruz. He couldn't go, we told him that.

'You will be killed, Sebastião,' I said. 'You, of all people—everybody knows you work for the UN. You were on television every night as the UN translator.'

He shook off my hand. Others pulled him aside and told him the same thing. His family was either dead, or in the hills, or in one of those trucks or ships everybody had been forced onto over the previous two days. To go outside now—for Sebastião in particular—would have been suicide. He knew that, but wanted to help his family—to at least try. But he didn't go. The UN staff he worked with pulled him into the office and spoke with him.

While all this was going on through the day, Ian Martin would not come out of his office and we were not allowed to see him. I asked Brian Kelly, who had become the acting UN spokesperson, for a comment or a report, and he replied stiffly: 'The attitude of everybody here is that we'll stay as long as humanly possible and ride this thing out. We are not here to preserve ourselves, we're here to do a job.

'We're going to maintain our responsibility to the people this mission was ordered to help,' he said. And I could see by his manner that he would sacrifice himself if it came to that.

>-+-+>-0-<+-+-<

SCATTERED REPORTS from around the country said that several local centres were burning and being depopulated. An American Catholic nun from Aileu said the town had been burning when she left the day before, and the people were being ordered onto trucks.

'There never was many militia in Aileu . . . It is the army,' she said by phone from the airport, where she was waiting to be evacuated.

>-+-+>-0-<+-+-<

ELEVEN JOURNALISTS and UN staff were leaving the compound in the Indonesian military truck for the airport to catch the evacuation flight. They were told to lie down in the back of the truck and soldiers stood above them, lining the sides. As they left, the level of gunfire reached such an intensity you couldn't hear yourself talking. I was in the middle of an interview with an Australian radio station, and I let the phone fall away from my ear, the noise was just too loud.

The Indonesian police were being relieved of their command at the compound, and were registering their displeasure at the order by emptying their remaining ammunition into the air above the compound. Martial law had officially been declared by the Indonesian military and the role of protecting the UN had fallen to the army. Fresh troops from Kostrad Battalion 502 had taken up positions and were replacing the police around us.

Those evacuating were caught in the middle of the barrage and lay terrified in the back of the truck as it drove through the burning remains of the centre of town. Gunfire followed them along the road to the airport. Later, I saw footage of their faces on a video taken in the back of the C-130 once the evacuation flight took off. There was not a trace of joy or relief there. They looked drawn and exhausted. Their eyes were downcast as they thought about the fate of the East Timorese they'd left behind.

After the military took over, the regular phone lines were cut off, and mobile phones started working only occasionally and only on a certain network. Satellite phones had become the only real means of communication with the outside world.

><+>-0-<+>-<

BY WEDNESDAY 8 September, I had developed some semblance of a routine. I had worked out where to have a wash and get a cup of coffee in the morning, and the shooting didn't seem to bother anybody as much any more. We interviewed the first people to come into the compound that day with what was now becoming a very familiar story—the continuing destruction of Dili.

An Australian consular official came into the compound to tell us they would be flying two planes out to Darwin that day. They would be absolutely the last two flights out, he said. The consul staff would all go on those flights, leaving only a few military advisers, who would go to the compound. He knew some of us wouldn't leave and gave me a backpack with a few essentials—tinned food, a bottle of whisky, some cigarettes.

His appearance and what he told me about what was happening outside made me almost physically sick. His face was grey from exhaustion and he was speaking rapidly, emotionally, flecks of spit coming out of his mouth.

'Those new Kostrad troops outside, I heard them talking. You know where they have just come from? Aceh. If they get the order, they'll come across those walls just to steal the cars. They don't care.'

At that point, one of the Australian military attachés stormed up. 'Get away from those fucking journalists,' he boomed at the consular official. 'You can stay here and die with them or come with us.' He was shouting, using his officer's voice.

The official followed after him, saying goodbye quickly.

Lindsay Murdoch was standing next to me.

'That's it, I'm leaving,' he said, and went off to collect his things.

A few others did the same. I was trembling. I knew all about what the Indonesian army had done in Aceh. They had been killing members of the Free Aceh movement in that province at the other end of Indonesia for years.

If the exchange between the consular official and military attaché was designed to scare the last of the journalists into leaving, it certainly worked for me. I had to go and sit in a toilet for 20 minutes to pull myself together—but I still couldn't bring myself to leave.

The decision to leave or stay turned out to be academic, anyway. Those journalists who had decided to go were forced to stay—a communication problem meant no-one ever came back to pick them up. Late that afternoon, we heard the last aircraft had left without them.

AMERICAN JOURNALIST and long-time East Timor activist Alan Nairn had slipped out of the compound that morning and when he returned, he told me what he'd seen. It was chilling. He described the soldiers in the nearby suburb of Villaverde looting the houses. Short, muffled bursts of machine-gun fire sounded in houses, as if the soldiers were killing the people inside. Several large buildings in the centre of town at that time were still in flames and he heard the thud of incendiary bombs going off.

He came across two terrified old people in their home. Soldiers had been there, but had left them alone because they were old.

He had seen groups of militia on motorcycles and young Timorese men diving over fences to get away from them. Otherwise, the city was deserted.

Nairn wasn't identified as a foreigner because of his dark skin—he's half Puerto Rican. He had also draped himself in a red and white Indonesian flag, in the manner of the militia. His appearance had fooled a small East Timorese girl he passed coming back into the compound—she spat at him.

THE INDONESIAN military seemed to be thoroughly looting the capital after they had removed the majority of the people. Ric Curnow, then working for the UN, went down to the dock with some of the UN civilian police, escorted by the Indonesian military, to see if they could get access to the supplies in the UN warehouse.

He said there had been about 30 to 40 fires burning, mainly public buildings. TNI soldiers were loading trucks, emptying other buildings. The main shopping area had been totally destroyed. There were about 4,000 people waiting on the dock, surrounded by militia and some police. The dock was covered with abandoned possessions, the wind blowing them into the sea. Mattresses, chairs, boxes—whatever people had thought to get together, as armed men ordered them to leave their homes immediately.

Ric described militias brandishing machetes and guns at the UN vehicle; a whole family trying to pack all their belongings onto a motorcycle; people picking through the rubble of the destroyed shops. And, less than one kilometre away from the compound, the UN workshop and vehicles were on fire and the building next to the UN communications centre was burning. The transmitters the UN had used were probably destroyed, Ric thought. They had been; we found out later that the whole UN contingent had been relying on three satellite phones for communication with the outside world.

A FIVE-car convoy was sent down to pick up supplies from the UN warehouse at the dock. They were escorted by two trucks of Indonesian military, one in front and one behind. They had only managed to load 68 boxes of water into the pick-up truck when about 50 militia approached and opened fire. The convoy left, leaving the warehouse open.

'When we were trying to drive away, the militia tried to smash the windows [of the vehicles] with clubs and machetes,' said one of the drivers, Ronnie Wahl, a Norwegian UN worker.

It was also rumoured that one of the UN military liaison officers had almost been abducted during the confrontation.

I was working in the office of the UN logistics personnel when the convoy returned. Hearing what had happened at the warehouse, one of them began to cry, punching the desk. He was a hardened UN veteran who had worked in Rwanda and Sierra Leone—he knew what the loss of the warehouse meant. They had no supplies. These guys were in charge of supplies, and they now knew the UN presence in the compound was unsustainable.

That afternoon, the UN personnel began to act very secretively. None of it was lost on the East Timorese, who watched as the different groups of UN personnel were called into closed meetings, section-by-section.

We all knew something was going on. The implications of the loss of the warehouse meant only one thing, and Brian Kelly confirmed as much.

'We have been trying to get to our supplies for the last two or three days,' he said. 'We estimate we can probably hold out for four days. We have been totally blocked.'

The logistics department had returned from its meeting. They would not look me in the eye when I walked in to get my computer, and they had already begun packing. There was to be an evacuation, and it didn't look like it would include any Timorese.

I was shocked, and went to get some kind of confirmation. Other journalists had already demanded to see Ian Martin, and were arguing with his security people when I walked by. They got nothing, just a vague promise of a briefing later.

Downstairs I saw the humanitarian officer, Patrick Burgess. He had always been reasonably straight with the press. But that time he gave me nothing. All he said was, 'Look, it's New York's decision. I hate it as much as you do.'

That was enough confirmation for me to know what was about to happen, and I swore at him viciously. They planned to leave without their local staff, and the East Timorese in the compound who had put their trust in the UN were about to be abandoned.

I was told to wait until we got some sort of official comment before I reported on the evacuation. They told us nothing for at least two hours. All we received were the downcast looks of those UN workers who had been informed of the decision and had been given the job of telling their local staff that they might or might not be included.

It was horrible to watch the apprehension on the faces of the East Timorese UN staff who waited in small groups, talking among themselves, to be informed of what was going on.

Worst off were the students and pro-independence people who had sought refuge in the compound. Nobody from the UN made any attempt to explain to them what was planned. Panic was slowly rising among them. They knew if the UN left they would be sitting ducks for the militia and the military, who knew exactly where they were.

As the afternoon wore on, TNI soldiers from the new guard outside started wandering in through the gates and circulating among the refugees. Nobody could stop them. They were armed and were supposedly our protectors— they terrified the refugees by telling them the UN was about to leave them behind.

The TNI looked pleased with themselves. They were casing the buildings and the vehicles, choosing what they would take for themselves and, at the same time, making a mental note of who was inside the compound.

FINALLY BRIAN Kelly called a press briefing at about 6 pm. The few staff who still remained in the public information office stood behind him, looking at the ground as he made his announcement. The Timorese staff, including Sebastião, were nowhere to be seen.

'There is going to be an evacuation,' he said. 'We will begin departing at 7 am for a 10 am departure from the airport.

'Local staff have the option of joining the 205 international personnel who will be evacuated, including all the civilian police and military liaison officers,' he said flatly.

It was a tremendous blow to everyone. The whole mission was going to be abandoned, and the 2,000 or so other East Timorese in the compound were going to be left to the mercy of the Indonesian military.

It still wasn't clear whether the Indonesian authorities would allow the local staff to join the evacuation—that was still being negotiated. We were told the Australian army would be securing the airport, arriving on the planes sent to take us out.

'There are 167 local staff here, and it has been made very clear to them that local staff and their dependents are going to leave with us,' Kelly continued, his face tight with emotion.

Only hours ago, he had still been taking calls from international media, calmly reiterating the UN's commitment to the East Timorese and declaring the intention to stay.

Now they were being ordered out in shame. Kelly was almost in tears as the journalists present loudly expressed their disgust with the decision.

⊷⊶⊷

AFTER THE briefing, panic did set in among the refugees in the compound. Some journalists, myself included, immediately informed those Timorese we were personally acquainted with of what was about to happen. Jacinto, who had come to the compound with us from the Tourismo, asked me to tell him the truth as soon as I stepped out of the briefing. I did. I had no choice—it was his life that the UN was putting under threat. I felt an obligation to let him know it.

He listened as I phoned through the report on the evacuation to Australia. He became very thoughtful, and then he said he would have to go to the hills behind the compound. The gunfire around the compound hadn't ceased, and tracers were still being shot into the hills. We looked up there and I had nothing to say. Then Jacinto smiled and said he had worked for the UN at the start of the mission but quit when he realised he could make more money with journalists. I said I'd see if I could get him on the list.

Sebastião was furious. I found him sitting with a group of students, telling them what was about to happen. As a UN worker, he was on the evacuation list, but the people he was sitting with were not. He was also supposed to keep quiet about the evacuation, but he told me he had to give these people some warning. They were students who had campaigned for independence; many refused to work for the UN because that would have required they be publicly neutral. Then, having believed the UN statements regarding its commitment to stay, come what may, after the ballot, they were being cruelly dumped in the worst possible place at the worst possible time. Very few of us could look these people in the eye.

Antero and Cico from the Students Council were sitting with another group of students at the front of the public information office. They were having an animated conversation when I sat down.

'I suppose you would be wanting quotes about our situation,' said Antero, always sarcastically good humoured, but now more than a little bitter.

There was no chance these guys would get on a flight, and he would probably have to try his luck on the hill.

'How about you start your story like this,' he said. 'There will be a genocide tomorrow as the East Timorese are abandoned by the international community.'

I wrote it down, almost too ashamed to look at him.

'It will be like the Holocaust, they will simply kill all of us here as soon as you leave,' he said.

Another student piped in with, 'How dare you gamble with our lives like this—you have gambled and lost, now we will die.'

They laughed at these suggestions—there was nothing else they could do. They would have to decide by morning what their plans were. If the UN left as announced, they would probably be killed by the soldiers if they stayed in the compound.

'You have to go or you will be killed tomorrow,' said Antero when I suggested I might try and stay—more to make myself feel better about what was going on than really meaning it.

But all over the compound UN workers, civilian police, military police and journalists were saying the same thing. That they wouldn't, *couldn't* leave. Most considered the consequences of a swift departure in the morning too grave to live with. Nonetheless, at a meeting of the UN civilian police called by Commissioner Mills at around 6 pm, the police were told to pack their things; they would be leaving in the morning.

Australian police officer Wayne Sievers was in charge of organising transport to the airport. He was ordered to organise the convoys for the following morning; we were all going to evacuate. He told me later what happened in the meeting with Mills.

'He told us to pack our things, we were going to evacuate the next day. He was challenged by one or two of our people.'

Kendelle Clarke, a policewoman from Melbourne, recalled expressing her deep concern for the fate of the locals to Mills, and him making it clear in no uncertain terms that he felt there was no alternative course of action.

Confidence among everyone in the compound was at an all time low even before this. The Australian government position, as expressed by Commissioner Mills in a briefing to the police, was that the UN police who had been attacked by the militia and TNI and Polri (Indonesian police) in Liquica on the day of the ballot announcement—when the American Earl Candler had been shot—had put themselves in that position by getting caught in crossfire between two hostile groups. 'Everybody knew that was not the case,' said Sievers.

'The Aussie police were so fucking angry at the thought of leaving all of these people here, they organised a petition to inform the leadership they were not going to leave. It was a way of saying to the bosses, "You can go, but we are going to stay."'

The decision was a hard one—people were thinking of their partners and children.

'Some of us were of the view that if we did stay and there was not a resolution, there was a better than even money chance that Indonesian army intelligence would send the militia over the wall for us,' he continued.

It was what everybody in the compound was thinking. Commissioner Mills was in regular phone contact with John Howard. It was clear the Australian government supported the decision to leave the East Timorese to their fate.

A petition of most of the civilian police and some UN personnel was hurriedly put together. More than 100 foreigners were prepared to stay—even though the water, power and telephones had been cut and the food was running out—whatever the situation.

〰〰〰

ALL THAT evening people were hurriedly packing and giving supplies to those staying. Anything—food, money, clothes, flak jackets, backpacks—they might need to get to safety up the hill and away from the soldiers. People gave car keys and instructions to where cars had been left; notes to friends and relatives were pressed into hands, to be sent from Darwin. Everything was final and nobody doubted the fate of those who remained.

The UN staff were especially bitter about the order to leave and very generous to the refugees. For three months they had worked with East Timorese staff as they were harassed and threatened by militia and military. They had constantly reassured them of the power of the international community and the UN, and told them not to be intimidated.

Indeed, that was the main message of the entire mission in East Timor—the UN had told the East Timorese to vote according to their heart, despite the constant violence. Posters printed in three languages—Portuguese, Tetun and Indonesian—saying the UN would not abandon the East Timorese after the ballot still hung all around the compound. The East Timorese had believed the international community would not abandon them, and responded with 98 per cent of all those eligible voting in the ballot and 78 per cent of those voting for independence. Now, after all that, the UN was just going to walk out and leave them in the middle of a destroyed and depopulated city, surrounded by those who were still looting the place.

⊳─⊷─○─⊶─⊲

THAT NIGHT, Indonesian troops sauntered around the compound with their guns trained on the refugees. Outside one office, two crying East Timorese women, one with a baby in her arms, pleaded with UN officials to take them. It was a scene repeated a hundred times around the compound. Other groups of men stood around shaking their heads and swearing. Everywhere, refugees stared at passing foreigners with looks of despair, pleading and anger.

I couldn't face them. Suddenly, my white skin marked me as one who was now going to abandon them.

'They don't care that tomorrow is open season on these people,' said one Swiss UN worker. 'This is like Srebrenica all over again, when we helped separate the men to be killed and the women who were raped when we left,' he said.

His comment rang in my head. I had to file something, anything, to describe the chaos and sense of betrayal. The computer's battery had died and I had to surreptitiously unplug someone else's computer and use its lead—we were running on generators, and there wasn't much power. I ran the line outside. Behind me, journalists were arguing with each other about what to do.

I signed the petition, the draft of which stated simply: 'We the undersigned foreign media wish to express our deep concern about the sudden termination of the UN presence in East Timor and urge the UN Secretary-General to urgently reconsider this decision. We would give our warmest support to all efforts by the head of UNAMET to prolong the stay of the UN mission and to avert the imminent humanitarian tragedy.'

All the journalists who remained signed it, and it was going to be presented to Kofi Annan's representative, Ian Martin—if he ever came out of his office.

East Timorese were talking loudly about what to do, raising their voices. The panic the UN didn't want was happening.

Still, the gunfire around the compound continued; and the tracers still hit the hill and the fires still burned outside. The Indonesian troops had started lighting piles of tyres on the road outside, and the thick black smoke drifted across the compound.

I began to write. I tried several different leads, but the only one that seemed to adequately convey the situation was Antero's semi-mock suggestion: 'There will be a genocide tomorrow as the East Timorese are abandoned by the international community.'

Behind me, the other journalists continued to debate what to do—whether the Indonesians would kill them if they stayed on after the evacuation, or if we could somehow call their bluff, like we seemed to have done until now. Maybe this time it wasn't a bluff at all.

A bullet ricocheted off a nearby car and nobody even turned around. They kept arguing and I kept writing, sitting on the ground.

Getting the story through was a nightmare. The battery on the satellite phone was dead and, when I finally got it plugged in and facing the right direction, I realised how late it was—the Sydney office had closed, Jakarta had closed, and I didn't have any other numbers for Associated Press.

Someone suggested I call New York directory services, and I got the number that way. I dictated the whole piece to an understanding but confused copytaker in New York who seemed absolutely horrified by what was happening. The only place I could get a signal on the satellite phone was in the open area in the centre of the compound. When the shooting died down, the New York copytaker could hear the shouting and arguments of both the East Timorese and the foreigners in the background.

By the time I had finished, it was past midnight and I was exhausted. I went back inside and poured myself a whisky. Jose Belo came in and I apologised for not looking for him when I gave away my food. The supplies were pretty much gone, as everybody had given away what they had. He told me not to worry, because there was no need to leave. He could wake me early and we could go up the hill. It wouldn't be too bad, he said, he knew a way where there was no shooting. I feebly told him I would decide later, and Jose knew what I meant. He looked at me in disgust for a moment, and said, 'You are just like the rest of them. You will leave tomorrow. But you know you don't have to.'

He walked off.

Outside, journalists were still arguing with UN officials. They were trying to present the petition we had signed to Ian Martin.

Still holed up in his office, the UN head seemed oblivious to the chaos his decision to evacuate had unleashed on the compound. He refused to come out and speak to the journalists or the East Timorese who had come to see him.

I went to sleep on an army stretcher someone had left outside the public information office.

Brian Kelly roughly shook me awake. It was 2 am and Ian Martin wanted to make an announcement.

'Come on, get up. We can't make an announcement without the wire services there, can we?'

He was cheerily acknowledging that there were no other wire service reporters left.

Half asleep, I climbed the stairs to Ian Martin's office. There were people crowded all along the landing and on the top of the stairs, and Ian Martin stood outside his door, as if afraid to allow this angry crowd into his office.

'I am glad to announce there will be a delay of 24 hours in the proposed evacuation,' he said, and then went on to say there would be more details in the morning.

He wouldn't tell us why the decision had been reversed, but he did admit that more than 100 UN staff had expressed their desire to stay.

I filed the news on the satellite phone. The compound had gone quiet. Refugees sat in small groups, talking quietly or sleeping. A few minutes after I'd filed, the shooting around the compound stopped altogether for the first time in four days. Over the next few hours, more refugees left to go back up the hill. They didn't believe the UN could protect them and had realised, even though there was a reprieve, the UN in New York, and at a certain level, here placed little value on their lives.

That Wednesday night left a stain on relations between the UN and the East Timorese that will be forever hard to remove.

A LINE of Indonesian troops could be seen walking along the hills behind the compound in the morning. Only the occasional shot sounded in the air and it seemed to be relatively quiet. But everybody in the compound looked up nervously at the figures in camouflage deployed high on the hills behind us. This meant there would be no way out for the refugees. Previously, the Indonesian military had just been shooting at the hill, but now they were patrolling it.

In the schoolyard, Indonesian soldiers lazed around on the UN vehicles parked there and refugees still sat inside some of the buildings. They were mainly women and children. A nun introduced me and another journalist, Joanna Jolly, to some young girls who had just been brought in by the military. The day before, they had tried to come down to the compound in search of food but were shot at by the soldiers. There had been nine of them—they didn't know what had happened to the others.

The girls told us how they'd seen four naked bodies— two men, two women—on the road about one kilometre from the compound the day before. When they passed that spot 24 hours later, as the military escorted them to the compound, the bodies were gone. They told us they had been to Dare, but there was no food there, so they had tried to come back.

The nun told us how the police had told her that the last departure to West Timor was tomorrow, and anybody who didn't leave then would be killed. They also told the girls that UNAMET would soon be gone.

Joanna and I wandered up to the checkpoint which was manned by soldiers sitting around with weapons ready, but seemingly pretty relaxed. Beyond the barricades further up the street we could see military or militia go past in trucks or on motorcycles. The soldiers laughed and spoke among themselves. They talked about who would be the first to rape Joanna the following day when they came into the compound. It was a nasty scene and the soldiers enjoyed it. They could see that I understood what they'd been saying, and that just encouraged them.

><><><><

'WE WANT to get out of here in a straightforward, dignified way,' said the large American security adviser we'd just been introduced to. The man looked every inch the CIA man we were sure he was, but he was given some title by Brian Kelly that I didn't even bother to write down.

'We want no breakdowns in security,' he said.

'And just so there is no lack of clarity, journalists are banned from leaving the compound. I don't want you out there. They don't want you out there.

'We are remaining with a very small contingent, which gives us a very different security problem,' he said, looking each of us over to see who was going to give him trouble. Once again, some people tried to argue and the conversation went along the lines of, 'How dare the UN tell us what we can and cannot do.'

These objections led the man to announce that any journalist who wished to remain after the following morning's evacuation would not be able to seek shelter in the compound. It was deal time, and the Indonesians had made it clear to the UN that they would only agree to the UN evacuating local staff if the journalists were out of the way.

Some of the other journalists had taken advantage of the relatively peaceful morning and snuck out of the compound and into the city. Two had just been brought back by the police, and another three—two Dutch and one American—had walked down past the markets before being told by the military to return.

They described a totally empty and destroyed downtown area. The only sign of life seemed to be Indonesian military systematically looting buildings and loading trucks.

One of the chief political analysts for UNAMET, Geoffrey Robertson, explained what was happening.

'We are drawing back to a minimum plausible presence,' he said. 'This is to fulfill our obligation to the people of East Timor and to provide as much protection as we can to the IDPs [internally displaced people—refugees].'

He admitted that the pressure from the staff in the compound had been the main reason the redeployment was postponed, and said UNAMET's feeling was that 'the reduced number of staff here will allow us to continue to operate and do whatever is possible in these extreme circumstances to fulfil our mission.'

They were taking out the local staff and most of the international staff the following morning. The rest, about 80—mainly police and military—would remain to provide some kind of shield for the refugees.

>—+—+>—0—<+—+—<

THE AUSTRALIAN army attaché, Colonel Ken Brown-Rigg, drove his four-wheel drive into the compound. Isa Bradidge, the Christian activist, who had refused to leave all those months ago when the militia threatened Australians, and his East Timorese wife Ina, holding their eight-month-old baby, got out. I had already reported that Isa was missing; I'd last seen him before the ballot and he'd told me he would stay with his family. He looked terrible. He was drawn and nervous, dirty and shaking. He told me how he'd been stuck in the Polda police headquarters for the last two days, hidden by his family as militia searched through the refugee-filled complex looking for him and pro-independence supporters.

The police complex was where people had been ordered to go as their houses were destroyed. It was on the western edge of Dili and from there, thousands of people were packed into trucks and sent west. It became a massive transit camp for those being forced out of Dili, and since the ballot announcement, had held around 20,000 people at any one time.

He had ended up there on Tuesday after being stuck in the middle of town.

'I had a flat tyre,' he explained, 'a militia throwing petrol on my car wanting to burn it, another saying he was going to kill me, and about 15 people and a dead pig in the back of my ute.

'There were shops on fire, and people breaking windows and dragging stuff out of burning buildings. It was just like, "what did I do to deserve this?"' he told me, laughing at the insanity of the situation.

A truck had come along and he'd escaped with his wife to the police headquarters. But there, things were worse. His wife's family hid him under a blanket while militia searched for him for two days. The police did nothing to stop the militia going through the compound, looting the refugees' possessions and taking away those they'd identified. For two days all they had to eat was a bowl of noodles between them. There was no food out there, he said, meaning the whole city. His wife said she had seen many bodies in the cells at the police station.

━━◦◦◦◦◦━━

ISA HAD taken shelter in Belo's residence on the first night after the announcement, but then they'd returned to their nearby house. Forty militia had arrived in his street and started burning houses. His wife, a distant relative of Eurico

Guterres, had gone with Isa to the militia headquarters to try to stop them. Eurico had told them to get out as soon as possible—he could not control what was going to happen. Isa said Eurico had appeared distraught and helpless.

'I've lost count of the number of times people have tried to kill me in the last few days,' Isa said. 'They hate us, they hate the UN. They say the ballot was rigged. They want us dead and gone.'

At one point, he had gone out to the airport to try and board one of the Indonesian military C-130 transport planes that were taking people to Kupang, but the military had told him to go back to Polda. They told him they were there to protect the airport against foreign forces landing.

FURTHER ALONG the balcony of the public information office sat the Korean photographer whose few words about the trip to Maliana had alluded to a similar horror. Next to him was an Indonesian journalist who some people believed was a spy. He had come in with the Korean and he said they had gone to Maliana together; he had the same dull, shocked stare.

PAT BURGESS, the UN humanitarian officer, came to talk to some of the journalists about what he'd been hearing. An aid worker he had contacted in Atapupu, the port just over the West Timorese border where many of the ships were depositing people, saw militia meeting the boats. She saw one man being tied up and killed in the back of a truck as soon as he disembarked. She reported that young men in the rapidly filling camps had their mouths taped up or were not given food or water for days. Other reports were of militia killing people in refugee camps in Kupang, and of 70,000 people arriving in those camps, and more than 40,000 in Atambua across the border.

Nobody was able to confirm what had happened in Suai, but there were reports that all the priests had been killed along with the refugees in the church. But there was no way to confirm it—anybody who had stayed in Suai was either militia or dead.

The accepted figure was that at least 200,000 had been forced across the border since Monday. It was only Thursday, and that was only the estimate of those who had crossed by land.

Isolated in the compound, we got only those snippets of what was happening in the rest of the country. It was usually delivered by some shocked individual brought into the compound by the police. Whether they were Timorese or foreign, they all had the same shocked expression or a curious way of staring straight ahead as they recounted a story, as if they were watching it all over again. There were a lot of people like that among the refugees.

<hr />

I SPOKE to Brian Kelly on behalf of Jacinto, and he said they could organise to get him out.

As it got dark, the firing at the hills started again. Jose Belo left to meet Max Stahl, who had done some filming of the refugees attempting to climb to the tenuous safety of Dare. The eerie green night-vision footage that was seen all around the world the next day showed a child falling in the dark as the flashes of tracer rounds shot across the sky above him.

Hundreds left the compound that night, easing pressure on the UN. We were speculating whether that was why the Indonesian troops had pulled back from their positions on the hill, to allow the refugees to pass that way. They still continued shooting at them, however.

Some of the Australian military liaison officers invited me to their area of the compound for a drink. We sat up at the back of the compound looking down on the crowded area still full of vehicles and people, and talked about what was going on. They talked about 'hot extractions' by helicopters under fire from the hills if things went wrong. They mentioned the ease with which the Indonesian military or the militia could lob grenade launchers into the compound, creating chaos among the refugees.

I was thinking, again, that as employees of the Australian government, they had agendas. Tonight that agenda must have been to make sure the journalists left. I still don't know whether they were speaking honestly, but the precariousness of our situation from a military point of view was obvious. Later, I was told it was the military liaison officers who had recommended the total evacuation the day before. They had reasoned, after the attack on the warehouse in full view of the Indonesian military escort, that they could in no way even advise on security any more because it had ceased to exist.

The explanation one officer gave regarding the general course of events made sense: 'The Indonesian military is doing this all for two reasons. Firstly, they have to be able to show their own people—that is, the Indonesian people—the consequences of separating from the country; and secondly, this chaos, however stage-managed it's been, certainly does mean the Indonesian military can allow peacekeepers in without losing face. It is all an exercise to justify to their own people that the militia, not the military, are the threat to peace here, and they have been the ones who have destroyed the town because they didn't accept the result of the UN vote.'

It was a logical argument and the fact that no foreigners had been killed up to that point in the violence seemed to support it. As did the systematic way we had been targeted and rounded up from the first attack on the Mahkota on the Saturday afternoon, which by then seemed so long ago. We were all so used to our new reality of being shot at in the compound for so many days. More than 2,000 foreigners had been evacuated without incident and, as it turned out, only one German priest had been killed in those last few days.

⊱─◦─◦─⊰

I CALLED the office one last time for the day, and told them I was planning to leave. They were glad; they'd been asking me to leave for days—they didn't want blood on their hands. Just as I was about to hang up, they mentioned they'd had a report that the school next to the compound was under attack—were any details available? I felt like telling them they should try going into that school at night themselves. I was sick of it, but went anyway.

It wasn't under attack. The 'guards' from Kostrad had started burning tyres and a house over at the far end of the school. It had panicked those refugees still in there, and, of course, the burning was accompanied by volleys of gunfire.

It was like they were closing in. I saw Antero and Cico for the last time—they were leaving for the hills. They could have got themselves onto a plane like Jacinto had, but Antero simply said, 'I can't run now. How long will it be before I can come back, and then will everybody be dead?'

Nobody spoke of peacekeepers any more. As far as everybody was concerned, the international community and its interest in East Timor would cease once the last of the foreigners left.

I climbed the water tower at the back of the compound. Buildings were burning at the nearby university. What looked like a particularly fierce fire was coming from the grounds of the military headquarters. The whole skyline was lit up with fires but the power was out in most of the town. Strangely enough, we could still see the arc of lights that led up to the statue of Jesus on the point outside of town. The Indonesians had built the statue as a gift to the Catholics of East Timor, who hated it for the simple reason that the Indonesians had built it. It was one of the few things the Indonesians didn't try to destroy.

<hr/>

UNABLE TO sleep on that last night, I plundered a bottle of wine and sat out near the wire overlooking the school. The fires were burning and the guns were still firing tracers. Half asleep and a bit drunk, it was all starting to look beautiful, and I stood up to walk forward. It would be easier to die from a stray bullet than leave, I remember thinking. Instead, I heard the crackle of a two-way radio and an American voice behind me: 'Ahh, we've got a problem out here on the wire. I think I can deal with it—over.'

It was the civilian police, still working.

The Indonesian military trucks started to arrive early and the local staff accompanied by UN police were the first to go. Not all the journalists were leaving, and a few were still painfully trying to make up their minds in the morning. Dutch journalists Irene Slegt and Minka Nijhuis, who had covered East Timor for years, refused to leave, along with Marie Colvin from the *Sunday Times*. They all ended up joining the next evacuation.

Max Stahl had already gone up to the hills two nights previously, and was still there, sending Jose Belo back with the tapes which we took out. Jose was going straight back up there to work with Max. Robert Carroll from Macau also stayed in East Timor; he left the compound that day to go to Dare, and he ended up very ill, contracting a dazzling array of tropical diseases. Alan Nairn stayed after the final evacuation and was arrested, alone, by the Indonesian police in the deserted compound.

AROUND 80 UN staff ended up staying until the final evacuation four days later, when the majority of the refugees in the compound were airlifted to Darwin. Just 12 UN staff remained in Dili. But we didn't know the refugees would be evacuated then. The first news we got from the compound after we left was that militia with grenades had entered the schoolyard and were stealing vehicles, unhindered by the Indonesian troops stationed around the perimeter. A militia had come up to the gate of the compound and threatened to throw a grenade across the fence if the UN did not give him the keys to their cars.

Indonesian troops lined the sides of the evacuation trucks going out to the airport. The town was ruined and quiet. Almost all the buildings on the way to the airport were gutted, and militia waved their weapons at the trucks. A few cars loaded with goods headed west, but there were mainly just soldiers standing along the road. The police headquarters looked like a rubbish dump, full of discarded luggage and broken-down cars.

There were still a few thousand people camped out; they were the only civilians we saw. Others said they could smell burning flesh from the fires that still sent huge columns of black smoke into the sky, but I can just remember the Indonesian troops being ambivalent about whether I stood up or not. They had told us to get down because of militia snipers, but at the last moment I think they couldn't be bothered with the farce any more. They weren't protecting us from militia—they were escorting us out of town like hostages.

▻⧫◇⧫◅

AUSTRALIAN TROOPS stood on the tarmac and around the still-intact VIP lounge at Dili airport. There was a brief moment of tension when some Indonesian air force troops tried to take from Carmela Baranowska the tapes filmed in the compound and finally of the destruction from the back of the truck.

Inside the terminal, Australian troops checked our scrappy luggage, searching it thoroughly. They got to me and wanted to see what was in my pockets. Everything of importance I owned was in my pockets—money, passport, papers, notebooks, addresses, everything—they were bulging. Did I really have to empty them? I assured them I had no intention of harming anyone. They were insistent. I was furious at them, with their body armour and headset communications. Where the fuck had they been and why the hell turn up now when everything was over—when the place had been destroyed and the people were all gone?

If it was so easy to secure the airport, where the hell had they been? I threw my stuff on the floor. But they just whispered into their headsets and one of them said, 'Calm down, you're safe now.'

That wasn't the point, but I was too inarticulate with rage to say anything; I bent over and picked up my remaining possessions from the floor.

CHAPTER ELEVEN

20 September 1999
Darwin, Australia

AMID THE MASS of Australian troops who were queuing, milling about, shouting orders, and checking and loading up equipment underneath the gum trees beside the tarmac at Darwin's military airbase in Winnelie, two soldiers were embracing; one was crying. They looked awkward, loaded up with backpacks, guns and the 15-kilogram body armour all the troops were wearing. They were obviously scared, and one was reassuring the other as they waited their turn to board the C-130 transports that had been leaving all morning, carrying the first batch of troops bound for Dili.

Australian Prime Minister John Howard had been out there that morning, wishing them well, basking in the reflected glory of the peacekeeping deployment that his government had maintained was unnecessary since the outset of the UN process in May.

The only people who had accurately predicted the

devastation of East Timor were the Indonesian military and militia leaders themselves. They'd been threatening and planning to destroy East Timor for months if the result of the ballot was for independence.

Those of us who were in East Timor, despite the constant warnings and signals of what was about to happen, had been caught by surprise by the extent of the killing, depopulation and destruction that had been carried out around us. In the end, the United Nations, foreign governments and the media either ignored the obvious warning signals or figured the violence was a fair price for the East Timorese to pay for their independence.

⊱⋅⊱⋅○⋅⊰⋅⊰

TEN DAYS before the Australian troops departed, we had landed after our evacuation. It was immediately obvious how much international attention had become focused on the chaos that had engulfed East Timor. Banks of television cameras and journalists greeted us. Some of us stopped to talk, but I was too tired, drained and scrambled, and just pushed through to get outside, past them.

That day, Friday 10 September, protests calling for peacekeepers to be sent to East Timor had attracted the largest crowds in Melbourne since the Vietnam war. Thousands more people had marched in Sydney and Brisbane, and protestors had blockaded the offices of Indonesian airlines, the UN and John Howard. Public opinion in Australia had demanded that something finally had to be done to stop the destruction and the killing and, with the result of the ballot so clear, the government was not in a position to ignore it.

Internationally, pressure had increased on the Indonesian government to allow peacekeepers to move in. Indonesia responded with a message that if foreign troops arrived, they would be resisted by the Indonesian military. Protests and pressure came from Australia, New Zealand, Britain, Malaysia, Thailand, the Philippines, Canada, France, Sweden, Portugal and Singapore, all of whom had offered to send troops to participate in a peacekeeping mission to restore order in East Timor.

Following the announcement of the United States' support for the mission at the APEC conference held in Auckland, New Zealand, that weekend, Indonesian President B.J. Habibie faced the prospect of Indonesia becoming a pariah state. With a multibillion-dollar series of loans through the US that propped up Indonesia's failing economy at stake, he finally made a decision. Late on Sunday 12 September, he made an announcement in Jakarta: 'I called the United Nations Secretary-General Kofi Annan to inform him about our readiness to accept international peacekeeping forces from friendly nations to restore peace and security in East Timor.' The Australian Defence Minister immediately responded that troops would be on the ground as soon as five days later.

▸┤◂▸──0──◂▸┤◂

THE FOLLOWING Tuesday, 14 September, the rest of the 1,450 refugees from the UNAMET compound landed in Darwin along with all but 12 of the UN staff. Those 12 had stayed on in Dili, but they had abandoned the compound and moved into the fortress-like Australian Consulate building.

We continued to get sporadic reports from the two journalists who had fled to Dare along with the refugees. Robert Carroll was rapidly succumbing to severe bouts of malaria and dengue fever, and his commentaries became

more and more disjointed. But, despite his illness, he hero-
ically continued working.

Max Stahl reported that the military was moving closer
to Dare and told us about a continual series of deaths as
people, desperate for food, ventured down to Dili.

'Four died yesterday in Lahane [a southern suburb of
Dili at the base of the hills] going down to get food and one
woman was wounded,' Max told me through an unreliable
mobile phone connection. 'Two children died in a clinic
near Dare. Large areas of Dare have been abandoned
because of the proximity of TNI. The killing yesterday was
done by the military—the militia were with them, but the
killing was done by TNI.' It was a typical report from that
week. But isolated in Dare, the two could only report a
fraction of what was happening. The UN officials in the
Consulate building reported that the looting of Dili was
continuing in a methodical manner. Trucks piled high with
goods moved out along the main road heading west.

<hr/>

IN DARWIN, it wasn't hard to pick the people who had just
been evacuated. One night, outside a beer garden full of
UN personnel and journalists, somebody started a Harley-
Davidson. Half the crowd jumped and ducked, and drinks
went flying. The days of gunfire had rattled everybody.

Now safe in Darwin, most of us wanted to go straight
back. There had been too much killing for any of us to be
glad about leaving, and so many people we knew were still
there. There was also our anger that the Indonesians' plan
had worked. They had removed foreign witnesses, giving
them the breathing space to thoroughly destroy East Timor
and remove the evidence of their atrocities before we had a
chance to record it. I kept thinking about the bodies in the

street that were there one day and gone the next, and the smell of burning corpses noticed by others as we had left on the trucks to the airport.

Darwin was crawling with journalists from all over the world trying to get into East Timor. When my name wasn't on the list to go in with the first wave of troops, I began to make plans with Richard Lloyd Parry of the *Independent*. We considered hiring a fishing boat to take us across the 500-kilometre stretch of the Arafura Sea that separated Darwin from the south coast of East Timor. Luckily, after we complained to the Australian military and a few strings were pulled, we were both included in the military pool and the plan was abandoned.

The 30-odd journalists in the military pool were ordered to go to Norcom (Northern Australia military command) headquarters on Sunday 19 September. We would be leaving in the morning. Body armour, helmets, water bottles, rations and sleeping mats were handed out to those who wanted them, and I laughed when I heard someone ask for a full uniform. If the peacekeepers were going to be resisted by the Indonesian military, I remember thinking, that was the last thing I wanted to be wearing.

⊢◆○◆⊣

WAVES OF C-130s were taking off and landing when we arrived at Dili's Comoro airport. Australian troops were everywhere, lines of them marching out to set up a perimeter, unloading planes, setting up positions, smashing down fences and stringing up communication wires and barbed-wire barricades. The noise and dust were incredible as the planes landed, taxied, unloaded and took off without even turning off their engines.

But through it all, it was hard not to notice the stench of

human faeces rising from the now smashed-up terminal building. Thousands of refugees had passed through there, waiting for the Indonesian military C-130s that had taken them to Kupang in West Timor at a rate of 10 flights a day since we had left on 10 September. But that didn't turn out to be the reason for the smell. As we were soon to find out, virtually every public building that hadn't been destroyed by the Indonesian rampage had been defaced with the most basic of insults—they were all smeared with shit.

OUTSIDE IN the carpark, Indonesian soldiers sat in their trucks watching the Australians unload and set up. British special forces troops that had arrived with the first Gurkha detachment of 50, roared around the carpark in open vehicles mounted with machine guns. They ignored the Indonesians who watched, and the Australians who laboured, sweating, setting up their positions, and headed off in the direction of town. Out the front of the terminal, I saw Max Stahl unshaven and covered from head to toe in black soot and dirt. He immediately asked for a drink of water. The Australian soldiers looked at him as though he was insane.

Max had taken hours to get down to the airport from Dare. He said that although the TNI were only shooting into the air at night as intimidation, the East Timorese who tried to return to Dili were still being killed.

'I saw one man shot by TNI yesterday with my own eyes,' said Max, who had been with the man going back to Dili to look for food.

East Timorese pro-independence leaders sheltering in Dare had told him they believed the militia had pulled out of certain regional towns and were then moving out through the capital, making the situation very fluid. Truckloads of militia were still in the centre of Dili. He couldn't say much else—he'd spent all morning trying to film what he could of the arrival, but had been avoiding militia. He ran off to find someone to take his film back to Darwin.

Another civilian vehicle pulled up. In it was Robert Carroll. He looked terrible, his face was pale and dirty, and he was shaking. We spoke in a hurry and he ran off to find a satellite phone or some other sort of communication. For days, his mobile battery had been dead and he hadn't been able to send through anything but the briefest report.

Driving his car was João Sarmento, the quietly spoken secretary from the Students Council. He told me how they had hidden the car in a dry creek bed to stop it being looted and had siphoned petrol from destroyed vehicles to get down to the airport.

'The young children under five are dying now in Dare,' said João. 'A lot of us have been sick—there is no food, no medicine. Here in Dili, there is nothing, everybody has left.'

He also looked like he'd lost a lot of weight, and his eyes bulged, wide with fear and fever. He told me he had been sick with malaria for a week.

'We didn't have too much trouble getting here,' he said with understatement. 'There were still militia in the Balide and Becora areas [to the east and south of the city centre] and near the Australian consulate [just down the road to the city from the airport] but otherwise they seem to have gone.'

'In Comoro, they seemed to be burning down their headquarters,' said João.

The two students in the car became nervous. The Indonesian soldiers were watching us with interest, and they wanted to get out of there even though there were Australian soldiers everywhere.

>-+-+>-0-+<+-+-<

BEHIND ME on the other side of the terminal, television reporters were already talking into their cameras, reporting the landing. I walked out past where the Australians were already dug-in on the road that runs out of Dili to the west and the border. Trucks piled with belongings still headed out of town. Red and white Indonesian flags were draped over the bonnets to identify them to militia who, we were told, were still manning checkpoints in Liquiça 30 kilometres away.

A group of around 40 East Timorese sat on their belongings by the main road. 'We are waiting for trucks to take us out of here,' said one 11-year-old boy who was wearing a looted Brimob police vest. The others—young boys, women and old men—were all wearing the red and white bandanas of the militia as some sort of protection against the militia who were still forcing their exit.

TNI soldiers lounged in the shade with weapons ready, ignoring a man who angrily shouted at the refugees for talking to reporters before racing off on a motorcycle. The refugees laughed when he had gone.

'Militia, Aitarak, they go Atambua,' they said as I walked away.

There was rubbish everywhere and the road into Dili was littered with junk, old tyres, furniture, a few smashed vehicles and, beyond that, no traffic, just rising smoke from a few fires in town. Most of the buildings were burnt down. Even with the peacekeepers arriving, there wasn't much to keep these people in Dili. A building started burning furiously a few hundred metres from the Australian post; thick, black petrol-driven smoke drifting towards the Australians. There were TNI soldiers further up near the road. Nobody seemed to know or care why the building was on fire, it was just another game between the militia or the TNI and the Australians.

THAT NIGHT, we stayed in the airport, sleeping on the ground. A plane-load of journalists had been flown in by the British forces, annoyed at the low representation of British media among the Australian pool, and they had moved into the looted Tourismo hotel.

In the morning, I saw an American photographer, Anastasia Vrachnos, who had been in Dili a few days before the peacekeepers. She had been staying with the Indonesians and was leaving, and suggested I use her driver, Florindo, and his motor scooter. I went into town.

All along the foreshore, refugees were living in shanties of wood, plastic sheeting and scraps of roofing. At the dock, now secured by INTERFET, Australian ships were landing at one end and Indonesian troop transports loading at the other. Piles of refuse and a few people sitting under plastic sheeting here and there were all that was left of the thousands who had been marched down there and deported. The Hotel Dili was crowded with people whose homes had been destroyed. However, except for that small pocket of Dili, the place seemed deserted. The buildings were burnt out or smashed, the roads were covered in refuse, and only the occasional person wandered through the wrecked city.

At the Tourismo, the old waiter João stood crying at the gate. He hugged me and, laughing and weeping, told me how the militia had stolen, burnt and shot my motor scooter because they couldn't get the locks off, and had torched my room.

The hotel had been looted, but aside from my room, the ABC's room and the kitchen, it wasn't burnt out. The place was rapidly filling with journalists who were kicking down doors and claiming rooms, and the Australian army was trying to reserve rooms for the media pool as soldiers strung up barbed wire and 'secured' the place.

The Australians were commandeering the hotel, and arguing with the British who were already there. I grabbed a room. There was no power or water anywhere in the city, and the Australians had generators.

JOÃO FROM the Students Council watched me break in through the window of the room. He had come in with Robert Carroll, who had collapsed exhausted in my old burnt-out room. João was laughing at me as I tried to clean out the room. There was nothing but a bed frame and rubbish left. All the mattresses were gone; all the mattresses in the entire country seemed to have been looted or burnt.

He asked me for some food. All I had left was a tube of jam and some biscuits from the rations. João carefully spread some jam on a biscuit and ate it in tiny bites. He hadn't eaten anything for days. He had trouble swallowing, and carefully put the other biscuits back in his pocket.

Next door to the Tourismo was the police headquarters that was now full of TNI. Rows of looted motorcycles sat out the front and Maggie O'Kane, a correspondent from the *Guardian*, bought one from the soldiers who would soon be leaving anyway and were happy to take her money. Florindo was still at the front of the hotel, and journalist Joanna Jolly grabbed him and his bike and we rode through the new Australian checkpoints through the deserted centre of town to Dare.

There was no-one in the southern suburbs of Dili at the base of the hills. As we climbed the nine kilometres of steep, winding roads to the seminary in Dare, we started to pass small groups of young men waving at us warily near the top. The closer to Dare we got, the more people there were just standing by the side of the road or sitting in the trees, and by the time we reached the seminary there were people everywhere.

Everybody looked dirty, ragged and tired. Occasionally, someone would shout a greeting as we passed. There was no sign of jubilation or victory. The nightmare was still going on—the Indonesian military was still in Dili, the militia were still roaming about, and the majority of the people in Dare were still living in the open with no food.

The landing of the international force could be seen clearly from the hills. Just as they had watched the Indonesians burn and loot Dili from the mountains, they could now see the C-130 transports landing and taking off, and the fleet of naval ships that had moved in over the horizon at dawn on the 20th.

As soon as we stopped, people came to talk. One was Sabino Mendoza, a student who had fled the UN compound after they'd declared they would evacuate on that chaotic Wednesday night.

'In Dili it is still dangerous for us,' he said, 'and the pro-Jakarta people are still there, and there is still Indonesian military there.'

A small detachment of Australian troops had driven up to Dare that day and left again.

'We need a guarantee from the UN force before we can go back to our city,' he insisted. 'I didn't believe in the security of the UN compound, so I came here.'

I asked if he had seen anybody killed.

'Guido, he was in the house when they attacked us in Dili. We didn't get him. And there was Francisco Nascimento—the militia killed him with machetes in the

Hotel Tropical [their headquarters]. I saw them kill four people, then they burnt them in a house.'

Others crowded around and joined in.

Jose Ferrera told me they'd killed his family at their house, at midnight after the announcement. 'They came to my place in Mascarenas,' he said. 'First they killed my neighbour—the militia shot him with a gun—then they came and started shooting my family. In the morning, all the people moved to Dare—about 500 in our area.'

Aquilas Barros, a 21-year-old student, was fleeing Dili on foot with a crowd of people to Dare on 4 September. 'We got as far as the Balide bridge and about four people from our group were shot,' he said. One was a girl he knew, Francesca Tilman, 25 years old.

'We had to leave her body on the road. I tried to go back but there was too much shooting,' he said with the guilty tears of a survivor rolling down his dirty cheeks.

Almost every one of the more than 60,000 people in Dare had similar stories to tell about when they fled Dili only a little over two weeks before.

⊶•○•⊷

WE RODE further into the mountains; there were people everywhere. What had previously been a quiet back road behind the seminary was now lined with people and make-shift shelters. Vehicles, the only ones not looted by the Indonesians, were parked under the trees on either side of the road and people were living in them. Occasionally, a young man with a weapon would dash off the road or jump behind a building.

Falintil had some people in Dare to protect the refugees in case the militia and military did attack up the hill from Dili. But, as Australian INTERFET force commander

Major-General Peter Cosgrove had declared in Darwin, Falintil were, in theory, to be disarmed on sight, along with the militia—leaving the Indonesian military and the INTERFET force as the only two armed groups on the island.

It was a strategy designed to fit comfortably within the public and diplomatic fiction that we were dealing with a conflict between the militia on the one hand and Falintil on the other, exonerating the TNI for any part in the violence. The disarmament of Falintil was abandoned a few weeks later once the reality became clear.

SISTER LOURDES ran a clinic and orphanage behind Dare. It was crowded with children and she told us six small children had died in the last 24 hours.

'We don't have food or medicine for them,' she said, 'but if there will be enough food, this will be a good time for the people to begin a new life—otherwise there will be revenge.' She told us how they had stood looking down from the mountains at the planes landing and the ships arriving the day before. The people had been surprised and ecstatic that it was happening so soon—they had received no information about the operation.

IT WAS getting late, and we had to get back to Dili. The others went on ahead but I realised that mobile phones were working in the hills, so I filed a report working from my notebook. Florindo was getting increasingly nervous— the signal kept dropping out and it was getting late. Going back into town there was nothing on the road except the carcasses of dead dogs and pigs, shot by the retreating Indonesians. Every house at the base of the mountains was destroyed and the few people we had seen around earlier had left. It must have only been 4 pm but it seemed to be getting darker already, and smoke from a few burning buildings still rose into the air.

▻┅◆━○━◆┅◅

THERE WERE people everywhere at the Tourismo. The securing of the hotel by INTERFET had attracted Timorese who had been coming out of the suburbs to seek shelter near the Australian troops along the beach. Another plane-load of journalists had arrived on a chartered flight from Jakarta, and some more had arrived from Darwin that day. There was hardly any transport available, and the journalists were busy setting up their equipment or trying to find somewhere to stay, or just standing around talking. Road blocks were set up on either side of the building and armoured personnel carriers roared up and down the street. I paid Florindo and told him to come back in the morning.

▻┅◆━○━◆┅◅

FLORINDO WAS back within an hour. He was out of breath, shaking, and his clothes were torn. He was also bleeding from cuts on his arm and leg. He told me and Joanna that he had picked up a tall blond man who spoke good Indonesian from out the front of the hotel—a journalist. He had taken him to Becora—where the man wanted to go. Some Indonesian soldiers with guns on motorbikes in the middle of the road yelled out to him to stop, and he had tried to turn around. The bike was hit by their bullets and fell over. The soldiers kept shooting, so he ran; he didn't know what had happened to the white man. His bike was still out there—he had run all the way back here to tell us.

We wrote this down and went to Major Rob Barnes, the Australian in charge of the media pool. We thought it could have been Richard Lloyd Parry from the description, but he was found working in the hotel. Other people gathered around, and Gwyn Robinson from the *Financial Times* started questioning Florindo. Sander Thoenes, a freelancer who worked as their Jakarta correspondent, had arrived on that chartered flight and left his bags in her room and gone straight out. She hadn't even seen him, and he hadn't come back. For the next two hours, Florindo repeated his story to anyone who would listen. But everyone in the INTERFET media pool was accounted for; eventually he asked me to take him home.

Riding Maggie's bike with Florindo on the back, I turned a corner by the Villaverde cathedral in the destroyed centre of town. Australian troops screamed at us to stop and get off the bike. They swore and kept their guns levelled at Florindo and myself until I produced my ID. They had night vision on, and told me to turn off my light. They searched Florindo for weapons in the pitch blackness.

I turned off into the back streets. There was junk everywhere and I had to weave in and out of the wreckage of cars and furniture, burnt and twisted roofing iron, and collapsed walls of destroyed buildings that spilled onto the narrow alleys. The only sign of life was an occasional fire lit from rubbish, with one or two young men standing around and nervously peering into our headlight. The neighbourhood had been a so-called pro-independence area and was thoroughly wrecked.

I dropped off Florindo and became lost, ending up in a street of intact houses. Lights were on and people were sitting in living rooms and on verandas. Being in an intact area scared me—it could only mean it was an Indonesian part of town, and I sped off until an Australian patrol once again screamed at me to get off my bike as I turned another corner. They told me to get back to the hotel, adding they'd heard a report of a journalist in trouble in Becora.

I'd presumed they'd meant the one who had been shot off the back of Florindo's bike, but they were talking about another incident. Jon Swain from the *Sunday Times* had also gone to Becora, where he'd run into military and militia. His driver was whacked in the head with a gun butt and lost an eye. His translator, student leader Antero's brother Anacleto, was taken away by the military and never seen again. Swain and his photographer fled into the surrounding suburb. A phone call to his paper in London led to his rescue from the area using a helicopter and armoured personnel carriers from INTERFET. Sander wasn't so lucky.

IN THE morning I was woken by journalist Diarmid O'Sullivan. Sander hadn't shown up and Diarmid, who was a close friend of his, wanted me to find Florindo. Then Ginny Stein rushed past. They had found the body. Some Timorese had come in the morning and told her and others that there was a white man dead near the Becora church. When they got there, they found a body face-down in a pool of blood on the street. The notebook next to it contained briefing notes from the INTERFET public relations officer, Chips Hendriss Anderson, who Sander would have spoken to as soon as he landed.

Sander was freelancing for a Dutch magazine and apparently had a deadline that night. He had landed, dropped off his gear, spoken to the INTERFET spokesman and gone out to find out what was happening—like any decent journalist would. The only transport available would have been motor-bikes out the front with drivers. He had grabbed one—Florindo's.

Florindo explained what happened next.

'Near the Becora church about 4.30 pm, there were six guys on three motorcycles, they were in Indonesian uniform,' he said. 'They were about 200 metres away. They told me to stop. I tried to turn around. They started shooting. There were bullets all around, about 20 shots. I saw the journalist on the ground—I ran because I thought they would start shooting again.'

When Ginny went out there at about 7 am, Lyndal Barry, an Australian filmmaker, went with her. She told me later how when they'd first found the body it had been face down in the street. The nose and lips looked like they had been cut away with a knife. They were clean cuts, not from an accident like falling face down on the road, but from someone purposefully slicing off parts of the face. Ginny Stein also recounted that all his fingers were intact. She remembered because they flicked open Sander's notebook with a stick. It was lying near his outstretched hand, and all his fingers were there. The only people nearby when they went out in the morning were Indonesian soldiers. Lyndal went back with the Australian army to retrieve the body, around midday, and she noticed some fingers missing.

The body had been mutilated, but in the official report of the incident released later by INTERFET, and in all the official statements at the time, INTERFET continued to claim the mutilation was caused by either wild dogs or the motorcycle accident. It was little official lies like these, told by INTERFET only to save face for the Indonesian forces, that chipped away at their credibility from the start. In these circumstances it made me feel sick.

The average INTERFET soldier, I think, felt the same

way. A few days later, I was watching some Australians going particularly hard on some suspected militia they had picked up near the Aitarak headquarters at the Hotel Tropical. They already had the men under control—their hands were bound with plastic strips behind their backs— but they continued to push and kick them. Later, one of the soldiers told me they had found human ears in the pockets of some of them, and that was the reason for the treatment. But at the time, they couldn't tell us that, and we'd criticised them for their heavy-handedness.

SANDER'S DEATH broke the spell of white impunity. No journalist or international UN staff member had been killed in the entire violent pre-INTERFET period, although many had come close. I had always believed there were strict orders not to kill foreign nationals throughout the Indonesian military. With that disproven, we all felt very vulnerable. It affected the aid workers, too, and they put their plans on hold.

'It's always the same,' said Phillip Marker, a representative from World Vision, 'everyone rushes in, all enthusiastic, and then something like that happens, and it makes you think twice.

'It's hard to give out food when you are dodging bullets. We don't expect to start until next week.'

EARLY NEXT morning, Lindsay Murdoch gave Joanna and I a tip-off about what he thought was a mass grave. It turned out to be only one badly decomposed and maggot-covered body in the well at the back of the destroyed Carrascalão family home. The stench was horrible and replicated in the deserted Aitarak headquarters next door. We searched all the rooms but couldn't find the source of it. Across the street, an old woman pointed to some sacks in the small drainage canal and told us they were body parts.

All over town in the next few days, bodies turned up in backyards and gutters. It was hard to keep count. Relatives or people returning to town would move or bury them out of respect and hygiene, and when you compared notes with other journalists, you were never sure if you were talking about the same ones.

⊳⊷⊶⊙⊷⊷⊲

I WENT out to the Polda police headquarters. Inside the deserted offices, it was a mess. Identity cards, finger-print records, ration packs, smashed televisions, typewriters, riot shields, bits of discarded uniforms and empty ammunition boxes lay everywhere. In the office of Lieutenant-Colonel Sitompol, who had been in charge of the task force to provide the security for the ballot, a big human turd sat in the middle of his desk in the smashed-up office. Outside the building, Sitompol, who had just arrived from Kupang that instant, was talking to Maggie O'Kane. I asked him who was responsible for the shit on his desk and the destruction of the compound, trying not to laugh.

'I left the compound in the care of TNI five days ago,' he said, glaring.

So I had to ask if he thought it was TNI who shat on his desk.

'I left the compound in the care of TNI five days ago,' he repeated, 'we only removed some documents.' He looked around at his destroyed headquarters.

We asked about the story of the bodies stacked in the

cells and he insisted on showing us through the cell block. There was no sign of bodies but the cells were as wrecked and as full of junk as the rest of the place. I picked up a small notebook, which contained what appeared to be a list of the Ablai militia members in Same. One cell was stacked with spears and machetes.

Sitompol told us that 180,000 people had gone through the police compound during the violence on their way to West Timor. He told us how the police had worked 24 hours a day to help the refugees, and admitted that some of the 8,000 police in East Timor had joined in the looting.

'I helped save Bishop Belo,' he said. 'I saved, also, the personnel at the ICRC, but they say the police did not do anything.

'If I did not save Belo, and tried to fight the militia, 10,000 children would have been killed,' he said, referring to those who had been marched down to the dock at gunpoint.

It was easy to feel sorry for him. There had always been rivalry between the police and the military. The fact was there were only 8,000 police and there were more than 20,000 Indonesian military in East Timor in that period, and the police had often said that they were scared of the military.

But the number of incidents of direct police killings, or facilitation of militia activity or involvement in attacks on the UN meant they were not a neutral force as he was still trying to portray them. By his own admission, they had played a major part in the forced deportation to West Timor of around a third of the population, and the destruction of their headquarters by TNI was only what TNI were still doing all over town, and then to their own barracks, as they pulled out.

>-+-+>-0-+<+-+<

EVERYWHERE PEOPLE were starving and homeless, most still afraid to come back to Dili from the bush. I ran into Rui Lorenco from Kontras. He was walking dazed and barefoot through a destroyed suburb. He had lost everything and his feet were a mess from running barefoot from militia in the ruined city. He didn't even have a shirt on. He asked for food and I gave him all I had from the rations. When he started to eat, I could see tears welling up in his eyes from shame at his own wretched condition.

Up in Dare, Leandro Isaac looked more like a revolutionary than the neat civil servant he used to be. He had a beard, was wearing a dirty T-shirt and holding a long wooden staff.

A message from Xanana was being read to the crowd: 'You should forget about them burning your house. Those who follow the militia, we think they are stupid, but as Catholics, you must forgive them.

'Everyone has had family die, but you have to apologise. Everyone and to each other.' The leaders were concerned widespread reprisal killings would spiral out of control.

'When you see someone killing your wife or your children and burning your house, is it normal to hate them?' asked Armindo Maia, the former rector of the university who held a Masters in development studies from a New Zealand university. He was standing beside me, listening to the speech. I had never seen him out of a suit before, but here he was wearing suit pants cut into shorts and a torn white shirt that was so filthy with soot it was black. He scratched his scraggly beard in thought and said, 'You know, it is the worst colonial withdrawal ever. I don't know where you can find any parallel in history.'

We both stood there and ran through a few examples and dismissed them. He was right. Neither of us could think of worse.

On the way back to Dili, the historic Portuguese-era governor's residence on the hill was in flames. TNI soldiers had been guarding it when we passed on the way up to Dare.

▷─┤◄▷─○─◁├─◁

ON FRIDAY 24 September, INTERFET commander Major-General Peter Cosgrove held a joint press conference with Indonesian military commander Major-General Kiki Syahnakri in the Indonesian command centre, Kodim. We had never been allowed into that room before—it had been the central command room for Indonesian military operations in East Timor.

Behind the generals, their staff and translators at the front of the room, was the outline of three huge maps of East Timor. The shape of the half island was imprinted on the wall and shreds of paper showed where the operational maps had been hastily ripped down. The Australian and Indonesian troops guarding their respective generals eyed each other off. They were positioned around the room and behind the generals. The Australians, behind dark sunglasses, whispered into the small microphones around their necks.

The room was on the first floor and gave a clear view over the city where a few buildings continued to burn. Black Hawk helicopters circled the building and the din of their motors increased to a roar as they moved closer, as Cosgrove announced Syahnakri would speak first. Black Hawks screamed past the building as Kiki began to speak, so we missed the first few words.

He began by telling us how he had been appointed to restore security and impose martial law in East Timor on 7 September.

'I recognise in a quality sense I cannot fully control the situation here,' he said, through a translator. 'We cannot provide a peaceful environment here—I do believe command under General Cosgrove can make it happen here.'

He was asked when he would hand over control to General Cosgrove and he said some time in the following week, when the majority of troops had left.

He was also asked whether he was aware that his troops had assisted in the destruction, the deportation of the population and the killing.

'That report is true, but it happened before this martial law period,' he said. 'We will take legal action.'

And the Black Hawks swept in close to the building again, drowning out his words.

Then he spoke about the withdrawal of his men.

'The first phase is the military resort [garrison] here, total 7,000 men,' he said. 'Now we have 100 [left] in HQ of the command here.

'The second phase is the withdrawal of the five territorial battalions here, a total of 4,500 men. That will be completed tomorrow.

'The final phase we would like to reduce the number of available troops slowly.' And he was drowned out again by the thunderous noise of the helicopters.

There would still be another 4,500 Indonesian troops left after the first two phases, and it would be another month before they all finally left.

Cosgrove thanked Kiki and spoke. Someone asked if he was aware Indonesian troops were taking part in the destruction and had been involved in killings.

'It is beyond our authority to answer this,' he said, adding that the government of Indonesia had a commission for human rights that would be carrying out investigations.

He fielded questions from Indonesian reporters who quoted his Thai deputy commander, General Songkiti, as saying Australia was playing too large a part in the mission.

'Australia was the nation that was closest and had troops ready at the shortest notice,' said Cosgrove. 'Many more nations will be here to help those poor people without homes and food.'

Asked if there was a possibility East Timor would be partitioned, with the western part handed to the pro-Indonesian East Timorese leaders, as they were still demanding, Cosgrove simply replied, 'We never, ever deal with the political side. I don't want to answer this question on the orders of my mission.' The Black Hawks stayed away while Cosgrove was talking.

Kiki Syahnakri was asked about the militia and why he had failed to control them.

'During my period of time, no militia has entered this area,' he said.

Asked about the destruction and who carried it out, he said, 'The destruction happened before I controlled the situation in East Timor.'

He stated categorically that there were no Indonesian special forces left in East Timor.

Asked about relations with the militia and TNI, he said, 'We have identified relations between TNI and the militia. Even though it is something we both wish did not occur.'

He then told us that the TNI had arrested 47 people for militia activity, confiscated 22 homemade weapons and brought 12 of them to 'justice' already.

The Black Hawks moved in and the general's words were drowned out once again. The Australian troops kept whispering into their miniature microphones.

THE INTERFET troop strength by then was around 4,000, mostly Australians. Two hundred and fifty Gurkhas and their English officers and a detachment of British Special Boat Service troops were there too. All the INTERFET troops were stationed in the Dili area at that stage, and there were parts of town, such as Becora and Taibesse, where it was still not wise to go.

Outside the headquarters, when we tried to leave, the road back down to the waterfront was blocked by Australian troops. The helicopters were swooping low following the grid of the roads in the area. A house was ablaze near the crossroads, and armoured personnel carriers were following groups of soldiers who ran from wall to wall in full combat positions—clearing the area. They wouldn't let us pass and I had to wait until the media liaison officers, who had taken us there, went past in a Landrover so I could follow them through the checkpoints on the motorbike.

There was a screaming of commands over the noise of the helicopters, as soldiers dived over fences, kicked down doors and ran forward doubled over. They worked their way through the whole suburb like that. It was a massive show of force and the soldiers were taking it very seriously. We had to go the long way back to the hotel.

⊷⊶◇⊷⊶

AT THE hotel, another drama was in progress. The TNI soldiers next door were due to leave that afternoon, and some of them had been seen on the roof of the building pouring petrol all over it. They were going to burn it down, and the fire would probably take the hotel as well.

Armoured personnel carriers arrived and parked out the front, pointing their weaponry at the building. Black Hawk helicopters circled low, the noise so loud I could no longer hear the copytaker on my mobile phone as I shouted the story to him.

'We are requesting TNI to assure us that the house was safe due to my concern at the fire for the INTERFET location next door,' yelled Colonel Keith Jobson over the racket the helicopters were making.

We stood around and watched the TNI get themselves and their things together amid the noise and wind of the helicopters' downdraft. They didn't burn down the building.

Eventually, they marched outside and along the foreshore to the docks, followed by a throng of journalists, and Timorese who shouted abuse at them—all the way down to the docks past the Timorese living under plastic sheeting and corrugated iron on the waterfront, whose houses they had destroyed. Some Timorese shouted abuse and raised their fists, while some smiled and turned away. Young men ran after them throwing the occasional rock.

Another column of TNI marched down past the governor's office, and more out of the barracks across the road. East Timorese people were coming out of everywhere, screaming abuse as the troops entered the fenced-off dock area where the Indonesian landing craft were moored. Australian soldiers stationed along the fence faced out towards the crowd.

A group of young men were singing and jumping in a circle, doing the Timorese dance, the *tebe*—they put their arms around each other's shoulders in a circle that moves in and out. They were singing the student protest song—*Kole Lele Mai*—the loudest, hoarsest, roughest version I had ever heard. Some were just hurling insults in Indonesian at the soldiers, and a few threw a couple of rocks.

In the middle of them, I saw Jose Belo—screaming and shouting and jumping. He saw me and came over, screaming at the top of his voice in my face, 'They're fucking leaving! Liberation! They're leaving, they're fucking leaving!'

He kept repeating those words, laughing and yelling at the same time.

Somebody else started shouting, '*Viva Timor Leste! Viva Independencia! Viva Xanana Gusmão!*' And everybody joined in the shouting, punching their fists in the air.

There were no more than a few hundred people there. Most of them were students or young people who had just come back down to Dili from the hills, still ragged, filthy and skinny from their ordeal of fleeing the violence which had started exactly 20 days before.

Over and over again they kept shouting their *Vivas* as the Indonesians walked through the gates and up the ramps of the landing craft. Somebody said they could see Eurico Guterres on the large civilian ferry that had docked to take out Indonesians, and a torrent of obscenities in Indonesian was yelled in that direction.

The Australian soldier manning a machine gun on top of a gatehouse looked down on the ecstatic crowd and allowed himself the smallest smile.

THE FOLLOWING Tuesday, 28 September, I headed off to see the guerrillas. There were four of us, and we had got hold of a car.

INTERFET had sent convoys through to Baucau and Lospalos in the east, and they had returned to Dili with no problems. They were following what they called 'maximum force protection', whereby they would not move into an area permanently unless they could do so in such numbers as to overwhelm any opposition they might encounter.

Manatuto, the first major town east of Dili, was flattened—totally destroyed. A few people stood in the street and told us that the Indonesians had left. They were dirty and wanted cigarettes above all else.

We continued on. I was trying to remember where the turn-off to Waimori was and we stopped in a village. People came out of the wrecked houses after they realised we were foreigners. They asked lots of questions about what was going on. I used Maggie's satellite phone to call the office. They had just received my mobile phone bill—apparently it was astronomical—and wanted to put me through to the accountant. As I was speaking, the people started to run back off the road. Maggie and the others started running, too, and I looked up and saw a TNI truck coming towards me. I reacted slowly—the accountant was still talking in my ear—and I jumped over a brush fence and hid behind a small sapling. I crouched down as the truck stopped in front of us. Then I heard laughter. The truck was full of Falintil. They were laughing at me and my pathetic attempt to take cover.

Anico, whom I had met in David Alex's camp in 1997, was driving and he was laughing the hardest. They had just looted the truck from the deserted TNI base in Baucau and we followed them to Waimori.

At the checkpoint, the Falintil soldiers had new weapons—AK-47s, the type issued to police. A few were wearing bits and pieces of police uniform and some were wearing the high-crowned police dress hats. With their long hair and beards, they looked truly weird. They wouldn't let us pass and the commander berated Anico for a breach in security, and then finally agreed to let us continue.

Commander Falur ran up to our vehicle as we lurched into the camp.

'What's wrong, what has happened?' he asked, running along beside us until we parked.

'Nothing, we've just come to interview Taur,' I said, and he looked genuinely relieved.

He had just received news of the death in Lautem of a priest, two nuns and five civilians—they were horribly executed during an ambush by militia near Lospalos three days earlier. He thought we were fleeing militia.

'That Indonesian friend of yours, Agus, was killed—he was with them,' Falur said. We had talked about Agus and the film he had been making on Falintil before. It was the first I'd heard of his death. I hadn't even known Agus was in the country—I thought he'd left.

Apparently he'd been travelling with the priest and the nuns when their vehicle was ambushed by the Team Alpha paramilitaries from Lospalos. They shot the priest, made the nuns strip, then shot them. Agus tried to run with some of the other civilians and was shot down. A small boy who saw what happened was tied to a tree and sliced up with a machete. Their bodies were loaded back into the car, which was pushed into a nearby river. Those killed were later clarified by UN investigators as three Catholic brothers, two nuns, Indonesian journalist Agus Mulyawan, two church workers and the young boy who was a bystander.

Falur explained to us what was going on. There were still pockets of militia in Lospalos, Same, Alas, Ainaro, Suai and the southern port of Betano. They were trapped. TNI had assured them they would be sending boats to take them to West Timor but they had never arrived.

'We have seen more massacres and killing after they [INTERFET] arrived because they did not move out of Dili,' he said. 'On the 24th, 25th and 26th there was fighting in Betano and two Falintil soldiers were killed by TNI.'

The Ablai militia were still in the area and were still killing many civilians, Falur told us, angry it was taking INTERFET so long to move out of Dili.

Ordered not to fight by their leader, Xanana Gusmão, to prevent the conflict deteriorating into the civil war the Indonesian military were trying to create, the guerrillas were mostly forced to watch the destruction of their country from the four cantonment camps.

'It made me feel mad,' said Falur. 'I felt so sick and sad when I saw what was happening. But I must obey my commander, Xanana.'

But they hadn't stuck to the cantonment deal entirely. Falintil did engage the militia and the military to try to save the population in the nearby towns of Laleia and Manatuto.

'We went in there and they surrendered their weapons,' said Pedro, a senior guerrilla fighter and Taur Matan Ruak's assistant. 'The Indonesian police gave us all their guns without a fight, and we let them leave from Laleia. But it was too late, the town was destroyed and most of the population had left.'

As INTERFET forces were arriving in Dili, Falintil forces came under heavy shelling, and mortar and rocket fire as they tried to move down the hills to Manatuto.

'They were raining it down on us as they pulled out along the road. Three of our men were wounded, two seriously from explosions,' said Anthony, the Australian who had stayed in the camp all along. They allowed him to join them on that operation, but he still didn't carry a weapon.

He talked about the uncertainty of the last few weeks and how it had been very tense in the camp. The Indonesians had not tried to attack them, but they had been on high alert and when the UN pulled out from Dili, everybody had expected an attack.

Like everyone else, he looked like he'd lost weight. They were down to one meal a day. The yellow plastic wrappers of emergency supplies air-dropped to the camp by the international forces littered the dry river bed that served as a road to the camp.

'We had a lot of problems collecting it,' said Falur. 'The Indonesians got some of it, and the people here are not used to the preservatives, it gives them diarrhoea.'

As I was talking to him, I pulled out a packet of cigarettes and lit one. All eyes at the table followed my hand as I drew on the cigarette. I offered the pack; it was gone in minutes—they had been out of cigarettes for weeks.

'We watched from the hills as the Indonesians burnt everything they couldn't take with them in Manatuto. Food was covered in petrol and burnt in the street, along with all the cigarettes,' said Anthony, now smoking.

Falintil commander Taur Matan Ruak joined us after we'd had a basic meal of rice, buffalo intestines and monkey. Last time I'd been there, he'd offered me Australian red wine with a meal of Portuguese steaks. There was nothing like that now, and he seemed to want to play down Falur's reports of Falintil moving out of the cantonment. He was trying to control his men, make them stick to Xanana's orders.

It was a bad position, being in charge of an army that was not allowed to fight while its country and people were being destroyed around it. Taur, who had been fighting in the mountains for 24 years, since he was 19 years old, said he had known what would happen when the vote was declared.

'I know the Indonesians too well,' he said. 'They say peace and reconciliation, but they mean the opposite. All we could do was provide security to those they terrorised.'

Around 10,000 people had fled to the Waimori area

seeking the protection of Falintil. They were having a lot of trouble feeding them.

'We now control all of the area east of Dili except for Baucau and Lospalos where INTERFET are,' he said without a hint of victory in his voice. 'There are still a lot of militia in Ainaro, Zumalai and Suai. They are Mahidi, Kopassus and Lak Saur. We don't have any men down there.'

I had travelled to Waimori fresh from the euphoria of the Indonesian withdrawal in Dili and expected victory celebrations. But clearly the situation was not resolved, INTERFET was not deployed outside of Dili, and the convoys to Lospalos and Baucau had not properly secured the area. Large areas of the south and the west were still occupied and still terrorised. The thought of what the cornered militia were doing to the local population in those areas was not pleasant, and you could tell it bothered the commander.

>─◄►─○─◄►─◄

BACK IN Manatuto, someone shouted my name from the rubble as we passed on the way back to Dili. It was Quintão, my old translator. Wearing nothing but shorts, he was standing by the side of the road. He had worked for UNAMET but had fled to the hills rather than evacuate with them.

'What, you think I'm crazy?' he said. 'The UN were getting shot at—we thought we would get killed if we stayed with them. We went to Falintil.'

He wanted food—there was nothing in Manatuto. I said I'd come back in the morning.

Early the following day, I headed off on the bike alone after stealing some rations from the army at the Tourismo.

The road was totally deserted and it was a brilliant, sunny morning.

All the small fishing villages along the road were just charred wrecks. I stopped at one. Inside the burnt remains of a house there was a mass of flies. The stench told me what it was. There were three half-burnt bodies—the occupants of the house, probably killed for refusing to leave. I tried to take a photo but the smell made me gag and vomit. When I finished, I was shaking, holding on to a blackened pole in a destroyed house, on a deserted road in the blazing sun, with three grotesque half-burnt, half-decomposed corpses. It was totally silent except for the buzzing of the flies.

Further on I saw something in the sky and a cloud of dust approaching. It was the Lospalos INTERFET convoy. With a Black Hawk overhead and armoured cars at either end of the line of vehicles, they moved quickly through the destroyed landscape, as though oblivious to the evidence of the killing around them. This was maximum force protection heading back to Dili.

Armed men appeared on the road in front of me as I came into Manatuto. I slowed down, remembering Agus and the nuns and their horrible recent deaths on the deserted road further east.

They raised their weapons. It was Pedro, Taur Matan Ruak's assistant. They were Falintil, on motorbikes, riding armed through the deserted burnt-out towns.

'We are going to check Hera,' he said. 'We think Mateus is still there with some militia. Want to ride with us?'

I gave the rations to Quintão's uncle, who was waiting for me, and rode back to Dili, thankful for the escort.

EARLY ON Friday 2 October the Australians mounted what the INTERFET press release called, 'The biggest air mobile operation since the Vietnam war'—Operation Lavarack— to secure the western border. They moved nearly 1,000 men into position at the northern end of the border region and set up headquarters at the old Portuguese fort on the hill in the town of Balibo.

Luckily, I got a seat on a helicopter going down the next day. It was a very tense group of soldiers we went down with, and they made the dramatic gesture of fanning out and assuming firing positions when we landed on the football field opposite the fort in Balibo.

There was something perfectly symbolic about the choice of location for the base of this operation. The fort was the one from which José Ramos Horta had pointed to the Indonesian warships off the coast of Batugade in October 1975 and said, 'They are not there for fun you know.' That information came from one of the last reports put together by the five Australian-based journalists before they were killed in October 1975.

The next year, the Indonesians chose the small crossroads town of Balibo as the place to sign the official integration of East Timor into Indonesia as the republic's 27th province. Then it became a centre for pro-Indonesian rallies throughout 1999.

But that morning, the fort resembled a Vietnam war-era hilltop firebase, with coils of razor wire being erected, sand-bagged fortifications being built and guns being put in place. A stream of helicopters landed, then took off again with supplies and men. A column of around 80 vehicles arrived from Dili, with the ageing Australian armoured personnel carriers taking up positions on adjacent hilltops.

We went up to the fort and got the official statistics from the briefing officer. In Balibo, 80 to 90 per cent of the

buildings had been rendered uninhabitable (the withdrawing TNI and militia removed the roofs). Patrols were out at
all the known exit and entry points across the border. The
Indonesian troops present at the border town of Batugade
had fled on foot at the first sight of the Australians the day
before. The previous night, patrols had sighted and interviewed people not from the area; intelligence received there
was that some people were fleeing across the border;
suspected militia abandoned four homemade weapons,
which were seized.

'We are establishing a forward operating base to provide a
secure environment for people to move back into,' said the
briefing officer. It was all pretty straightforward. The people
had gone, forced across the border. The place was wrecked,
but in a more methodical way—they had taken care to
physically remove anything usable from the buildings, such
as roofing iron, plumbing, doors, wiring, anything.

As we filed our updates, a captain came up to the fort.
He wanted to show us what was in the house in which the
journalists had been killed—the right one, this time. There
was fresh blood smeared around the walls to about eye
level. Schoolbooks were scattered on the floor, along with
playing cards, perfume bottles, pillows and smashed beer
bottles. A Kopassus special forces emblem had been carefully drawn on the wall. Most disturbing of all were the
lipstick marks at waist level all around the room. They were
smudged and showed signs of having been made by a head
being forced against the wall.

'We are sealing off the area as a crime scene,' said the
officer. 'We suspect it has been the site of sexual crime.' He
was clearly disgusted.

The soldiers outside were also repulsed. Judging by the
furniture and possessions, it appeared to be the room of a
young schoolgirl who had been raped, said one.

The next morning we were told by the briefing officer that they had found something for us. An inhabitant, still there. We all trooped down to a small wooden hut with a thatched roof—one of the few buildings that hadn't been destroyed. A soldier knocked on the door and said in Tetum not to be afraid. Terry McDonald from the ABC got ready with his camera, and there were stirring noises from inside. The soldiers told whoever it was inside that they had food and water. The door opened very slightly, and a very old woman took one look at the Australian soldiers towering in her doorway, and closed the door again. They left the food there and we left. She was the only person still living in Balibo.

Next, a young man was brought to the guard post. He had been picked up at the border and at first was treated as a suspected militia. Domingos Dos Santos was terrified of the Australian soldiers, but the 24-year-old relaxed when Antonio from the Portuguese news agency LUSA spoke to him in a language he understood. He had pretended to be a militia at the border to be able to get close enough to slip through the three-kilometre zone that separated the Australian and Indonesian positions.

Domingos had fled his home in Dili after his uncle was killed by militia on the day the independence result was announced. Like thousands of others, he ended up in the West Timorese town of Atambua, 10 kilometres over the border.

'In Atambua there was Polri [Indonesian police], TNI, Kostrad, Aitarak, Saka, Loromonus and Dadurus Merah Putih, all armed with M-16s,' he said, describing conditions the thousands of East Timorese had to endure there. 'They told us they want to get everybody out of East Timor and they aren't letting them back in. They're saying there is going to be a war in East Timor and we can't go back till later. Nobody is giving us food or water.'

He also told us there had been a lot of people killed, and that they'd thrown their bodies into the sea, and that young men in the camps were being targeted.

At the Portuguese fort, the Australian commander, Lieutenant-Colonel Mick Slater, expressed his disappointment that the refugees had not started to return as a result of the Australian presence in the border area. Across the road near the playing field, supplies of food for returnees were being stockpiled in roofless buildings that were being covered with tarpaulins. At night, looking out from the fort using night vision, thousands of small cooking fires could be seen to the west. That was where all the people were— held in camps across the border.

Back in Dili, INTERFET spokesman Colonel Mark Kelly said that the international force had reached 6,000, with 4,000 of those being Australians. The total force of 7,500 would not arrive in East Timor until the end of October. He also said that he hoped the East Timorese people would return from across the border, but acknowledged international negotiations would have to continue to enable their return.

With the border sealed by INTERFET troops, it looked as though the militia in the south and south-west of East Timor were trapped.

I began making trips south of Dili, first to Aileu, and then to Maubisse where, on Tuesday 5 October, ABC reporters Tim Lester and Di Martin and I learned that INTERFET had already passed through in an armoured convoy that day. It was the first time that the forces had moved south into the areas where, we knew from the local people, militia were still active, and we reported the movement.

Jose Belo was down in Maubisse to collect videotapes sent from Max Stahl, who was in Ainaro further west where there was still militia activity. After we arrived back in Dili, both Tim and I got called in by the officers in charge of the media pool. We were told separately, and in no uncertain terms, that we had reported Australian troop movements and were risking Australian lives. Tim's management reprimanded him, but my bosses at AAP, to their credit, said it was a good story.

Jose Belo spoke to Max on the satellite phone in Ainaro, telling him things were happening and that I should get down there. I left with Jose and Joanna Jolly the next morning. Jose left us in Maubisse to take another batch of Max's tapes back to Dili. He looked worried as he said goodbye, even though Valentin, the guide we had picked up, said things were fine. We had only the vaguest information about where the militia were.

⊢•◆•○•◆•⊣

AT DUSK we arrived in Ainaro. In the destroyed town square, the only light came from piles of burning tyres on the street outside the trashed town hall. A woman was standing in the street, screaming. Her hair was unkempt, her dress ripped down the front and stained with blood that had also run down and dried on her bare legs. She had a Bible and was screaming phrases in English in a tortured, high-pitched voice. They were phrases about damnation and wrath and vengeance that, had she understood English, she would have picked to condemn what had happened to her and the town.

She was clearly unhinged and the effect was terrifying. We saw the shadows of men with wild hair and automatic weapons who were running into the destroyed buildings as we stopped the bike. Scrawled on the walls of the burnt-out town hall, anti-Indonesian graffiti in English said, 'TNI is the devil of destruction' and 'Indonesia worst imperialist go home'. The flag of Fretilin flew above the ruins. Max stepped out of the black smoke into the light of the burning tyres.

'Welcome to Ainaro,' he said, smiling slightly.

Max had been there for a few days and told us how the Australian convoy had passed through and spent the previous night in the town, but they had not spoken to him and had warned the locals not to approach them. As far as the troops were concerned, they were in hostile territory. Not that there were many locals left. Out of a population of roughly 4,000, there were only around 200 people left, mostly young men who slept in the hills outside of town every night for fear of the militia. After the Indonesian military left, the day before INTERFET landed in Dili, militia from Cassa under the command of Cançio Lopes De Carvalho attacked the nearby village of Maununu.

Max was staying in a barricaded classroom with an East Timorese doctor, Jose Antonio Gusmão Guterres, who had managed to survive the violence and was trying to tend the wounded. He told us what had happened when the militia attacked Maununu on 23 September.

'They came in shooting. People were washing, making breakfast, they were totally defenceless, mainly women and children,' said Jose. Twelve people were shot dead that morning and six were wounded, four so badly they would not have survived if they had not been evacuated in the next few days, the doctor said. The wounded included a pregnant woman.

He told us that the militia were either still in Cassa, 20 kilometres to the west, or had fled to the border in the face of the INTERFET advance. The few people remaining in Ainaro were still terrified of the militia returning, and the doctor was angry at both INTERFET and Falintil for not protecting them.

We heard through a satellite phone call we made to the AAP office in Sydney that two Australian soldiers had been shot in an ambush by militia in Suai that night. We could only presume that they were part of the convoy that had left that morning from Ainaro and was heading west to the militia stronghold of Cassa. The doctor told us there had been another militia attack in Hata Hudo, near Cassa, on Sunday 3 October. Apparently, all the militia who had been trapped in the southern port of Betano waiting for a boat to West Timor had travelled through there to join up with Cançio and his men before attempting to get to West Timor. They were cornered and desperate, and we barricaded ourselves inside the classroom attached to the church as it got dark. They thought the militia might be coming back to kill us before they left for West Timor.

In the early hours of the morning, we heard movement outside, then the sound of dogs howling. But it wasn't dogs howling, it was humans impersonating dogs, and then they started banging on the door. We all lay still on the hard wooden bunks where we had been sleeping (the mattresses, like everywhere else, had been looted), not daring to make a sound. After a while, they stopped howling and we heard the sound of running. Max got up and looked out the door. There was no-one there and we had no idea whether it was militia or not who had been making those frightening noises. None of us could get back to sleep.

On the way to Cassa the next morning, Max's bike broke down just outside of Ainaro. Nearby was a sheer cliff leading down to the river valley. In the 1970s and '80s the Indonesians had thrown many people to their death from that cliff, and it had been renamed by the people. They called it Jakarta 2. Apparently, the Indonesian soldiers would tell the people who were to be killed that they were taking them to Jakarta; instead, they were thrown over the cliff.

There was fresh blood on the top of the cliff, and two bodies visible below. Max, stuck in Ainaro with no transport before we arrived, had hiked down there and found the two with bound hands and stab wounds, and smashed bones from the fall. It looked like they'd been dead for about a week, he said. He had found the bodies of other people who had recently been killed and had heard of many more.

When we were finally on our way down the hills to Cassa, we passed through deserted villages where the stench of decomposing corpses was interspersed with the fresh smell of the tall grass and trees. We didn't stop to look; it had become commonplace—in even the smallest hamlet or village, you'd find at least one body. That seemed to be the pattern. As they arrived, the troops or militia killed at least one person to terrorise the rest into getting on the trucks going to West Timor.

⊳⊶⊷⊙⊶⊷⊲

THERE WAS a small knot of people on the main street of Cassa. Behind them, furniture and smashed pieces of wooden buildings, fences and petrol drums lay all over the road. The people were armed with spears and were very nervous. The militia were gone, but they were expecting them to return and they guarded small road blocks made of junk, armed with their spears.

We walked through the town to the church. It was looted and destroyed: near the cross behind the altar, there was blood on the floor, and the statue of Mary had been stolen.

Armandio De Jesus came over and started talking to us. He had returned to Cassa the day before. When he'd arrived in the afternoon, the place was deserted and everything was a mess. Armandio had worked for UNAMET in Cassa. He had been involved in a fight with a militia who had been trying to take weapons from the Brimob at the UN polling station just before the voting began. The UN police had taken him to the local police station for his own safety. When the UN evacuated, he went to the forest around the town and hid, along with about 100 other young people. He told us that the militia had left on Sunday after attacking the village of Hata Hudo. They left in a convoy of 14 trucks, motorcycles and six looted UNAMET four-wheel drives from Same and Ainaro. According to Armandio, who had watched from the mountains, there were about 200 militia and 500 civilians in the convoy that headed off in the direction of the border.

'The militia promised the people here they would drop their families in Atambua and then they would return to kill those who stayed,' he said.

That same convoy was carrying at least 80 automatic weapons, according to those in Cassa, and was heading for the West Timorese border, 70 kilometres west. According to the local residents, INTERFET's force of Australian troops followed through early Wednesday morning visiting Cassa and Zumalai further west. On Wednesday night, the clash between INTERFET troops and militia took place; as a result, two militia were killed and two Australian soldiers were wounded along the same route to the West Timorese border.

At the time, the Australian army was reporting to the press in Dili that a militia convoy had left Cassa at dawn on Wednesday, heading for the border. INTERFET had apparently shot out the tyres of one of the trucks and injured four militia as they attempted to run an INTERFET road block near Suai on the way to the border. Nine were detained by INTERFET and sent to Dili. Dozens more were disarmed and taken by Australian troops to the border. As those troops returned to Suai, they were ambushed by militia. One soldier was shot in the neck and another in the leg and the wrist. Two militia were killed as the Australians returned fire. That was the official version.

According to rumours I'd heard later in Dili, the convoy had been escorted by a truckful of TNI troops. They had led them into the ambush and had opened fire themselves after the militia opened up. I was told that the soldier wounded in the neck told the doctor operating on him that he had emptied the whole clip of his Steyr into the TNI truck as it sped away. He was positive that he had hit some of the Indonesian troops who were in the back. There were other inconsistencies between what I was hearing from the locals and the story the military gave us about the clash, such as the timing of the militia departure from Cassa and the arrival of the Australian convoy in the town. That was the same convoy we had been reprimanded for reporting the whereabouts of earlier in the week. We were never given a clear picture by the Australians of what happened that day. The East Timorese I spoke to in Suai later told me of the deaths of Indonesian soldiers in the clash.

One thing was clear, and that was that Cançio Lopes De Carvalho, the Mahidi militia leader, had got away. The same man who had established his authority back in February by slicing open a pregnant woman's belly in public, was allowed—and possibly escorted to safety— across the border by the INTERFET soldiers based in Suai. Months later in Dili, soldiers told me and other reporters stories of escorting militia with blood still on their machetes across the border during this time. But that was off the record and not to be reported; they would clam up as soon as you pestered them for specifics.

Outside Cançio's house in Cassa, there was a fire smouldering in a pit on the football field where he had held his rallies. Armandio called me over. He tapped his spear on the blackened steel frame of a chair. Loops of wire ran around the chair and part of a human backbone fell from under the wire when he moved it with his spear. There were more bones in the smouldering pit.

'They tied him to that [chair] and set him alight in front of the whole town on the soccer field,' he said.

They had done that to a young man just before they'd left, to ensure those in the town accompanied them to West Timor. Five hundred of them had.

Max was going through the wreckage of Cançio's house. The militia leader had obviously gone to the effort of destroying his own house rather than leaving it to be used by those who had defied his order to flee with them to West Timor, who he had vowed to return and kill. Max had picked up an exercise book from the house. It was your normal, cheap Indonesian exercise book with a picture of the Spice Girls on the cover. It turned out to be Cançio's notebook for learning English, and in it was written a series of phrases in English and the translation into Indonesian. But these weren't the normal notes your average language student would make. The only one I wrote down was, 'Attack the weak, avoid the strong' but there was a whole string of notes he had made to himself. In the same notebook there were lists of people labelled 'employed by Indonesia but pro-independence supporters', and the home villages of those named were written beside them.

━━◆━○━◆━━

WE RODE up an impossible track of loose rock to the village of Hata Hudo which the militia had attacked the day they left Cassa, Sunday 3 October. It was deserted when we arrived. The people had heard our motorbikes and thought we were the militia returning, and had fled to the surrounding forest. They slowly emerged from behind the blackened uprights that showed where the village had been before it was destroyed. They were mostly women and chidren, with the few men present carrying spears and traditional swords.

'There was a lot of shooting when they came,' said Aniceto Xavier, a 31-year-old who seemed to be in charge. 'The victims are still here in the jungle,' he said, referring to those wounded from the attack. He told us how the militia had killed six people and one of them, an old woman, had been decapitated and her head left on a petrol drum in the middle of the road. The militia had been looking for food but had also continued to try to make people leave for West Timor. The people fled and were still living in the mountains. They complained about the heat in the day, the cold at night and the lack of food. Many people were getting sick.

As I sat down to read out the story over Max's satellite phone, I found I couldn't talk properly. We had run out of water long ago and my throat was dry. A woman handed me a coconut and I drank the milk, then she handed me another and another. It was the only food they had in abundance.

Max wanted to keep going to Suai, but I was scared. I thought the militia could still be stuck between the border and Cassa, trying to avoid INTERFET. After what I'd seen and heard that day, I didn't want to run into Cançio. I could just imagine turning a corner and finding him on the road. I remembered Cançio's enraged eyes when he had been asked why he had disembowelled the pregnant woman back in Balibo all those months ago. I didn't want to have to face them again, so I left with Joanna and headed back towards Dili, leaving Max to the last lawless and barbaric part of East Timor.

ー◦ー

RIDING BACK to Cassa we got a flat tyre, but we had no choice but to keep going. The day was almost over and we rode slowly through the deserted villages that reeked of dead bodies. There was no-one alive around. In Ainaro, one of the young guys with a looted weapon and police webbing directed us to his family's house. In the middle of the destroyed town, as they prepared to walk back up to spend another night in the safety of the hills, the whole extended family sat around and chatted with us over weak coffee while the young men fixed the tyre. Two of them had been in Australia and they all had relatives there, and I found myself talking, of all things, about the pros and cons of certain Melbourne suburbs.

In the dark, riding across the freezing hills to Dili, the people along the mountain road shouted *Dibuna Saja* over and over again as we went past. I couldn't remember what it meant and neither could Jo. I thought it meant under or over or something like that, but trying to keep the bike on the bad road was occupying all my attention. Later, we realised what they had been shouting as we went past—'Just kill them'. Hopefully they had thought we were militia.

The next day, Tim Lester and Di Martin from the ABC were heading down to Suai. We had all heard that there had been a massacre in the church, but what that meant hadn't really sunk in and the uncertainty of the whereabouts of the militia down there in the south-west was still fresh in my mind. I didn't want to go back to Suai.

They were among the first journalists to get to the church in Suai where the priests, nuns and refugees had been killed on 6 September, the day after the UN evacuated the town. The INTERFET soldiers down there had found only six bodies washed up on the beach, but the locals told them Indonesian soldiers, police and militia had killed more than 400 people who had sought refuge in the church grounds. They were the last of those who had started looking for sanctuary at the church on 25 January when it all began with the panic following Cançio's first round of killings in Zumalai and Galitas. The people present at the church when the killing happened were mostly women and children, because they had believed the military and the militia would not kill women and children, only the men. The day before the killings, there had still been around 1,000 people in the church grounds, but many men had fled.

They didn't find the bodies of the dead in Suai—they had been removed and taken to West Timor. But the evidence of their deaths and the remnants of their disposal remained.

'They took the bodies and threw them onto the fire. They used the trucks to roll over the bodies, to drive over the bodies,' said a witness.

Di walked through the classrooms in the church compound with an Australian doctor, John Cooper, who assessed the remains. 'The big classrooms were probably full of a couple of hundred people who lived in there. They've thrown the bodies in here on top of burning schoolbooks and clothes and things, and what's left is the shape of the bodies and their clothes. Under the clothes, there is still a sort of pooling of blood, here, that was lying under the bodies that they've carted off. There's one there, there's one over here,' he said on the tape as they walked. Outside, amid the personal effects and documentation of those who had lived there, there were more blood stains and torn clothing. Tufts of human hair were caught on debris. The actual bodies had been collected by Indonesian security forces and militia two days after the killings.

Andrew McNaughtan was also in Suai and ran through

the evidence of the killings in the steeple of the half-built cathedral that overlooks the church compound—evidence that was soon lost to weather and the passing of time before an investigation was conducted.

'We're one floor up the top of the church steeple and we can see now really clear evidence of the victims of this massacre,' he said. 'There's blood that dropped on the scaffolding. It would have had to have been litres of blood, I suspect. You can see it on the cardboard, you can see it on the steps. These poor people have staggered down or been thrown down or fallen down.

'When you come out here you can see one body or more had been dragged over here towards the edge and, unless I'm very much mistaken, from here they've thrown them— that's where you can see the blood below.

'And if you hang out, you can see the scrape marks that are on the bottom directly below here, and I think you can see blood here and here. There, the bodies have been thrown from here and crashed onto the ground below— probably about 20 metres from here.

'You can see how those hiding in the top of the church would have been absolutely terrified in the moments before being shot or hacked or whatever—dragged to their deaths from this church steeple. If you hang out, you can actually see. If you look down, it becomes very clear. There are scrape marks and blood all over the place.'

A few days before the ballot, Andrew and I had gone to see Father Hilario in Dili before he returned, for the last time, to Suai. I remember being annoyed with Andrew because he wanted to ask very specific questions about the killings around Suai we had reported way back in May. Hilario had not paid any attention to the questions and had simply said, 'They will kill us, those of us in the church,' and Andrew had stopped talking. We asked him if he could possibly stay in Dili and he had said no, he had to return to Suai, and the meeting was cut short. He had a long day's drive ahead of him, and wanted to get moving.

Jose Manuel Da Silva, a witness to Hilario's murder, spoke to Di.

'When the Indonesian military came here, Father Hilario was there and he said to the people, don't cry, we are ready to die now,' Jose said. 'They told him, don't speak any more. If you speak any more, we will shoot you.'

Hilario was then shot. The other two priests were also killed—Father Francisco and an Indonesian priest newly assigned to Suai, Father Dewanto.

Jose said he recognised Hilario's killer as an East Timorese member of the Indonesian military. The TNI were accompanied by Indonesian police and 10 carloads of militia from all over East Timor, including Aitarak from Dili. All of them took part in the killing of those in the church grounds.

Jose escaped by hiding in a 44-gallon drum after running out to the back of the church. As he hid, he heard the voice of the local garrison commander, Colonel Sugito—the same commander who had sat in on Ian Martin's meeting with the local leaders in Suai when he visited for the first time in June; the meeting after which Ian Martin said he was pleased with the 'assurances' he had received regarding security from the local military. And now, Colonel Sugito was shooting people.

The night before the massacre, Father Hilario had called the UN compound in Dili predicting the killings and asked for some form of assistance. He had received no response. Fathers Hilario, Francisco and Dewanto's bodies were exhumed from a common grave in West Timor in December by an Indonesian human rights investigation team. When they carried out the exhumation, they wore flak jackets, afraid that militia, who still controlled the area near the border on the western side, might try to shoot them.

REFUGEES STARTED returning from West Timor on flights supplied by the United Nations High Commission for Refugees (UNHCR). Over 270,000 people were in West Timor and access to the refugee camps was almost impossible for journalists and, in many areas, for aid workers, who were usually chased out of the camps. Militia would throw rocks or beat them, or smash the windows of their cars if they saw them anywhere near the camps. The stories of killings and rapes in the camps and the targeting of pro-independence people were the norm for that period.

On 10 October, I heard Pedro had come back on one of the first refugee flights from Kupang, and I went out to see him in Becora. His guesthouse, the Villa Harmonia, was a burnt shell, and I found Pedro out the back of the building. He was sitting down, without a shirt on, and didn't even rise to greet me when I walked in. All I got was a simple 'Hey John,' as if I was just dropping around to see him like I'd always done when things were quiet.

I'd brought some ration food, thinking he'd need something, but he just picked it up without looking at it and put it in the cupboard behind him. The cupboard was full of ration food, and I almost wished I hadn't given him so much. Hunger makes you selfish, and I had thought at the time that Pedro, the scammer that he was, probably had more than me. But those kinds of thoughts were quickly dismissed when he started speaking.

He had put so much effort and money into turning his house into a hotel, and now it was all gone. He looked almost like he was going to cry when I stupidly asked when he was going to start fixing the place up. His children were all safe, that was the main thing, and he didn't really want to talk about anything else. I told him I'd seen his daughter Lola in Darwin after she was evacuated with the UN, and tried to make a joke about how she had seemed to have some Australian guy in tow who she seemed to have firmly in place, paying for all her shopping.

It fell flat. I think it just reminded him of where he'd been and everything that had happened. I didn't tell him how, on that horrible Wednesday night in the compound, Lola had grabbed my arm and asked me if I thought everything would be okay. I'd said yes, even though I knew at that stage that it didn't look like the Timorese were going to be evacuated.

Pedro didn't really want to talk, so I got up to leave. He told me to come back later and he would tell me about what happened in West Timor. He knew that was what I'd wanted to ask about, but when he said that I felt like saying that it wasn't the reason I had come around. But I just left it and said I'd be back later.

I went back later with Jo and felt a deep resentment towards her when she got straight to the point and asked about conditions in West Timor. This is Pedro, I thought, not just anybody—I lived in his house, he used to lend me money when my cheques didn't arrive, he was questioned on my behalf by the Intel—if he doesn't want to talk about it, leave him alone. But I turned on my tape recorder and listened with interest to his answers.

He had returned to his house in Becora after the announcement. The three Australians from Melbourne were still there, and he felt almost safe while they were there, even with the heavy gunfire around the place. On the Monday morning after the announcement, the Australian ambassador, John McCarthy, had come out to pick up the Australians for the evacuation. Pedro had asked him if he could go, because he was going to be targeted for his involvement with foreigners. McCarthy, as were his orders, had said no. Only foreign nationals were allowed to be evacuated.

As the Australians left, Pedro's security disappeared.

'There was no time, you just had to leave the house,' he said. 'We went to the church near here, Becora church, then we left the church at 11 o'clock to go to Kodim. It was the same time they burnt the Bishop's house, so it was not safe to stay in the church, either.'

'There was burning and shooting everywhere. It was a very hard time. We were shepherded to Kodim, and stayed in Kodim just on the road. There were many dead people on the road. I saw about three. I didn't see all of them, I was scared so I stayed in the middle. People were pointing them out. I think I saw about three persons.'

They stayed one night at the military headquarters, Kodim, but some people were shot and there was panic, so he went to the Polda police compound to spend the next night.

'The next day, they forced people to go to Atambua, but there was no vehicle and you had to find your own trans-portation to go to Atambua. But how can you do this? And we were scared to even go 10 metres, so we just stayed there waiting for a vehicle to turn up and take us to Atambua. Nothing happened, and the next day the army took us to the airport from Dili to Kupang. I was lucky; if I went to Atambua I may have been killed in Liquiça because I've been with IFET many times to these places, I've spent many days there, they know me,' said Pedro.

He flew out with his wife and youngest children on the Wednesday on an Indonesian military C-130. He was hidden by the priest in Kupang, Father Herlando, and wasn't able to leave the building. It was too dangerous. If he had been recognised, he believed he would have been killed.

'I don't know how many flights they had each day, but 150 people in one plane. I don't know how many flights, but for four days they evacuated,' he said.

'Many people hid in the church and many people hid us in their houses. Kupang is full, there are Timorese people in the market and everywhere. I never went out, but my wife saw them. I went once to organise my visa to get out of Kupang, but it was hard. Even to go to the airport was hard.

'Many people they killed, they took away. They would blindfold their eyes and tie their hands and they would be taken to a place and killed. It happened all over West Timor.'

Pedro heard many stories of people being killed or taken away by the militia in West Timor, and heard the cars of the militia come and take people away on two occasions.

'In many places, people have been taken away, but the refugees there cannot say anything about it because they are also scared. It is still going on,' he said. He also said that if militia in East Timor were killed, revenge would be taken on the refugees.

Everything of value was taken from the refugees, just as anything left behind in East Timor was trucked out before INTERFET arrived.

'All the looted stuff is taken to the border and put on boats and taken to Java. We didn't expect this, we thought something would happen, but not this. The situation was a robbery. They were attacking people and taking things away. It wasn't any fight at all. They were killing people and taking away things.'

To register for the evacuation flights meant exposing himself as a pro-independence supporter, but Pedro took the chance.

'The people in Kupang said, okay we want to die, but at least we die in East Timor, we don't want to die in Kupang. Everybody was in such a hurry to go back home. When the multinational force came, everybody was so happy they had come. Yesterday, before we came, I organised with the boys to write on T-shirts "*Timor Lorosae*, Home Sweet Home, there is no place like home, Kupang, Sept 1999". It was nothing political, we just wanted to show we wanted to go home.'

Pedro was lucky to get out of West Timor. His experience there was typical of that of the roughly 280,000 people who were forcibly deported. According to Indonesia, at the time of writing, there were still between 80,000 to 100,000 refugees in West Timor.

▸━◂▸━०━◂▸━◂

TENSION CONTINUED on the Western border. On 10 October, Australian troops approaching the border post of Motaain were fired upon by TNI, Indonesian police and militia. One Indonesian police officer was killed and two others wounded by the Australian return fire. On the same day, Australian troops finally moved permanently into the wrecked and virtually deserted town of Maliana.

The Australians had billeted themselves in the shells of the old market buildings across the road from the deserted UN compound in Maliana. They camped out in the roofless buildings and, by the time we arrived there a few days later, they were settled in and people had begun to return from the hills. Paulo Maia, the only surviving CNRT representative in Maliana then, had already set himself up in the building next to the UN compound. He told me 300 people had been killed in the area, and they had taken the bodies and thrown them into the sea. He told us that those who had led the killings, Indonesian police commander Budi Susilo and TNI commander Lieutenant-Colonel Burharnudin Siagian, had fled to Atambua and were still there. He insisted that the people who had been killed after seeking shelter in the police headquarters after the UN evacuated had been killed by the police from Kontingen Lorosae—the special Indonesian police unit formed to provide security for the ballot.

The day I was there, Paulo told me how there were still militia in the village of Aidabasalala, east of Maliana, and that they had raped women and killed 20 young men in the last few days. The militia had taken the 400 people in the village hostage. 'Why they continue, we don't know,' said Paulo. 'They were trying to move from Atabae to West Timor and got stuck.' He told me they were under the command of an Indonesian TNI lieutenant, Yusuf Sutrisno from the Maliana garrison, and an East Timorese SGI operative, Paulo Goncalves.

The CNRT told us that they had passed this information on to INTERFET who at that time were moving SAS troops into position. They, of course, would tell us nothing about the operation, but the following day the SAS attacked and the last group of militia in East Timor surrendered after they had fired on an INTERFET patrol. The return fire killed three militia and wounded four. It was the last major action for INTERFET inside East Timor.

⊢⊣◆⟩─○─⟨◆⊢⊣

ACROSS THE border, Eurico and João Tavares were telling the refugees still stuck there that they had 50,000 TNI and militia in training and they would attack INTERFET. They were also telling the refugees INTERFET and Falintil would kill the refugees if they returned.

＞−＋＋＞−０−＜＋−＋−＜

OUTSIDE THE deserted UN compound, I saw one of the translators I had known who had worked for the UN in Maliana. He had just come down from the mountains after fleeing Maliana on 2 September in the afternoon just as the destruction of the town began. He greeted me excitedly; he was emotional and wouldn't let go of my hand. I was the first white person he had seen from the pre-ballot time. He told me they were afraid of the Australians because they 'don't know which ones are militia and which ones are the people,' and they treated everyone with suspicion.

'We don't know about our families,' he said. 'Most of us here are just boys. We don't know about our brothers, mothers, sisters. We think they've gone to Atambua. We don't know what has happened—everybody has gone.'

＞−＋＋＞−０−＜＋−＋−＜

THERE WAS a group of about six young men standing in the darkness as we spoke English. I was writing down what he was saying, but I couldn't remember his name, so I asked him. He grabbed my arm tightly and said intensely, with tears in his eyes, 'John, you must be joking. Remember in 1998 when we tried to have the dialogues here and you were here with Andrew and Quintão, and remember Siagian threw us out of town. Then you came to Viqueque and in Dili, in Santa Cruz, in November . . .'

He ran through all these events at which I'd been present, and the people who I'd been there with. I remembered them all, but I still had to say I couldn't remember his name.

He was crying when he told me that everything in his life was gone, destroyed—his family, his friends, his job with the UN, who packed up and left him to die. His whole town was now a smashed ruin occupied by soldiers who were suspicious of him. Then he came into town and I was the only person he saw who was a link with that past—the first days of the student movement—that had, for him, led to this total devastation—and I couldn't even remember his name.

He was still crying when he told me to forget about it, and apologised for getting upset. He was just tired, he said. When I asked him what he would do now, he repeated he was tired and would rest, and the small group of young men trudged off into the darkness to find somewhere to sleep.

>–+–◆–0–◆–+–◄

INTERFET MOVED into the Oecusse enclave in West Timor on 20 October, completing their mandate to secure the territory of East Timor.

Postscript

By late December 1999, things had become quiet in Dili. The INTERFET mission had reached full deployment— 9,941 personnel from 16 nations. Australia was the most heavily represented with 5,570 personnel on the ground. The Australian Defence Minister, John Moore, arrived for a one-day visit. He travelled directly to the enclave of Oecusse, then secured by Australian troops from 3rd Battalion Royal Australian Regiment. Geoff Thompson and I were the only Dili-based reporters to join the press who had travelled with the minister from Australia and we flew down to Oecusse in an old UN-chartered Russian helicopter.

At the briefing given by the troops based in Oecusse, it was announced that they had discovered a mass grave containing the bodies of around 50 men near the village of Passabe on the southern border of the enclave.

The commander handed over to the Battalion intelligence officer, a captain, who in great detail and with the aid of a relief map of the enclave, told the minister and Major-General Cosgrove how TNI and Polri troops had been involved in the round-up and killing of the pro-independence supporters whose bodies had been located in the graves. The captain told us how the site was so close to the border with West Timor that the TNI, Polri and militia who carried out the killing probably thought they were in West Timor.

Immediately after the briefing, we asked the Minister for a response to the 'revelation' that TNI and the Indonesian police had been involved. He replied that there was no firm evidence of that and the allegations of their involvement had yet to be confirmed, and he refused to make a comment on who was responsible for the 50 dead.

Despite having just sat through the same briefing as we had, and having heard what the captain had said, the Minister would not admit that what the Australian army captain had been able to discover about the killings was true. TNI were not to be publicly blamed for the killings, not by the Australian government. We filed the story anyway, without the Minister's comments.

On 14 December, the Indonesian Inquiry Commission into the Violence in East Timor, KPP HAM, held a press conference in Dili following their second trip to East Timor since the violence surrounding the Indonesian withdrawal in September. They stated: 'KPP HAM has found that TNI was involved in the establishment of most of the militias in East Timor; SGI, a notorious combat intelligence unit, dominated by Kopassus members, was heavily involved, to set up, arm and coordinate the militia in each of the regencies; information that KPP HAM has got, strongly indicates that high-ranking officers of TNI and Polri actually commanded this operation.'

The report continued: 'From several major cases that are now being thoroughly investigated, such as the massacres in Liquiça, Maliana, Suai and Bishop Belo's house in Dili, KPP HAM has found similarities of pattern of joint TNI and militia operations. The similarities were clearly shown by the involvement of TNI and Polri units to plan, prepare and actually do the killings. TNI and Polri units have also been found to be involved in collecting, dumping and burying the bodies from the massacres, as well as in cleaning the scenes, in order to hide proof and evidence. In most of the cases the speed, scale and level of coordinated works that have been conducted to carry out such atrocities, KPP HAM believes it cannot have been done without the deep involvement of TNI and Polri structures as well as the use of their facilities.'

Perpetrators of the crimes in East Timor were named by the commission as being all those high and middle rank TNI and Polri officers who served in East Timor, as well as the civilian authorities, the *Bupatis*. The leaders of the following militia groups were named as responsible for atrocities: Aitarak (Dili), Besih Merah Putih (Liquiça), Halilintar (Bobonaro), Dadurus Merah Putih (Bobonaro), Mahidi (Ainaro), and Team Alpha (Lospalos).

KPP HAM eventually published lists of those responsible, 32 people in all. They included Indonesian armed forces chief General Wiranto and head of the Udayana military district, which included East Timor, General Adam Damiri. In February 2000, Indonesian President Abdurrahman Wahid forced Wiranto to resign his post as head of the armed forces, which he did after a brief stand-off. Those others named have been forced to attend hearings before the inquiry, but at the time of writing, no charges had been laid by KPP HAM and no sentences passed.

At the time of the stand-off in Jakarta, Aniceto Guterres from Yayasan Hak in Dili was still pushing for justice to be done. He had survived the violence and was back working, along with Joaquim and the other human rights workers in Dili. They had to find a new office, because the old one had been destroyed. Aniceto warned that the push from Abdurrahman Wahid for an Indonesian court to hear the case against Wiranto as recommended by the KPP HAM report could be part of a plan by the civilian and military powers in Jakarta to avoid an international tribunal.

'TNI has never acknowledged responsibility for what happened in East Timor to the international community,' said Aniceto. 'The army is trying to keep the legal procedure in Indonesia to avoid the tribunal. It would be too humiliating for the generals. Maybe Wahid and Wiranto have cut some kind of deal.'

But Aniceto's hopes for a United Nations–sponsored international war crimes tribunal appeared to be in vain. UN officials in East Timor believed that the difficulties of getting an international war crimes tribunal for East Timor approved in the security council would stop it going ahead, and to date it has.

'Russia and China would not agree because it would leave them open to international investigation of their actions in Chechnya and Tibet,' said one UN official.

'There is no chance at this stage of the kind of international tribunal originally envisaged by some members of the international community, such as those that were set up in Rwanda and Yugoslavia,' said UN human rights chief in East Timor, Sidney Jones. She resigned in frustration at the process in mid-2000.

United Nations Secretary-General Kofi Annan visited Jakarta and arrived in Dili on 17 February. In Dili, he said: 'It is essential that those who committed crimes be brought to justice.'

He implied that the UN would be satisfied if the Indonesians conducted the trials themselves. 'The Indonesian judicial process should be transparent and meet minimal international standards.'

He told reporters in Dili: 'I think the message here is that impunity should not be allowed to stand and those responsible are going to be put on trial.'

Following this, the Indonesians started hearings in Jakarta. Wiranto was interviewed by the commission in Jakarta, but many of the other potential suspects did not turn up to their interviews. In July 2000, the commission travelled to Kupang and Dili to conduct interviews with suspects and witnesses. They said they would indict suspects in a few days. However, international human rights organisations were already calling the process too slow and ineffective.

◦───◦───◦

COLONEL TONO Suratman, who commanded TNI forces in East Timor for most of the period of the militia build-up and violence, was promoted to Brigadier-General and spokesperson for the entire TNI after his service in East Timor. Comments he made to the *International Herald Tribune* on 28 June 2000 had an eerily familiar ring to them: 'There are some rogue elements from within the security forces that are not acting professionally. They are taking sides and we are going to replace them.'

He was talking about Ambon and the TNI role in the religious violence there, but the statement could have easily been from East Timor 12 months before.

Major-General Adam Damiri, the man who Eurico Guterres once said was the only one from whom he took orders, was promoted to Operations Assistant of the TNI's general chief of staff, who also oversees the army operations in North Maluku—an area also racked with Indonesian military-inspired and maintained religious violence.

In January 2000, I travelled to Kupang aboard the *Patricia Anne Hotung*, a boat donated to the East Timorese by Hong Kong millionaire, Eric Hotung. It was being used to repatriate refugees. I managed to interview Eurico at his house in the West Timorese capital. He had put on weight and looked tired, but he was still surrounded by his men, some of whom I recognised, and they still appeared very well off. There were many four-wheel drives in the street outside the comfortable house.

Eurico started by declaring that the ballot was unfair—the UN was not neutral. He told me he wanted to return to East Timor, that he was just a simple refugee. He warmed to his theme and started behaving as he always had, as though I agreed with his statements. His men nodded and laughed at the appropriate times. He said that Falintil and CNRT were acting like the winners when his rights were being ignored. He laughed when I asked if he was afraid of appearing before the KPP HAM commission.

'I demand that UNTAET and KPP HAM explain to us about the human rights abuses carried out by the Timorese from 1959 to 1975,' was all he would say.

He told me he was going to Jakarta the next day to make those demands, but he never left Kupang. He railed against Falintil and the UN.

'It's bullshit Falintil never carried out violence. The UN is not fair. They must take responsibility for all the destruction. UNAMET must explain about the unfairness of the mission. I told Ian Martin that the situation was not safe to have the ballot—he must take responsibility.' He went on to tell me he had called Alexander Downer and the Australian army, and told them to send the peacekeepers in, but they had said they had to wait. That got a big laugh from his men.

<hr />

EURICO APPEARED untouchable in Kupang, still the well-paid protégé of the military. In March he'd had a run-in with the local Indonesian police when he shot at their vehicle, and they tried to arrest him for unlawful possession of a weapon. At the first hearing, he threatened to get his men to burn down the courtroom if the case was not adjourned. It was adjourned. At the second hearing, in July, he appeared with 300 militia outside the court, and argued successfully that as an Indonesian government-employed militia leader he was allowed to carry a weapon. The case was dismissed.

In the meantime, Eurico had recorded a pop song that blamed UNAMET for the destruction of East Timor and lamented how the UN had divided the people of East Timor. It was surprisingly popular and copies of the tape brought back from Kupang were circulating in Dili in April.

Cançio Lopes De Carvalho was still in Kupang in January as well. The local paper reported he had threatened to burn down Kupang if the Indonesian government kept supporting the repatriation of refugees. Around January, the repatriation started slowing down. Over 150,000 people had returned to East Timor in the previous three months of 1999, with ships, planes and trucks provided by the International Organisation for Migration, contracted to the UN and coordinated by the UNHCR. It slowed down quickly, leaving an estimated 120,000 East Timorese still in West Timor, where they'd read daily reports of INTERFET atrocities and pro-independence reprisals against those who returned. The reports were fantasy, but they seemed to work.

Photographer Matthew Sleeth, with whom I was travelling, found Cançio staying in a cheap motel. Matthew convinced him to pose with his pistol. He said Cançio seemed to be a nice guy. I didn't go along; I didn't really want to meet him again.

On another trip to Kupang in February, I found out how the militia were making ends meet. They were selling their weapons to Ambonese Christians embroiled in the religious conflict in Ambon. One of Eurico's men, Agostinho, took me out to the Tuapukan refugee camp near Kupang, where the majority of the East Timorese, TNI and their families were staying. After we gave him $50, he started telling us how they had killed Mau Hudu. He had gone to the Hotel Maya where Mau Hudu was staying in September, and shot him in the legs. They had then driven him back to the East Timorese border, killed him and thrown his body across. He told us this as we were driving back from the refugee camp. He then turned around in the car and said to me, 'And you, we were looking for you but we couldn't find you. We wanted to kill you.'

I must have looked shocked, because he laughed and whacked me on the shoulder. 'Don't worry. That was then, it is all over now.' Later, watching an old video, I recognised him standing in full TNI uniform next to Eurico at the rally on 17 April. Agostinho had then gone and taken part in the killings at the Carrascalão house.

━━━━◆━○━◆━━━━

BACK IN East Timor, we waited around for INTERFET to pull out, after which our news organisations would follow. People slowly put their lives back together. Sebastião returned from Australia with all the other East Timorese flown out in September. He started back at the new UN administration, UNTAET, biding his time until he organised a scholarship to study abroad.

Pedro opened a restaurant opposite the floating hotel that the UN brought in to house their staff in the destroyed capital. He did a roaring trade until he raised his prices so much that people stopped eating there. He closed down and moved on to other ventures.

Jose Belo began work as the Associated Press television stringer for Dili after he was recommended by Max. Most of the other students found work with the burgeoning NGO community, as their language skills were in high demand. But the rest of the population struggled on with an unemployment rate of roughly 90 per cent at the end of 1999.

In Liquiça, there was a map on the wall of the UN civilian police office. It had pins stuck in it where they had exhumed bodies and others where they thought bodies were buried.

'We have in this area over half the identified bodies in all East Timor, and this is only one district out of a total of 13 districts,' said Steve Minhinett, the English police officer then in charge of the investigations. 'We will probably be looking at around 230 bodies of militia victims from the information we have from the people here.'

The map showed clusters of pins around the sites of the road blocks that were on the road west from Dili to the border for months. They were mostly finding bodies with stab wounds. But some had no wounds at all, indicating they'd been buried alive. 'There was so much violence in this town, half the time we only have to talk to the cleaner to find out where the bodies are,' he said.

Steve had only arrived in East Timor in November 1999, and was gone by April 2000. The information he compiled on bodies was not matched up with that compiled by INTERFET, which was not checked against that collated by UNAMET, whose records had apparently been destroyed in the evacuation from the compound. In January, INTERFET stopped quoting figures to the press, claiming that it was all being done by the UN police under the UNTAET administration. The police claimed they had not received the information from INTERFET and directed enquiries to the newly established UN human rights team. The human rights team said they had not received the figures from the police.

The rough figure always quoted is around 1,500 to 2,000 people killed in the September violence. But a trip to Suai revealed that the UN representative down there was unaware that there had been any violence in the area before the church massacre, where she said only 100 people had died. Nobody had accurate records of the violence throughout 1999, and the lowest estimates were always quoted. The evidence had literally been washed away in the wet season. Indonesia was being let off the hook.

Major-General Peter Cosgrove, deservedly on some counts, became something of a star for his handling of the whole mission. He was named Australian of the Year in 2001. Before he handed over command of the forces in East Timor to the UNTAET administration on 23 February 2000, he granted interviews to those who wanted to speak with him one more time before he left.

When I asked about the figures and the numbers of those killed, he responded that 'there was simply a natural caution about making pronouncements over guilt or the facts of the case before these were established.

'We would have been very derelict and negligent, not to say perhaps even malicious, to have started to pronounce on detail we did not have,' he said. He did admit—on the record—that 'we needed forensic investigators in here earlier than they arrived—now that's a matter for history, but they are here now and they are working hard.'

At that point he asked me to turn off my tape recorder.

'Look, you know as well as I do our job was not to come in here and accuse the Indonesians. That is the job of the international community,' he said. He was annoyed.

And he was right, of course, but it seemed he was implying the entire truth was not being told for the sake of smoother bilateral relations between Indonesia and Australia.

Indonesian President Abdurrahman Wahid visited the UN-administered East Timor on 29 February 2000. His visit was marred by a noisy and angry protest by 300 youths. They were demanding the president release the details of the death of commander David Alex and four other pro-independence leaders who had 'disappeared'. Wahid agreed to provide details after Xanana Gusmão intervened personally to disperse the demonstration. The details were never forthcoming.

On 24 July 2000, a New Zealand peacekeeper, Private Leonard Manning, was shot dead near the border with West Timor in the southern region near Suai and his body was mutilated. His ears were cut off. The UN command revealed that they believed the ears were removed to collect a bounty that had been offered to militia by the Indonesian military to kill peacekeepers in order to maintain an unstable situation on the border. (It was not the first time that such a bounty had been offered. In February, a failed militia ambush on UN civilian police in Oecusse was supposedly planned with the same aim. That was foiled by local East Timorese who disarmed the militia. As a result of this incident, the UN allowed police to be armed for the first time.)

Kopassus uniforms and equipment were found near the site of the killing of Private Manning, leading many to believe it was the work of special forces troops determined to destabilise the situation.

Visiting Dili on 5 August to oversee the deployment of four Black Hawk helicopters on the border, to beef up the Australian forces in light of the new threat, Australian

Defence Minister John Moore told reporters: 'Clearly, the militia today is better trained, better disciplined and are acting more coordinated than ever before.'

Moore called on Indonesia's government to fulfil its promise to empty dozens of refugee camps in West Timor, which had been used as training and recruitment grounds by militia gangs.

'The instability on the border is primarily due to a large number still in the refugee camps, and it's up to the Indonesian government to move these people along,' he said.

He was still not going to directly address what was going on: TNI were responsible for the killing by training and arming the militia and, as many people in East Timor believed, carrying out the killing themselves.

The organisation in charge of repatriating the 120,000 East Timorese still in West Timorese camps, the IOM, announced a week-long suspension of its operations on 2 August following an increase in tension and hostility to their employees after the shooting of the New Zealand UN soldier. Acts of intimidation included the wearing of Indonesian uniforms or the red and white bandana symbolising loyalty to Indonesia outside the camps, and threats to burn down houses or to kill humanitarian workers. 'Because of deteriorating security in the last several weeks, UNHCR has been forced to undertake a cooling-off period and take a low profile in the camps,' said Ron Redmond from UNHCR.

On 6 September, in the West Timor border town of Atambua, three UNHCR humanitarian workers were killed. The three—a Croatian, an Ethiopian and an American—were beaten and hacked to death by a group of militia that attacked their office. Their bodies were doused with kerosene and burned. The group was said to be angered at the death of a militia commander from Suai, Olivio Mendoza Moruk, whose body had been discovered near the town the day before. The militia blamed the international community for his death.

Within four days all 462 UN and relief workers and their dependents were evacuated from West Timor, temporarily halting the relief effort to assist the 120,000 East Timorese still in West Timor. International condemnation for the killing was swift. The UN passed a resolution demanding that Indonesia disarm and disband the militia gangs and bring those responsible for the slayings to justice.

Indonesia responded by declaring it would take all measures to disarm the militia and arrested six militia in Atambua, accusing them of the murder.

At one disarmament ceremony in Atambua on 25 September, Eurico Guterres ordered his men to seize the weapons that had been handed in. For this he was later arrested and taken to Jakarta on charges of inciting a riot. His trial in the North Jakarta district court in early 2001 became something of a cause for nationalist Indonesians who hailed Eurico as a patriot, and supporters gathered daily to wave red and white Indonesian flags and proclaim his innocence.

In late March 2001 his lawyers demanded the weapons charges against Eurico be dropped on the grounds that he was a patriot, not a criminal, at the same time the prosecutors recommended one year in prison for him so that even if found guilty, he would be free by the end of the year, taking into account his time already spent in police custody and under house arrest in Jakarta. The Indonesian authorities however, refused a request by United Nations authorities in Dili to hand him over for questioning.

In March 2001 charges against the six militia suspects were downgraded from manslaughter to 'mob violence resulting in death' by the prosecutors in the case who recommended sentences of two to three years in prison. Their lawyers argued that the deaths of the UN workers were not premeditated and that was why the lighter sentences were fair. At the time of writing, Indonesian authorities still had not charged anyone for the violence that erupted in East Timor after the UN-supervised independence ballot on 30 August 1999.

In January 2001 the first person was sentenced in the newly established UN civil courts in Dili for crimes carried out during the Indonesian withdrawal. Judges from Italy, Burundi and East Timor sentenced 22-year-old João Fernandes to 12 years in prison for the murder of a village chief in the police compound in Maliana in September 1999. João had admitted to the killing, carried out whilst he was a member of the Dadurus Merah Putih militia group. The 50 or so militia being held by the UN civilian police in Dili were also due to be charged and charges were also laid against serving members of the Indonesian military.

Only those militia who had been detained in East Timor after the arrival of the peacekeepers and those who had returned from West Timor faced any threat of punishment for their crimes in East Timor. The militia leadership were not among them. Cançio Lopes De Carvalho and his brother Nemezio were still in Kupang from where they expressed their desire to return to East Timor and face charges. They said they feared for their lives in West Timor from their former Indonesian bosses and wanted the protection of the UN in exchange for information on who was responsible for the violence in 1999. At the time of writing their safe return to East Timor had not been fully negotiated.

The TNI leadership responsible for the operation seem

to have put East Timor behind them and are continuing with matters at hand. Major-General Adam Damiri, the last Indonesian military commander to be in charge of the eastern Udayana military district while it still included East Timor, was afterwards assigned to Aceh at the other end of Indonesia. In March 2001 he was made responsible for deploying thousands of Indonesian troops to quell the growing GAM (Free Aceh Movement) separatist movement. Over 1000 deaths had been attributed to the Indonesian security forces in that province in 2000 by Indonesian human rights workers working there. In December 2000 and in March 2001, the Indonesian police and military were also accused of the murders of Indonesian human rights workers in two separate incidents.

While the country prepared for its first elections to be held on 30 August 2001, and its transition from a UN-administered territory to full independence, another 224 refugees arrived on 23 March from Kupang aboard the *Patricia Anne Hotung* along with rumours that the repatriation service would soon cease.

For the estimated 80,000 East Timorese still in the militia-controlled camps of West Timor the nightmare continues.

Acknowledgements

I am indebted to those East Timorese who continually helped journalists like myself in circumstances that very often put their lives at risk.

Specifically I would like to thank: Pedro Lebre and his family; Sebastiao do Rego Guterres, Quintao Gaspar, Joao Sarmento and Antero Bendito Da Silva and the students of the East Timor Students Solidarity Council; Jose Antonio Belo; Rui Lourenco; Joaquim Fonseca and the staff of Yayasan Hak. Many other East Timorese, most of whose names I did not record, assisted me in my time in East Timor and many such as John Maulano, Fathers Hilario and Francisco from Suai, Mau Hudu, Jose Andrade and Commander David Alex were killed during the period covered in this book. It is to them and the thousands of unrecorded victims of Indonesian rule in East Timor that this book is dedicated.

I would like to mention the assistance and support I received from ETISC in Darwin which enabled me to continue working. Also the help of many individuals involved in the East Timor campaign in Darwin such as Vaughan Williams, Ilana Eldridge and Sonny Inbaraj. In the production of this book I was assisted greatly by material and advice offered by Jill Jolliffe and H.T. Lee, in the editing by Daniel Pedersen, and in corrections and Portuguese spellings by Meredyth Tamsyn. Hazel Flynn of Random House Australia had the patience and persistence to help me see this project through and Anne Walsh inspired the initial idea for this book. Lastly I would like to thank the influence of my late father Dr Sigitas Martinkus who, as an exiled Lithuanian, was unable before his death to return to his then occupied homeland. He taught me the consequences of international political expediency and the effects on the lives of those it sacrifices.

Index